Running

Visual Basic™

for Windows™

SECOND EDITION

Running Visual Basic™
for Windows™

ROSS NELSON

A Hands-On Introduction to Programming for Windows

PUBLISHED BY
Microsoft Press
A Division of Microsoft Corporation
One Microsoft Way
Redmond, Washington 98052-6399

Library of Congress Cataloging-in-Publication Data
Nelson, Ross, 1957–
    Running Visual Basic for Windows / Ross Nelson. -- 2nd ed.
      p.   cm.
    Includes index.
    ISBN 1-55615-564-6
    1. Windows (Computer programs)   2. Microsoft Visual Basic for
Windows.   I. Title.
QA76.76.W56.N4585   1993
005.4'3 - - dc20   93-13651
                                                  CIP

1 2 3 4 5 6 7 8 9 FFG 9 8 7 6 5 4

Distributed to the book trade in Canada by Macmillan of Canada, a division
of Canada Publishing Corporation.

Distributed to the book trade outside the United States and Canada by
Penguin Books Ltd.

Penguin Books Ltd., Harmondsworth, Middlesex, England
Penguin Books Australia Ltd., Ringwood, Victoria, Australia
Penguin Books N.Z. Ltd., 182–190 Wairau Road, Auckland 10, New Zealand

British Cataloging-in-Publication Data available.

Acquisitions Editor: Michael Halvorson
Project Editors: Maureen Williams Zimmerman, Nancy Siadek
Technical Editor: Dail Magee, Jr.

To Margaret Hannah Nelson

Contents Overview

Table of Contents

Acknowledgments

I'd first like to acknowledge the Visual Basic project teams—both the team who originally conceived and implemented it and those who have continued to improve it. Clearly, this book would not have been written without the inspiration provided by this innovative product and its developers.

I would like to thank Claudette Moore for her encouragement and support. At Microsoft Press, Eric Stroo's enthusiasm and the comments of Mike Halvorson and Mary DeJong on the initial drafts were very helpful. Mary Renaud also deserves recognition for modulating my occasionally wild-eyed prose, and Dail Magee, Jr.'s careful technical edits and corrections saved me from embarrassment. Thanks as well to Nancy Siadek and Maureen Zimmerman for their work on the new edition. There are a lot of other people at Microsoft Press who work behind the scenes typesetting, creating artwork, proofreading, indexing, and so on. I've never met you, but please accept my appreciation for the work you've done.

Finally, I must mention Rufus (under the equal time provision) and give special thanks to my friends, especially John and Elsa Nimmo, who cheerfully put up with my grousing about deadlines and editing and occasionally being missing in action.

Introduction

The Microsoft Visual Basic programming system for Windows is an exciting advance for anyone who is involved in writing Windows-based applications. With its event-driven programming engine and innovative, easy-to-use visual design tools, Visual Basic lets you take full advantage of the Windows graphical environment to build powerful applications quickly.

But if you're not an experienced programmer, you might be wondering whether Visual Basic is for you. Maybe you've mastered an application such as Microsoft Excel or Microsoft PowerPoint and want to do even more with your computer. Perhaps you're just looking for a new challenge, and computer programming sounds interesting. Or, better yet, you've discovered that no commercial application does exactly what you want, and you're thinking of trying to write a program yourself to fit your own special needs.

If any of these suppositions hit the mark, you're holding the right book. *Running Visual Basic for Windows* is a primer on Visual Basic programming. It will not transform you into a computer scientist, a wily hacker, or an up-and-coming software engineer. But it will show you how to use Visual Basic to convert your ideas into functional programs for your computer, to solve problems that you need solved.

Why Visual Basic? To understand what Visual Basic is all about and why it has generated so much excitement in the world of graphical computing, let's first look at a bit of history.

A Look Back

The earliest programming languages were designed in the 1950s and were created primarily for solving complex mathematical problems. They were rather bewildering to the average person, but this didn't present a serious problem, as computers were found only in major research institutions. Eventually, of course, people realized that computer technology could be useful for more than math, and computers began to be a common sight in businesses and universities. As more people began to use computers, the esoteric and complicated languages used for programming became more of an obstacle.

In response, a language called BASIC was developed at Dartmouth College in the early 1960s. The original version of BASIC (an acronym for Beginner's All-purpose Symbolic Instruction Code) was a very simple language, designed especially to make it easy to learn to program. A whole generation of programmers cut their teeth on BASIC and used it to write an amazing variety of programs.

BASIC's simplicity also made it small, and size was important when computers also began to get smaller. The MITS Altair, which ushered in the microcomputer revolution, appeared in 1975. Bill Gates and Paul Allen, cofounders of Microsoft, took on the challenge of developing a version of BASIC for the Altair that would run in the 4 kilobytes of RAM available on that computer. This version of BASIC eventually developed into the most widely used product in the personal computer industry.

Over the years, this programming language was enhanced and developed. When the early micros gave way to the IBM PC, Microsoft's GW-BASIC set the standard. Later the demand for faster, smaller, and easy-to-use software led to the development of Microsoft QuickBasic. QuickBasic brought BASIC into line with the programming language technology of the 1980s, but an even bigger change was on the horizon: the graphical user interface (GUI).

With the advent of Microsoft Windows, PC users were able to work in an intuitive, graphically rich environment. A graphical user interface made applications much easier to learn and use. Instead of learning to type lengthy commands, users simply chose an option from a "menu" with a click of a mouse button. Multiple windows on the screen let users run more than one program at a time. Dialog boxes appeared when a program needed information or decisions from the user.

Although this environment was wonderful for the user, life was suddenly a lot tougher for programmers. They now had to create and program windows, menus, fonts, dialog boxes, and a multitude of other elements, even for the simplest programs. Thus, when Microsoft Windows was introduced, programmers were simultaneously excited and depressed—excited because Windows gave them a platform for writing graphical, user-friendly applications; depressed because it made their work much more complicated.

A simple program to display a message on the screen could be written in four lines by a programmer working under MS-DOS. A similar program for Windows required two or three pages of code and involved learning to control fonts, menus, windows, memory, and other system resources. But the benefits of Windows for the end user were unquestionable, and people were buying programs written for Windows in record numbers. So professional programmers bit the bullet and began writing those pages and pages of code.

Many believed that Windows heralded the end of the amateur programmer. In the MS-DOS world, professionals in noncomputer fields were commonly able to learn enough programming to write simple applications that helped them with their jobs, streamlined tedious calculations, or organized data quickly. But could anyone do that in Windows, where the programming demands were so complicated for even the simplest applications?

Programming for Windows with Visual Basic

The answer came in 1991, when Microsoft introduced Visual Basic. The Visual Basic programming system packages up the complexity of Windows in a truly amazing way. Combining the proven capabilities of the Basic language with visual design tools, it provides simplicity and ease of use without sacrificing performance or the graphical features that make Windows such a pleasant environment to work in. Menus, fonts, dialog boxes, scrolling text fields, and all the rest are easily designed, and these features require no more than a few lines of programming to control.

Visual Basic is also one of the first computer languages to support event-driven programming, a style of programming especially suited to a graphical user interface. Traditionally, programming has been a very process-oriented, step-by-step affair, much like the instructions that make up a recipe: Beat the eggs, add the milk, stir in the sugar, bake for 20 minutes. One of the drawbacks of this style is that the person who writes the recipe (the program) is always in charge of what happens when. That might be acceptable for baking cookies, but in modern computer applications, the aim is to have the user in charge.

That's exactly what event-driven programming does. Instead of writing a program that plots out every step in precise order, the programmer writes a program that responds to the user's actions—choosing a command, clicking in a window, moving the mouse. Instead of writing one large program, the programmer creates an application that is really a collection of cooperating miniprograms triggered by user-initiated events. And, with Visual Basic, such an application can be written with unprecedented speed and ease.

The initial release of Visual Basic was a runaway success, selling tens of thousands of copies and winning awards from most of the major computer magazines. In the fall of 1992, Visual Basic version 2 was released, offering important new strengths and features.

With the release of Visual Basic 3, Visual Basic has become a mature programming system, complete with many powerful programming tools. Version 3 includes the following new features:

- Improved performance

- A database creation tool

- Visual data access with the Data control, so you can create data-browsing applications without writing code

- New OLE (object linking and embedding) control that allows in-place editing

- A collection of common dialog boxes that streamline common user-interface tasks

- The ability to create pop-up menus anywhere in your applications

Running Visual Basic for Windows will introduce you to Visual Basic version 3 and will help you develop the skills to do real programming. You don't need to know a lot of computer buzzwords to use this book, nor do you need to have programming experience. You must have Windows version 3.0 or later installed on your computer, however, and you should be familiar both with the Windows operating system and with one or more of the major Windows-based applications. It will be helpful if you have created macros for your spreadsheet or word processing program. And, finally, you shouldn't be afraid of a little algebra. This book contains no heavy math, but remember that computer languages were originally designed for performing mathematical computations; consequently, a little of that heritage remains in every computer language today.

Learning to program—in effect, learning a new language—does require some effort and a good deal of trial and error. It's a bit like learning to play the piano: You've got to practice your scales and arpeggios before you can play Chopin or Fats Waller. You won't be performing the programming equivalent of a Chopin concert when you finish this book, of course. Here we'll focus on the fundamentals; we won't cover everything there is to know about programming or even everything there is to know about Visual Basic. But you will be able to build some useful, nontrivial applications and adapt them to your needs. What's more, you'll be able to quickly take advantage of the capabilities of some other applications—Microsoft Word for Windows uses a version of Basic as its macro language, for example, and Microsoft Access (a new database manager) is based on the same technology as Visual Basic.

At the back of this book you'll find information about ordering a companion disk. The disk contains more than 70 forms, code modules, and project files—all you need to create nearly every application in this book.

The tools, power, and features of Visual Basic make programming skills accessible to a wider range of people than ever before—even within the complex world of graphical computing. Now it's time to put *your* computer to work for *you*.

1

A Head Start with Visual Basic

To demonstrate how easy it is to begin working with Visual Basic and how quickly you can learn to create useful applications, this chapter lets you dive right in and write a simple program. Actually experimenting with Visual Basic is the best way to get a feel for the tools you'll be working with, and it will also give you a hint of Visual Basic's exciting potential. After this bit of practical experience, Chapters 2 and 3 will offer you a more detailed look at the hows and whys underlying Visual Basic.

Installing and Starting Visual Basic

Like most Windows-based applications, Visual Basic comes with a program called SETUP.EXE, which installs the application on your computer's hard disk drive. The complete setup process is described in detail in the documentation that comes with Visual Basic; essentially, you follow these four simple steps:

1. Start Windows by typing *win* at the MS-DOS prompt and pressing the Enter key. Visual Basic works with Microsoft Windows version 3.0 and later versions.

2. Insert the disk labeled Disk 1 in a floppy disk drive.

3. Choose the Run command from the File menu in Windows' Program Manager. Type *a:setup* and press the Enter key if you inserted Disk 1 in drive A; if you are using drive B, type *b:setup* and press the Enter key.

4. Follow the instructions on the screen, and provide answers to Setup's questions about various installation options.

After you have answered all the questions and followed the instructions of the program, Setup will install Visual Basic on your hard disk and add a Visual Basic group window and icon to the Program Manager window.

The simplest way to start Visual Basic is to double-click on its icon in Program Manager. Alternatively, you can begin by double-clicking on VB.EXE, the Visual Basic file in Windows' File Manager. Also, you can start Visual Basic from the MS-DOS prompt by entering the command *win vb*, which starts both Windows and Visual Basic at the same time. All of these methods are illustrated in Figure 1-1.

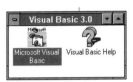

From Program Manager

From the MS-DOS prompt

From File Manager

Figure 1-1.
Starting Visual Basic.

Exploring the Screen

After you start Visual Basic, five windows appear on your screen, as illustrated in Figure 1-2. (On your initial Visual Basic screen, the windows might overlap; in Figure 1-2, the windows have been resized and repositioned so that all of them can be clearly seen.) At the top of the screen is the main window. It contains the standard File and Edit menus and other menus for Visual Basic, as well as a Toolbar. In the center of the screen is the form window, a large empty window titled Form1. Directly to the left, you see a palette window called the Toolbox. To the right of the form window is the Properties window, and, below that, the Project window appears.

> *Tip: In Figure 1-2, all applications other than Visual Basic are minimized to icons. Keeping applications minimized helps to avoid screen clutter. You might find it helpful to choose the Minimize On Use option from Program Manager's Options menu. When this option is selected, Program Manager automatically minimizes itself whenever you start a new program.*

I can almost hear you muttering, "This could be complicated." Indeed it could. But the key to managing complexity is organization, and the Visual Basic environment is designed to keep you organized. Let's take a look at each of the windows.

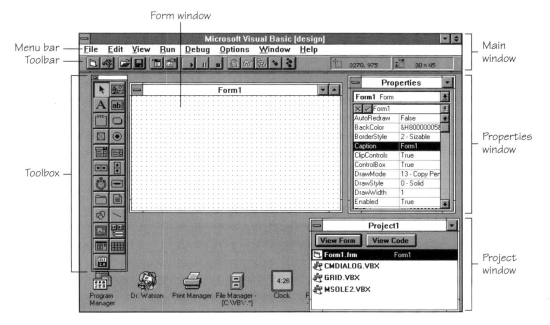

Figure 1-2.
The Visual Basic startup screen.

The Main Window

The main window contains the menu bar, with eight drop-down menus. One of the most important, especially while you're learning Visual Basic, is the Help menu. From this menu, you can access a tutorial that introduces you to Visual Basic, find information about how to contact Microsoft's Product Support services, and explore the comprehensive Visual Basic online Help system.

When you choose Contents from the Help menu, for example, you see a list of all the categories of information contained in the online Help system. By clicking on underlined phrases in the various Help screens, you can move to the specific sections and topics you need to see. When you choose Search from the Help menu, Help displays a dialog box that lets you specify a particular topic and move immediately to the Help information on that topic.

In addition, Help provides context-sensitive information. If you need to know more about a button, a dialog box, a window, an error message, or any other element as you are working in Visual Basic, simply press the F1 key when the element is highlighted, and Help will immediately display the appropriate information. (A more complete description of Visual Basic's Help system can be found in Chapter 8.)

The main window also contains the Toolbar. The buttons on the Toolbar, shown in Figure 1-3, are shortcuts for frequently used commands. For example, instead of opening the File menu and choosing the Open Project command, you can simply click on the Open Project button.

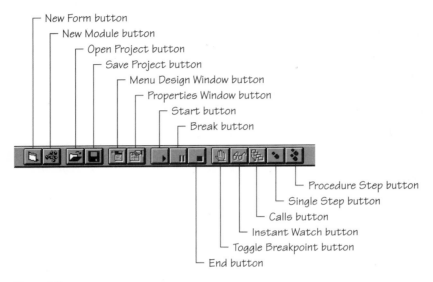

Figure 1-3.
The Visual Basic Toolbar.

Finally, to the right of the Toolbar in the main window, you'll see two display fields that indicate the location and the size of the currently selected object in the form window.

The Project Window

The Project window contains a list of all the files required to run the Visual Basic program you are creating. Although you haven't started yet, four entries appear in the Project window, as you saw in Figure 1-2. The first is the filename Form1.frm; its label (Form1) indicates that the file is associated with the form window called Form1. If you save the form on a disk without changing the name, Visual Basic uses the default filename Form1.frm. An application can be made up of many forms, each of which is stored in a separate file. (Because the files are separate, a form can also be shared with other applications.)

The three additional entries that appear in the Project window are the filenames CMDIALOG.VBX, GRID.VBX, and MSOLE2.VBX. The filename extension VBX indicates that these files are Visual Basic extension files. When you load an extension file, you add supplementary tools to the Toolbox palette (discussed in the next section).

The Project window also contains two buttons, labeled View Form and View Code. By default, Visual Basic displays the corresponding form when you choose a file in the Project window. This view lets you design the *user interface* for your application—the part of the application the user sees and interacts with. If you click on the View Code button in the Project window, the *code* for the selected file appears in a different window. Code refers to statements in a programming language; the process of programming is called *coding*. When you create a program in Visual Basic, you divide your work between the form design, which the user will eventually see, and the coding, which controls the operation of the program. To switch from the code window back to the form, you can simply click on the form to activate it or click on the View Form button in the Project window.

The Form Window and the Toolbox

A *form* is a display area that corresponds to a window that you will see when your application is running. When you start a new project, Visual Basic creates an empty form and titles it Form1. As you design your application, the form serves as a canvas on which you can draw various parts of the application. The components of the application that you place on the form are called *objects*, or *controls*—picture boxes, option buttons, and scroll bars, for example. (Incidentally, Visual Basic considers the form itself to be an object.)

The controls are created from the Toolbox palette, which is shown in Figure 1-4. Each control is represented by a Toolbox icon, or tool. Most of the tools you see in Figure 1-4 are built into Visual Basic. (Chapter 5 describes the standard tools in

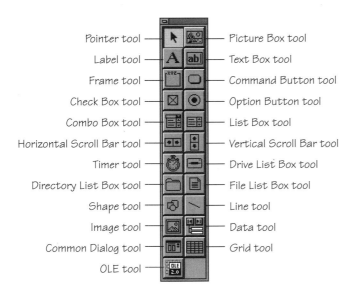

Figure 1-4.
The Visual Basic Toolbox.

detail.) As mentioned earlier, however, the Toolbox can be extended to include additional tools. Each file with a VBX filename extension in the Project window provides one or more new tools for the Toolbox. The Grid tool, the OLE tool, and the Common Dialog tool, for example, come from the files GRID.VBX, MSOLE2.VBX, and CMDIALOG.VBX that are included by default in your project file. The Microsoft Visual Basic Professional Edition offers additional VBX files and gives you the ability to create new extensions (if you are a C or Pascal programmer). A number of third-party software packages are also available.

You design the appearance of your program by choosing controls from the Toolbox and placing them on a form. When you are designing an application, Visual Basic operates very differently than it does when you are running the application. In the design phase, Visual Basic provides tools to help you create display objects and write your program. You interact with the objects on the form by altering their size, position, and other attributes. But the objects are not active, and your code doesn't execute—for example, if you place a scroll bar object on a form, you can change the size and position of the object, but it can't be used to scroll anything.

When you run the finished application, however, Visual Basic removes the design tools. The window layout is fixed, the objects on the screen can be activated, and the user can interact with the display in the ways you've designed. The application takes over, and Visual Basic executes your program statements. (In the title bar of the main window, Visual Basic lets you know whether you are designing or running an application.)

The Properties Window

Visual Basic *properties* are formal mechanisms for describing the attributes of an object. In the real world, I might ask you, "What color is that cow?" In Visual Basic, I would ask instead, "What is the value of the Color property of that cow?" The answer, in both cases, would of course be "purple." Breed is another typical property of cows. Expected values, or settings, for the Breed property could include Guernsey, Holstein, and Hereford.

Every Visual Basic object has specific properties, whose settings control the appearance and behavior of the object in an application. Some properties are restricted to certain values. For example, the Visible property of an object can be set only to True or False (that is, the object is either visible or invisible). Other properties, such as the caption of a form window, can be set to almost anything. Note that you don't have to set every property of every object; the default values of many properties are often perfectly acceptable.

Although many properties can be altered both at design time and when the application is running, the Properties window, shown in Figure 1-5, is active only at design time. You can activate the Properties window in several ways: by simply clicking on it, by choosing the Properties command from the Window menu, by pressing F4, or by clicking on the Properties Window button on the Toolbar.

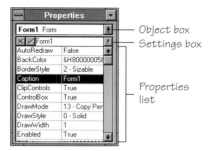

Figure 1-5.
The Properties window.

The drop-down list box at the top of the Properties window is called the Object box. It displays the name of each object in the application as well as the type of object. Initially, the Object box contains information for the form only; but as you add controls to the form, Visual Basic adds these objects to the drop-down list in the Object box.

Below the Object box, you'll find the Settings box and the Properties list. The Properties list allows you to scroll through a list of all the properties of the object displayed in the Object box and to see the current setting for each property. When you select a property from this list, its current setting appears in the Settings box above the Properties list. To change the setting, you can either type a new entry in the Settings box or choose a new predefined setting from a drop-down list, depending on the specific property.

To demonstrate how you can use the various Visual Basic windows to create an application, let's design your first project.

Creating a User Interface

As a first project, let's create a program that simply measures elapsed time, much as a stopwatch does. A stopwatch has a button that you click to start timing, another button that lets you stop the timing, and a face on which you read the elapsed time. You can use this model as a basis for your program. In Visual Basic, a form will serve as the watch face and the location for the start and stop buttons. To begin designing your application, you'll need to examine and modify some of the form's properties.

Setting the Form's Properties

When the application is running, the form will be presented in a standard application window. If you want this window to resemble those displayed by other applications written for Windows, it should have certain similar attributes. For example, one attribute shared by Windows-based applications is that the application's name appears as a caption in its title bar. In Visual Basic, many such attributes are controlled by the properties of the objects.

To begin setting the form properties, first select the form as the current object by clicking anywhere in the window labeled Form1. Now look at Visual Basic's Properties window, where Form1 is displayed in the Object box. To change the form's caption, click on the Caption property in the Properties list. The current (default) caption, Form1, will appear in the Settings box. Type *Stopwatch* as a replacement caption. As you type it, this new caption is displayed both in the Settings box and in the title bar of the form window.

Notice the two buttons to the left of the Settings box, which are marked with an X and a checkmark. The checkmark button confirms the setting you enter in the Settings box; clicking on this button is the equivalent of pressing the Enter key. Clicking on the X button cancels your current entry and restores the previous setting in the Settings box.

When a selected property can take on only a restricted, predefined set of values, the Settings box acts as a drop-down list box rather than as a text entry field. Scroll through the Properties list, and select the Visible property, for example. The down-arrow button beside the Settings box now becomes active, meaning that the settings for the Visible property are restricted to those available in the drop-down list. If you click on the down-arrow button, the list drops down to show the settings True and False, as shown in Figure 1-6. Be sure that the Visible property is set to True.

Figure 1-6.
Setting the form's Visible property.

Another property related to the form's appearance is BorderStyle, which controls whether or not the user can resize the display window when the application is running. Because the Stopwatch application will have a fixed appearance, its window should not be sizable. Select the BorderStyle property from the Properties list, and then set the property to 3 - Fixed Double by selecting this entry from the drop-down list in the Settings box. (Fixed Double specifies that the window will have a nonsizable border and no Minimize or Maximize button.)

The Name property

Every Visual Basic object has a property called Name. When you set the Name property, you give the object an identity that you can use within the program to refer to the object. In a form window, you can access an object by clicking on it. In the code portion of the program, you must refer to the object by the name you have assigned with the Name property. (Note that the Name property and the Caption property are different: An object's name is its identity in your program's code; an object's caption is what the user sees on the screen—the identifying text that is displayed in the application window.)

In the Properties list, select the form's Name property. Its default value, shown in the Settings box, is Form1. Edit the Name property of your form by typing the text *MyForm* in the Settings box.

> **Note:** *When you change a form name, Visual Basic reflects that change in the list of filenames displayed in the Project window. Remember that the definition of each form is stored in a separate file. When you save your application, you can choose any filename you like for your form, but Visual Basic will suggest a default filename based on the form name.*

Adding Display Objects

Let's return to the form design to create the buttons that start and stop the timer:

1. Click on the Command Button tool in the Toolbox, and then move the mouse pointer to the blank form window. The cursor changes to a crosshair, indicating that you are in a drawing mode.

2. Position the cursor in the upper left corner of the form.

3. Hold down the mouse button and drag the cursor downward and to the right.

4. Release the mouse button.

When you release the mouse button, Visual Basic creates a command button object in the rectangular area delineated by the drag operation. Your command button should resemble the one shown in Figure 1-7.

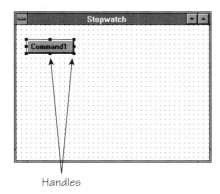

Handles

Figure 1-7.
A newly created command button.

After you have created the command button, the Pointer tool again becomes the active tool in the Toolbox. When the Pointer tool is active, you can edit the form by moving objects and by resizing them. To move an object, simply drag it to the new location. To resize an object, drag one of its handles (shown in Figure 1-7) to expand or shrink it. If the handles aren't visible, click on the object to select it.

Now create a second command button, this time using a shortcut: Double-click on the Command Button tool in the Toolbox. Visual Basic creates a button of default size and places it in the center of the form. Position and resize the second button so that both buttons appear on the left side of the screen and are the same size.

These two buttons, now labeled Command1 and Command2 by default, will serve as start and stop buttons for the Stopwatch application. For clarity, you should assign their captions accordingly. To set these button properties, you follow the same process you followed for setting the form's properties:

1. Click on the top command button to select it.

2. Select the Caption property from the Properties list in the Properties window.

3. In the Settings box, change the setting to Start.

4. Click on the bottom command button and change its Caption setting to Stop.

Even though you have just changed the captions, you should also change the names of the buttons so that you can refer to them easily in your program code. (Remember

Choosing Names

It is not absolutely necessary to rename the buttons in the Stopwatch application you are creating, but you will find that referring to btnStart in your program is much clearer than referring to Command1. T.S. Eliot cautioned: "The Naming of Cats is a difficult matter"; the same is true of objects in programs. You might decide that short names are easy to type, or you might find it convenient to let the system supply a default name. But when you return to a program six months after you wrote it, it could be very difficult to determine exactly what the program is doing if you haven't selected meaningful names.

You should also try to use a consistent naming convention that supplies both context and description. The names btnStart and btnStop, for example, have a three-letter prefix that identifies the type of object in your program code. In English, we often use descriptive phrases to establish context—for instance, rather than simply mentioning "Cardinal Fang," I might refer to "my cat, Cardinal Fang," to avoid any potential confusion between my cat and some ecclesiastical official. In Visual Basic, however, you cannot refer to "the button named Start," so it's useful to compress the context (btn) and the name (Start) into a single identifier (btnStart).

that the Caption property and the Name property are not the same; changing one does not affect the other.) Click on the top button and select its Name property. In the Settings box, change the default name Command1 to btnStart. Then click on the bottom button and change its Name property setting to btnStop. (See the sidebar titled "Choosing Names" on the previous page.)

Completing the Display

Now that you have positioned the user controls for the Stopwatch application on the screen, you need a place to display the results produced when the program is run. Let's add several text boxes to the form:

1. Double-click on the Text Box tool in the Toolbox to create a text box. The text box will appear in the center of the form.

2. Move the text box to the upper area of the form window, to the right of the command buttons.

3. Using the same method, create two more text boxes, arranging the three boxes as shown here:

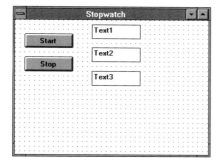

4. Use the mouse to "grab" the lower right corner of the form window and resize the form so that it fits snugly around the buttons and text boxes.

You need to give these new objects names. Click on each text box and change its Name property setting, using the name txtStart for the top text box, txtStop for the middle text box, and txtElapsed for the bottom text box.

You also need to remove the default text that appears inside the boxes. For each text box, select the Text property from the Properties list, and delete all the characters in the Settings box. This action sets the value of the Text property to empty (a zero-length text string).

All the necessary elements for the user-interface portion of your application are now in place. In fact, you can "run" the application as it currently exists. Choose the Start command from the Run menu, click on the Toolbar's Start button, or press the F5 key. The Toolbox palette disappears, as does the design version of the form, and the

Stopwatch window is displayed, as shown in Figure 1-8. You can move the window around on the screen, and you can also click on the Start and Stop buttons (although nothing will happen, because you have not yet written the Visual Basic statements that compute the elapsed time). Choose the End command from Visual Basic's Run menu or click on the End button on the Toolbar to quit the application and return to the Visual Basic design environment.

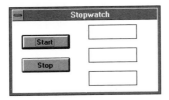

Figure 1-8.
The Stopwatch application window at runtime.

Writing Code

Coding—writing the language statements that control a program's operation—is the heart of programming. Now that you've completed your application's interface, you need to make the program work. Because you will be writing commands in the Visual Basic language, it is reasonable to think of those commands as controlling the computer, although they do so in an indirect manner. To understand this notion, consider a jet airplane.

When the pilot of a jet wants to fly higher, he or she must pull back on the control stick in the cockpit of the plane. The effect of this action is to alter the position of the plane's elevators, and the jet begins to go up. In a modern jet, no physical connection exists between the stick and the elevators. When the pilot pulls back on the stick, a sensor measures the distance the stick has moved and sends a signal to a hydraulic device that repositions the elevators. From the point of view of the pilot, however, the stick controls the plane. It's not critical that the pilot know whether a 1-inch pull of the stick translates to a 5-degree swing in the elevators' position or a 10-degree swing; it's sufficient that the pilot knows how the plane responds to the change.

Like the pilot of the jet, you are at the controls of your computer, and Visual Basic is your instrument panel. The following section concentrates on giving you a "cockpit view" of the system—that is, how it looks to a Visual Basic programmer. A lot is going on under the surface, of course, but for the moment we'll simply focus on an overview and save discussion of the relevant details about the underlying system for Chapters 2 and 3.

Event Procedures

You have already learned about the properties of objects and how these properties can be modified to affect an object. In a somewhat similar manner, each object can be associated with a collection of procedures that are executed at specific times. A *procedure* is a group of statements in the Visual Basic programming language. The statemt nts in the procedure are executed when the procedure is run. All the executable code you write will be encapsulated in one kind of procedure or another.

Every procedure associated with an object is tied to a particular *event,* or action, and therefore is called an *event procedure.* Events include actions such as Click, an event triggered when the user clicks the mouse button, and Resize, an event that occurs when the user changes the size of a form window. Events occur only at runtime, not during design. For every object, a number of events can be triggered; these are described more completely in Chapter 5.

Let's return to our Stopwatch application. In the form window, double-click on the Start button. Visual Basic will open a *code window* like the one shown in Figure 1-9. The code window's caption is MyForm.frm, which indicates the relationship between the code and the form. The code you enter in this window will be stored in the same file that contains the form's display objects.

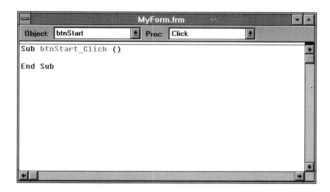

Figure 1-9.
A Visual Basic code window for Stopwatch.

The Object box in the upper left portion of the code window displays the name of the object you selected: btnStart. The Procedure box (abbreviated as Proc) in the upper right shows which event procedure you are editing. Because you have not yet selected a procedure, Visual Basic has chosen a likely default, the *Click* event procedure. The procedure shown in the code window is the one that will be executed when the user clicks on the Start button while the application is running. Although you have not written any code, two statements already appear in the text portion of the code window:

```
Sub btnStart_Click ()

End Sub
```

When you created this command button, Visual Basic created a set of default event procedures for the object. As you might guess, the default procedures do nothing; they simply consist of a procedure declaration (the first line) and the statement marking the end of the procedure (*End Sub*).

Procedure declarations

In the procedure declaration, the keyword *Sub* identifies the beginning of a procedure. Next comes the name of the procedure—in this case, *btnStart_Click*. Following that is a set of parentheses, which completes the definition. (The parentheses aren't used in this procedure, although they must be included; we'll discuss their function in a later chapter.)

The name of a procedure serves to distinguish it as an event procedure. Not all procedures are event procedures. You can create a procedure in Visual Basic and give it any name you like—even *Spot* or *Puff*, if you are so inclined. But an event procedure must be named according to the following rules:

■ The first part of the name must match the name of an object you have created on the form (or must be the word *Form*, when the relevant object is the form itself).

■ The last part of the name must be an event name.

■ The two parts must be separated by an underscore (_).

For the *btnStart_Click* procedure, the associated object is the Start command button (btnStart), and the event is the Click event. When the program is running, the scenario goes something like this: The application is hanging out at the corner CRT, waiting for something to happen. Along comes Jane User with her mouse. She moves the mouse pointer over the image on the screen and clicks. Windows kicks the application in the pants and says, "Hey, do something!" When Visual Basic figures out that the click occurred on top of the button named btnStart, it goes looking for the *btnStart_Click* procedure and executes the statements in that procedure. As a programmer, your job is to decide what those statements should be.

To get a feel for how this works, type the statement *Debug.Print "Hello, sailor"* in the blank line between the *Sub* and *End* statements. The code window should now look like this:

```
Sub btnStart_Click ()
    Debug.Print "Hello, sailor"
End Sub
```

The *Debug.Print* statement tells Visual Basic to write text to a special window called the Debug window. Press the F5 key to leave design mode and start to run the application (such as it is). When you click on the Start button, the words *Hello, sailor* are written to the Debug window.

Now choose the End command from Visual Basic's Run menu. Visual Basic will halt the application and return to design mode, where you can continue designing your application. (Before moving on, remember to delete the *Debug.Print* line from the *btnStart_Click* procedure.)

> ***Tip:*** *Notice that keywords such as* Sub, Debug, Print, *and* End *appear on the code window's screen in a different color than the rest of the code does. Visual Basic flags different parts of the code with various colors to make individual components easy to find. You can control the colors that are used by choosing the Environment command from the Options menu. This displays the Environment Options dialog box, in which you can set both the text color and the background color for keywords, identifiers, comments, and a number of other code elements.*

Variable declarations

When the user clicks on the Start button in the Stopwatch application, the program must figure out what time it is (the starting time). Then, when the user clicks on the Stop button, the program must subtract the starting time from the ending time to calculate the total elapsed time. Of course, you need to write the code that enables the program to perform these actions.

Visual Basic uses a function named *Now* to provide the current time. A *function* is a special kind of procedure that returns a value. (Visual Basic functions are closely related to the mathematical concept of functions. The Visual Basic functions named *Sin*, *Cos*, and *Tan*, for example, return the sine, cosine, and tangent of an angle.) When the user clicks on the Start button, your program must call the function *Now*, which returns a value—the current (starting) time. The program must then "remember" this value so that it can be subtracted from the ending time when the user

---

Visual Basic Is Watching You

If you happen to make a mistake while typing in the code window, Visual Basic might notify you by highlighting the mistake and displaying an information dialog box. This surveillance, called *automatic syntax checking,* occurs each time you press the Enter key. Visual Basic cannot detect all possible errors as you type, of course, but it does check for *syntax* errors—that is, mistakes in how the Visual Basic language is used, such as misspelled keywords, words out of order in a statement, incorrect punctuation, and so forth. If you type *txtStop..Text* instead of *txtStop.Text,* for example, Visual Basic will inform you of your mistake. You can turn off automatic syntax checking if you want: Choose Environment from the Options menu and set the Syntax Checking option to No in the Environment Options dialog box.

clicks on the Stop button. To save a value in a computer program, you must reserve a place for the value in the computer's memory. You can do this with *variable declarations.*

In the code window, click on the down-arrow button of the Object box to drop down the list of all the objects on the form. From this list, select the entry (general), which is the category for all code not associated with a particular object. Visual Basic then automatically changes the setting in the Procedure box to (declarations). (We'll refer to this throughout the book as the general declarations section of your code.) Now enter the following lines in the code window:

```
Dim StartTime As Variant
Dim EndTime As Variant
Dim ElapsedTime As Variant
```

These statements tell Visual Basic that you want to reserve storage for the starting, ending, and elapsed time values in the variables called *StartTime*, *EndTime*, and *ElapsedTime*. *Variables* are essentially names for reserved portions of computer memory. (More on this in Chapters 2 and 3.) The *Dim* statement tells Visual Basic what memory to reserve and what to call that portion of memory. The *Dim* statement is a *declaration* because it tells Visual Basic how the program should be set up.

Each of the three statements shown above declares a single variable, and all three have this form:

Dim *name* As Variant

Dim and *As* are *keywords,* reserved words that have special meaning for Visual Basic. The statements differ only because a different name must be provided for each variable. The keyword *Variant* tells Visual Basic to reserve enough memory for any kind of value. (You could use other keywords to make the declaration more specific. Using *Integer* instead of *Variant*, for instance, would instruct Visual Basic to reserve only enough memory for an integer.)

Executable statements

Now that you have reserved memory to save the time values, you can write the program's executable code. In contrast to a declaration, which sets up the program, an *executable statement* makes something happen when it is executed. For example, the *Debug.Print* statement you used earlier is an executable statement.

Terminology

If *Dim* seems like a rather silly word and you think something like *Declare* would be more appropriate, you are right. *Dim*, however, is short for *Dimension* and is an artifact of the earliest versions of the Basic language, dating back to the 1960s. As computer languages evolve, they tend to retain features of earlier versions for the sake of compatibility.

In the code window's Object box, select the btnStart object. Edit the *btnStart_Click* procedure by entering these statements between the line *Sub btnStart_Click ()* and the line *End Sub*:

```
StartTime = Now
txtStart.Text = Format(StartTime, "hh:mm:ss")
txtStop.Text = ""
txtElapsed.Text = ""
```

When your program is running and the user clicks on the Start button, these commands are executed. The first line of code uses the *Now* function to retrieve the current time and then saves it in the storage location named *StartTime*. The next line displays the time in the top text box (txtStart) by setting the Text property of this object; it also formats the starting time as hours, minutes, and seconds using a Visual Basic function called *Format*. The next two lines clear any existing display from the other two text boxes (txtStop and txtElapsed) by setting their Text properties to empty strings.

Now complete the program by selecting the btnStop object in the code window's Object box. Edit its *Click* event procedure as shown here:

```
Sub btnStop_Click ()
    EndTime = Now
    ElapsedTime = EndTime - StartTime
    txtStop.Text = Format(EndTime, "hh:mm:ss")
    txtElapsed.Text = Format(ElapsedTime, "hh:mm:ss")
End Sub
```

This procedure executes when the user clicks on the Stop button. First the *Now* function returns the current time, which is saved in the *EndTime* variable. The next line computes the elapsed time by subtracting the saved *StartTime* value from *EndTime*. Then the ending time and the elapsed time are written to the screen by setting the Text properties of the objects txtStop and txtElapsed. As it did in the *btnStart_Click* procedure, the *Format* function converts the time values to the format that displays hours, minutes, and seconds.

Running the Program

Simply press F5 to start the application. Use the "stopwatch" by clicking on the Start button, waiting a few seconds, and then clicking on the Stop button. You should see something like the result shown in Figure 1-10 on the following page.

You can click on the Start button again to restart the stopwatch. To close the Stopwatch application, click on the Toolbar's End button, press Alt-F4, or choose Close from the Control menu (the menu that appears when you click on the box in the upper left corner of a window, sometimes referred to as the system menu).

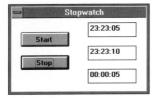

Figure 1-10.
Running the Stopwatch application.

Reviewing the Design

It's easy to get so caught up in the details of programming that you don't think about the user of the program. Let's look again at the design of the Stopwatch interface: two buttons, three text boxes. Pretty simple. But consider the person who doesn't know the purpose of the program. The terms *start* and *stop* are self-explanatory, but what information can be gleaned from three blank text boxes? One obvious improvement you can make is to label those boxes so that it's clear what information they provide.

The icon on the Label tool in the Toolbox looks like a capital A. Using the Label tool, draw a label object next to the top text box in the form window. You might need to resize the form and move the text boxes to the right to make room for the label. You can select all three text boxes at once so that you can move them as a group: Simply click on the top text box and then hold down the Ctrl key while you click on the other two text boxes.

Next click on the new label object, select the label's Caption property in the Properties list, and type *Starting Time:* in the Settings box. Then create two similar label objects next to the other text boxes, and set the Caption property to *Ending Time:* for one and *Elapsed Time:* for the other, as shown in Figure 1-11.

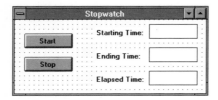

Figure 1-11.
Adding labels to the text boxes.

Any other design improvements to consider? Press F5 to run the application again, and then try clicking on the Stop button before clicking on Start. The application should respond in a reasonable manner to this user mistake, but instead you get a strange result: The ending and elapsed times are displayed with no starting time. You'll need to quit the application and return to design mode to fix the problem.

Given the current design, the simplest way to solve this problem is to disallow use of the Stop button until the user has first clicked on the Start button. In the form window, click on the Stop button to select it, and then select the Enabled property from the Properties list. Set the property to False in the Settings box. Now the Stop button will be disabled when the application first begins.

Open the code window and edit the *btnStart_Click* procedure to appear as shown here (adding the two lines that appear in color). You can use the cursor keys to move the insertion point in the code window, or you can simply click with the mouse to set a new insertion point.

```
Sub btnStart_Click ()
    StartTime = Now
    txtStart.Text = Format(StartTime, "hh:mm:ss")
    txtStop.Text = ""
    txtElapsed.Text = ""
    btnStop.Enabled = True
    btnStart.Enabled = False
End Sub
```

The new code reenables the Stop button after the user clicks on the Start button. It then disables the Start button, which eliminates another potential error: clicking on the Start button twice in succession.

To complete the changes, you also need to edit the *btnStop_Click* procedure, adding two lines as shown here:

```
Sub btnStop_Click ()
    EndTime = Now
    ElapsedTime = EndTime - StartTime
    txtStop.Text = Format(EndTime, "hh:mm:ss")
    txtElapsed.Text = Format(ElapsedTime, "hh:mm:ss")
    btnStop.Enabled = False
    btnStart.Enabled = True
End Sub
```

Figure 1-12 shows the final version of the application interface. In this illustration, the user has clicked on the Start button and the stopwatch is running.

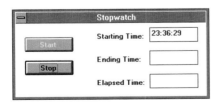

Figure 1-12.
The final version of the Stopwatch application.

The changes you just made were only a few of the many possible ways that the program could be improved. For example, because many stopwatches have only a single button, you could implement the program with one command button and change the button's caption from Start to Stop (or vice versa) each time it is clicked. You can probably think of other improvements.

Saving Your Program

You have one more practical concern: saving your program. In this case, your first step should be to select the filename CMDIALOG.VBX in the Project window and choose the Remove File command from the File menu. Repeat the process for the filename GRID.VBX and MSOLE2.VBX. Because you did not use these tools, you do not need to save the files as part of this project.

Now choose the Save Project command from Visual Basic's File menu or click on the Save Project button on the Toolbar. In the Save File As dialog box, shown in Figure 1-13, Visual Basic prompts you for the name of the file and the directory in which to save the form's code and its display layout, suggesting the default filename MYFORM.FRM (the name of the form plus the FRM extension) for the Stopwatch application. After you supply the necessary information, click on OK.

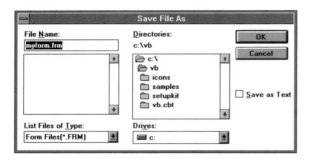

Figure 1-13.
The Save File As dialog box.

Next Visual Basic displays the Save Project As dialog box, shown in Figure 1-14, which allows you to save the project file. The project file contains the names of all the form files and some additional information about the project. (The Stopwatch application has only one form file.) Visual Basic will suggest the default filename PROJECT1.MAK for this application's project file. You can use a different filename, but you must include the filename extension MAK for project files. For now, save the Stopwatch application with the filename STOPW.MAK. (We'll return to this project in a later chapter.)

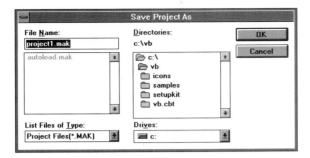

Figure 1-14.
The Save Project As dialog box.

To load and execute your application later on, you must first run Visual Basic. (To create a version of the application that will run like any other Windows executable program, without Visual Basic, you must compile the program, as you'll learn in Chapter 2.) Then choose the Open Project command from Visual Basic's File menu or click on the Open Project button on the Toolbar. The Open Project dialog box displays a list of all the project files (all the files with the extension MAK). Open the STOPW.MAK file by double-clicking on the filename in the list or by selecting the filename and clicking on the OK button. Press F5 to run the application, or, if you want to edit it further, open the form or code window by clicking on the appropriate button in the Project window.

2

Data and Instructions

You're undoubtedly familiar with much of the terminology used in the computer industry: bits, bytes, RAM, ROM, CPU, and so on. But if you have only a general idea of what these terms mean, the next few sections are for you. Understanding what's happening inside the computer is an important part of learning to program. You can, of course, simply "learn the rules" and do an adequate job, but a little additional knowledge can go a long way toward helping you be comfortable and productive with computers.

Computers and Data

Computers are tools for manipulating information, much as hammers and saws are tools for manipulating wood. Wood is measured in inches or centimeters; information is measured in bits. A *bit* is the fundamental unit that measures how much information can be transferred from one place to another. It is the atomic building block of the information universe. The answer to a question, for example, requires at least one bit of information—no bits, no answer. On paper, a bit is conventionally represented by the number 0 or 1. In a digital computer, a bit is represented by the existence or nonexistence of electrical current.

If you have 3 inches of wood, you know that you're dealing with a fixed amount of tangible material. But what does it mean to have 3 bits of information? It means, as Humpty Dumpty said to Alice, "just what I choose it to mean." As illustrated in Figure 2-1 on the next page, 3 bits could represent answers to the three questions "Is it bigger than a breadbox? Is it brightly colored? Can it sing?" (no, yes, no); a series of left or right turns (left, right, left); or any number of other examples.

The meaning of the information represented by bits depends on the context. To understand this, imagine that a friend walks up to you on the street and says, "Forty-two." Your immediate reaction is probably bewilderment. But if you had first greeted your acquaintance with a question such as "How old are you?" or "What's the frequency, Kenneth?" his response would have had an obvious meaning. Your question provides a context for understanding the answer. Alternatively, you might have just loaned your friend a copy of Douglas Adams's *Hitchhiker's Guide to the Galaxy,* and you would therefore understand the greeting "Forty-two" immediately. In this case, the context is inferred.

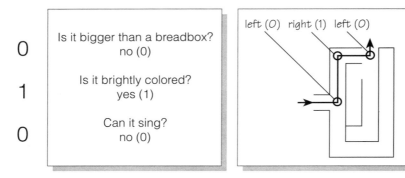

Figure 2-1.
Bits representing information.

In a computer, some contexts are more likely than others. One common context is numeric. Because bits are written as 0s and 1s, a group of them can represent a *binary number* (a value in the base 2 number system).

Representing Numeric Values

The decimal (base 10) number system uses ten symbols to stand for numeric values: 0, 1, 2, 3, 4, 5, 6, 7, 8, and 9. (Keep in mind that these digits are merely symbols; the Romans, for example, used the symbol V to represent the numeric value 5 and X to represent the value 10.) To represent a value greater than 9 in the decimal number system—10, for example—two of the symbols are combined, and the *positions* of the symbols are given special meaning. The progression of values represented by the positions, as shown in Figure 2-2, corresponds to increasing powers of 10. A decimal number that consists of more than one position is the sum of various powers of 10: The number 10, for instance, stands for the sum of 1 ten (10^1) and 0 ones (10^0); the number 423 stands for the sum of 4 hundreds (10^2), 2 tens (10^1), and 3 ones (10^0); and so forth.

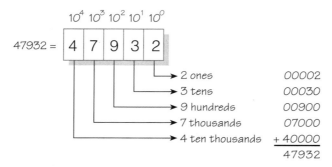

Figure 2-2.
Positional values in the decimal number system.

This general method of representing numbers can be used with bases other than 10. For example, the base 7 number system uses the seven digits 0, 1, 2, 3, 4, 5, and 6, and the value of each position increases by a power of 7, as shown in Figure 2-3. (A subscript following a number denotes the base; numbers without a subscript are assumed to be base 10 unless otherwise indicated.)

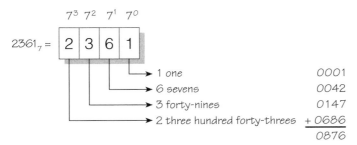

Figure 2-3.
Positional values in the base 7 number system.

Surely you're onto the game by now. The binary system uses two digits (0 and 1), and each position represents an increase in value by a power of 2. (See Figure 2-4.) For allowing computers to represent numbers, the binary system is just the ticket. You, of course, can do arithmetic in any number system just as easily as you can do it in base 10; computers must add, subtract, multiply, and divide using only binary numbers.

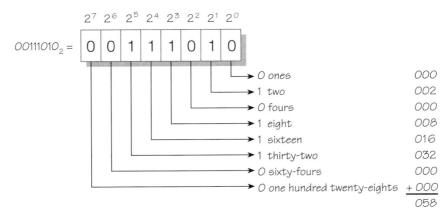

Figure 2-4.
Positional values in the binary number system.

Representing Characters

In most cases, it's insufficient to represent only numeric information. How can you move beyond the context of mere numbers? One possible way is to use a standard code. In International Morse code, used for sending telegraph signals, certain patterns of sounds represent letters of the alphabet: three "dots" in quick succession stand for the letter *S;* three "dots" followed by a "dash" stand for the letter *V;* and so forth. In much the same way that dots and dashes are combined to form a code, 0s and 1s can be combined into a code for computers.

The ASCII (American Standard Code for Information Interchange) standard specifies just such a code. ASCII code uses numeric values to define the standard English-language character set, including uppercase and lowercase letters, numerals, punctuation marks, and symbols. (As an aside, look for the Anglocentric ASCII to be replaced in the next decade with UNICODE, a standard that supports characters with nonroman alphabets such as Arabic and Cyrillic.) The extended version of ASCII used in most modern computer systems uses 8 bits to represent each letter, number, punctuation mark, and other codes used in textual data. Some examples of ASCII code are shown in Figure 2-5.

Character	ASCII Value (Binary)	ASCII Value (Decimal)
A	01000001	65
B	01000010	66
a	01100001	97
b	01100010	98
$	00100100	36
3	00110011	51
+	00101011	43
Z	01011010	90

Figure 2-5.
ASCII encoding of sample character data.

Remember, however, that merely examining a particular set of bits does not tell you the context. For example, the pattern 01000001 represents the letter *A* in ASCII code, but it is also the binary representation of the decimal number 65. The interpretation depends on the context. Sometimes you can take advantage of this, making use of the value as both a character and an integer. For example, the fact that each character has a numeric value means that you can test whether a character is uppercase by checking to see if its numeric value is greater than or equal to 65 (ASCII "A") and less than or equal to 90 (ASCII "Z").

Using Bits, Bytes, and Words

Using bits to represent information, a computer system can store or "remember" the information. Organizing memory on a bit-by-bit basis is inconvenient, however, because a single bit really doesn't represent much information. With the extended ASCII code, for instance, at least 8 bits are needed to represent a single character.

In fact, one character's worth of information serves as a standard unit of measure. This standard unit of 8 bits is called a *byte*. To refer to large quantities of data, the metric prefixes *kilo*, *mega*, and *giga* are added to the term *byte*. Because of computer scientists' fondness for powers of 2, a *kilobyte* stands for 1024 (2^{10}) bytes, and a *megabyte* stands for 1,048,576 (2^{20}) bytes. After the *gigabyte* (2^{30}) comes the *terabyte* (2^{40}), and then the *petabyte* (2^{50}). You don't need to be terribly concerned about what comes after that.

But a byte is not appropriate for representing most numeric values. The standard 8 bits can represent only the decimal numbers 0 through 255. Most computers therefore deal with data in chunks that are larger than a byte, to allow efficient arithmetic operations. The number of bits that a computer "prefers" to use is called the *word size* of the computer and is not standardized. Many mainframe computers and modern microcomputers have a word size of 32 bits, which accommodates binary numbers into the billions. (Although the hardware is optimized to use this word size, these computers are not limited to 32-bit values.)

Storing Information in the Computer

Figure 2-6 shows a simple block diagram of a computer. In terms of the diagram, you can think of *memory* as the box where bits are stored when the computer is running. For the moment, we'll restrict our discussion to the electronic memory called RAM (*random access memory*).

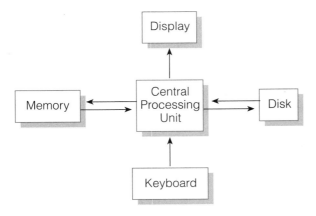

Figure 2-6.
A block diagram of a computer system.

You can think of RAM as a long row of boxes, with each box just big enough to hold 1 byte of data and each box identified by a number. For example, one might say, "Get me the byte of data in box 27441," or "Put the letter *g* in box 13." The identifying number of a memory location is called its *address*.

As you learned in Chapter 1, Visual Basic allows you to use names rather than numbers to refer to memory locations. (The computer is well equipped to use numeric addresses, but humans are more comfortable with symbolic variable names.) Each Visual Basic variable corresponds to a memory location, although in Visual Basic you can give a name to a collection of sequential bytes, rather than addressing each byte singly. In Chapter 3, you'll learn more about how Visual Basic stores and represents different types of data.

Computer Instructions

Let's look now at what your computer system does with the data it contains. Inside your computer, one or two chips act as the *central processing unit* (CPU). The CPU manipulates the data in memory according to a collection of instructions called a *program*. To enable the CPU to execute the instructions, the program must reside in RAM. Instructions, like data, must therefore be represented by sequences of bits.

The instructions tell the computer to perform simple, specific actions, such as adding, subtracting, comparing, or copying bits from one location in memory to another. Other instructions send information to external input/output (I/O) devices such as your hard disk or display monitor. For example, a particular bit pattern could represent the instruction "Add 1 to the number in memory location 732" or "Write the letter *M* to output device number 3." The bit patterns that control a processor differ from CPU to CPU. (This is why programs written for the IBM PC won't run on the Apple Macintosh, and vice versa.) The complete list of all the instructions that control a particular processor is called the processor's *instruction set*.

It is possible to write programs by directly entering the bit patterns that constitute each instruction. This method, referred to as programming in *machine language,* is rarely used. Somewhat more commonly, people program in *assembly language,* in which a special character string, such as *ADD* or *TEST,* corresponds to each machine language instruction. A program called the *assembler* translates the character strings written by the programmer into machine language, as illustrated in Figure 2-7. Although programming in assembly language is significantly less painful (and less error-prone) than programming in machine language, the programmer still must specify every instruction the processor is to undertake. The single act of accepting a keystroke from the keyboard takes dozens of machine instructions. Consequently, even the simplest program requires the execution of thousands of instructions, and complex programs consist of millions of instructions.

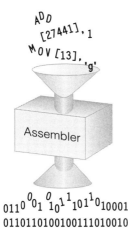

Figure 2-7.
An assembler at work.

Compilers and Interpreters

Special programs called *compilers* can help you avoid the burdensome detail of programming in assembly language. A compiler allows a programmer to write commands that are far more productive than assembly or machine instructions; one Basic command, for example, typically translates into many machine instructions. The programmer writes commands in the *source language* of the compiler, which then translates the source language into machine language. Common source languages in use today include C, Pascal, and Basic. Figure 2-8 on the following page illustrates how a compiler works.

To simplify, a compiler or an assembler reads a file of statements written by the programmer and produces a machine code file as output. The machine code program is then executed to produce the desired result. In the MS-DOS and Microsoft Windows operating systems, a file with the extension EXE or COM contains machine code and can be loaded directly into memory and executed.

Interpreters, which also translate source code statements, are similar to compilers. However, an interpreter translates a single line of source code and then immediately executes the resulting machine code. The interpreter then goes back to the source code and translates the next line. Figure 2-9 on page 31 contrasts compilers and interpreters. Another way to understand the difference is to imagine how the translation of a book into a foreign language differs from the "real-time" foreign-language interpreting provided by United Nations interpreters. The process of translating a book is similar to the job a compiler does: A translator receives the Russian edition of *War and Peace* and, after many years of labor, produces a new book with the same text in Urdu. The Russian-to-Urdu interpreter at the UN, however, deals with each spoken statement immediately, as a computer interpreter does.

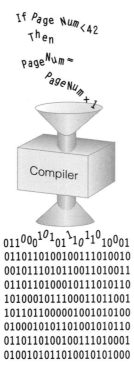

Figure 2-8.
Compiling source language into machine language.

Compilers and interpreters each have advantages. Compilers do their translation work once and then give you an executable file that can be run at any time. Interpreters give you quick feedback and can help you detect errors. Visual Basic contains both a compiler and an interpreter.

You have already encountered Visual Basic's interpreter. When you choose the Start command from the Run menu, Visual Basic translates the code you have written and begins to execute it. Chapter 8 explains how to suspend your program while it is running and issue commands directly to the interpreter in order to find and fix errors in your program code. When the interpreter is running, both the Visual Basic program and your application must be in memory at the same time.

You can also choose to compile your applications. A compiled application can run on any computer system that is running Windows; it does not require the Visual Basic program in order to work.

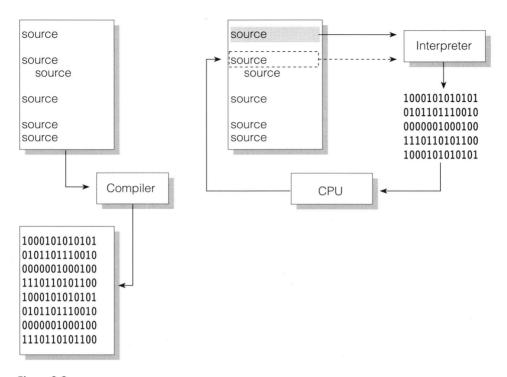

Figure 2-9.
Compiling and interpreting.

Compiling the Stopwatch Program

Let's try compiling the program you wrote in Chapter 1. If you are not running Visual Basic, start it now. Load the Stopwatch program by choosing the Open Project command from the File menu. Open STOPW.MAK, which is the project file for the Stopwatch program. To compile the application, choose Make EXE File from the File menu. In the Make EXE File dialog box, shown in Figure 2-10 on the following page, change the application title to Stopwatch. Set the directory to the location of your choice, enter the filename STOPW.EXE, and click on the OK button to close the dialog box. Visual Basic then compiles your program into machine code and writes it to the STOPW.EXE file.

Now try to run the compiled version of the Stopwatch program without Visual Basic. Exit Visual Basic by choosing Exit from the File menu. In Windows' Program Manager, choose the Run command from the File menu. In the Command Line text box of the Run dialog box, type the pathname of the Stopwatch program—for example, *\vb2\stopw.exe*—and click on OK. The application is loaded and executed.

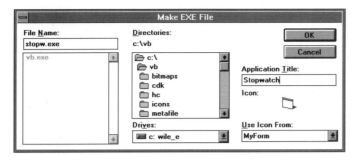

Figure 2-10.
The Make EXE File dialog box, which is used to compile programs.

You can give copies of the EXE version of your program to friends and co-workers, who will be able to run it even if Visual Basic is not installed on their computers. They will, however, need one additional file, named VBRUN300.DLL (which was added to your Windows system directory when you installed Visual Basic). Everyone who runs an application compiled by Visual Basic needs a copy of this file. (Because Microsoft explicitly allows you to distribute this file, you are not violating your Visual Basic licensing agreement if you give away a copy of VBRUN300.DLL with a compiled program.)

> ***Note:*** *Earlier versions of Visual Basic had files with similar names—for example, VBRUN100.DLL in version 1 and VBRUN200.DLL in version 2.*

VBRUN300.DLL contains a set of routines your program needs. Visual Basic doesn't compile every statement directly into machine code. Some statements—the ones that compute the current time, for example—are required so often that Visual Basic keeps a single copy of the necessary code available in VBRUN300.DLL. When your program requests the current time, the code in VBRUN300.DLL is executed. Because this file also contains the routines that handle basic elements such as windows and menus, even very simple programs need the resources provided in VBRUN300.DLL.

As you develop more sophisticated applications, you might need to include additional DLL files that are also part of Visual Basic. Visual Basic can help you create a setup disk (just like those provided in professional applications) that includes all the necessary components. See the programmer's manual section "Application Setup Wizard" when you reach this stage.

3

Variables and Constants

Chapter 2 raised the problem of determining whether a given piece of data is numeric, a character, or something completely different. Visual Basic helps you solve that problem by allowing you to specify various types of information.

Specifying Visual Basic Data Types

As you saw in Chapter 2, the bits 01000001 represent the letter A if the data is an ASCII character or the value 65 if the data is an 8-bit binary integer. You might resolve such ambiguity by developing special bit encodings for all sorts of information, but fortunately you are spared that task because Visual Basic defines a set of standard data representations, called *data types*. Figure 3-1 lists the names and characteristics of all the Visual Basic data types.

Name of Data Type	Description of Data	Range of Values	Storage Required
Integer	Numeric, integer	−32,768 through 32,767	16 bits (2 bytes)
Long	Numeric, integer	−2,147,483,648 through 2,147,483,647	32 bits (4 bytes)
String	Text	0 through approximately 65,500 characters	8 bits (1 byte) per character
Currency	Numeric, fixed decimal	−922,337,203,685,477.5808 through 922,337,203,685,477.5807	64 bits (8 bytes)
Single	Numeric, real	$\pm1.40 \times 10^{-45}$ through $\pm3.40 \times 10^{38}$	32 bits (4 bytes)
Double	Numeric, real	$\pm4.94 \times 10^{-324}$ through $\pm1.79 \times 10^{308}$	64 bits (8 bytes)
Variant	Adaptable	Any of the above	Depends on value stored

Figure 3-1.
Visual Basic data types.

The *integer* and *long* types are simple 16-bit and 32-bit integers, represented by binary values like the ones discussed in Chapter 2. Both of these types represent only numbers that have no fractional component. Integers require only 16 bits of memory but have a more restricted range than longs. (More on range in a moment.)

A *string* is a sequence of characters, each of which is represented with the ASCII coding scheme. A sequence that contains no characters is called an *empty string*.

The *currency* data type is specially designed to represent monetary values. A currency value always has a precision of four decimal places—that is, you can represent the value 11.1625 but not the value 21.00003. (The latter value would be rounded to 21.0000.)

The *single* and *double* types allow you to express floating-point numbers. *Floating-point numbers* (also called *real numbers*, or *reals* for short) represent values that have fractional components. The name *floating-point* comes from the "floating" decimal point, which can appear anywhere in the number, as in .000001, 356.876, and 100000.0. Contrast this with the currency type, which is an example of a *fixed-point* data type. Visual Basic also makes special use of the double type for encoding dates and times; you can find out more about this encoding technique in the Visual Basic reference manual.

Finally, Visual Basic includes the *variant* type, a sort of chameleon data type that can take on any value. Variants actually contain two pieces of information: a value, which can be any of the data types just discussed; and a code indicating the value's type (currency or string, for example).

Range

The most important characteristic of the numeric data types is their *range,* which limits the values a data type can take on. These limits are based on the number of bits used to encode the value. For example, consider Figure 3-2, which illustrates what happens when you try to count from 0 to 9 using a 3-bit binary number. With 3 bits, you can define only eight values. Consequently, some information gets lost, a condition referred to as *overflow* because the number of bits required to store the information overflows the number of available bits.

As a programmer, you must decide which data type to use for a given value. If you are writing very simple programs, you might reasonably avoid the question by always using the variant data type, which can represent any value. When your programs become more complex, however, you will need to choose more carefully, to deal with concerns of space and efficiency. (Variants are somewhat inefficient because Visual Basic must continually check each value to see what type it is.)

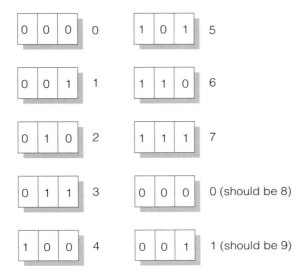

Figure 3-2.
Losing information as a result of overflow.

A Floating-Point Primer

When you work with floating-point numbers, you'll find that their precision is nearly as important as their range. Floating-point numbers have both a range, which defines the largest and smallest values they can represent, and a *precision,* which is the number of significant digits that a value contains.

Visual Basic stores floating-point numbers in a binary version of scientific notation. In scientific notation, values are expressed as a product of two numbers: a fraction and an exponent. In decimal scientific notation, for example, you can represent the distance between the earth and the sun as 5.84×10^{12} inches.

The fractional portion of a single is a binary value that expresses slightly more than 6 decimal digits of precision. The exponent allows the value to range from very small numbers (10^{-45}) to very large numbers (10^{38}). Doubles represent values of an even greater range (10^{-324} through 10^{308}), with approximately 13 digits of decimal precision.

If you find the idea of a 300-digit number having only 13 digits of precision a bit odd, consider this: The number 0.00000000017 seems very precise. In fact, that number has only 2 digits of precision. This is easier to visualize when you write the number in scientific notation: 1.7×10^{-10}. The fraction is only 1.7; the rest of the information (the exponent) tells you where to place the decimal point. As another example, consider the value 5.84×10^{12} inches. Although it represents a 13-digit number, you are concerned about precision only in the first 3 digits. The measurement could be off by thousands of inches, but the error isn't considered important.

This distinction between precision and range is subtle but important. Suppose you are hired by Immensely Big Megacorp to write a program that will keep track of the corporate accounts. This company takes in hundreds of billions of dollars in revenues every year. You might conclude that single reals would work nicely in your program because the range of a single extends to 10^{38}, which is considerably more than 100 billion (10^{11}). Unfortunately, you must be extremely accurate when you keep accounts, and the single data type doesn't have the precision to allow that kind of accuracy. If you started with an initial balance of \$121,734,240,722, for example, you'd need 12 digits of precision to represent the balance because each of the 12 digits in that value is significant. A single-precision real can represent a value in that range, but it can have only slightly more than 6 significant digits—that is, it could represent only the value 1.217342×10^{11}, or 121,734,200,000. Your first day on the job, and you've already lost \$40,722!

> *Note:* *Visual Basic's currency data type is perfect for dealing with monetary amounts. It provides 18 digits of accuracy and always keeps 4 of those digits to the right of the decimal point. A variable of the type double provides the same range and precision, but the currency type, which is fixed point and not subject to rounding, is preferable when you are dealing with dollars and cents.*

Of course, you needn't disdain the single data type if it is appropriate. For example, if you are working with physics equations and measuring the number of atoms in an ounce of silicon (approximately 6.02×10^{23}), a single-precision real will serve your purpose admirably—unless you plan to count the atoms very, very carefully!

Creating Variables and Constants

Regardless of its type, merely storing data in memory is of no use unless you can refer to it in some way. Visual Basic lets you give names to memory locations so that you can access the data stored there. A named memory location is called a *variable*. The *Dim* statement, which informs Visual Basic of your intention to reserve storage, has the following syntax, or form:

Dim *variable* [As *type*]

When you use this statement, you must type the keyword *Dim* (shown in roman in the syntax line) and follow it with the specific variable name you want to use (indicated in italics in the syntax line). The phrase shown in brackets is optional; if you use it, type the keyword *As* and then specify the type, without including the brackets. (More on syntax notation in Chapter 5.) For example, this line of code tells

Visual Basic to reserve enough memory for currency type data (8 bytes) and to refer to that memory location with the name *SavingsAcct*:

```
Dim SavingsAcct As Currency
```

By using the variable name, you can later instruct Visual Basic to store new data at that location, retrieve it, modify it, and so on. If you omit the *As* clause, Visual Basic assumes that the variable is the variant type.

You can look at variables as if they were containers or boxes. The *Dim* statement creates a new box of a certain size and gives it a name, as illustrated in Figure 3-3. When you use the variable name in a program, Visual Basic provides you with the current contents of the container (the value currently stored there). The program you wrote in Chapter 1 used three variables: *StartTime*, *EndTime*, and *ElapsedTime*. As the program executed, it stored data values representing current time and elapsed time in those variables.

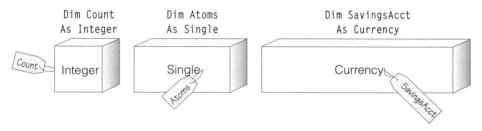

Figure 3-3.
Reserving storage with variable declarations.

When you reserve memory for a numeric variable, Visual Basic gives the variable an initial value of 0. But it's not a good idea to simply rely on this automatic initialization. Instead, if you want a variable to take on a value, you should assign it a value in your program. Explicitly assigning a value to a variable makes the program easier to read and avoids hidden assumptions. In addition, you should remember that automatic initialization is a feature specific to Visual Basic. If you convert your program to some other programming environment, the new system might not support initialization, and your program would no longer work.

From time to time, you will also want to use values that do not change—the value of *pi*, Avogadro's number, or the number of grams in an ounce, for example. Although you can use these numeric values directly in a program, it's easier to use a name such as PI than it is to repeat the number 3.1415926 each time it is needed.

For such fixed values, Visual Basic allows you to declare *constants,* which are reserved memory locations whose contents do not change (unlike the contents of variables). If you attempt to modify a constant, Visual Basic generates an error message. The *Const* statement declares a constant value and has this form:

Const *name* = *expression*

You don't need to declare the type of constant because Visual Basic simply determines the type based on its value: If you write *Const ANSWER = 42*, Visual Basic uses an integer; if you enter *Const FIRSTNAME = "Ross"*, it creates a string constant. (Names of constants are commonly written with all uppercase letters.)

Frequently some ambiguity exists about what type of constant Visual Basic should create. For example, the value 3.01 could be single, double, or currency. By default, Visual Basic chooses the representation that requires the least amount of memory. You can, however, force the issue by placing a special type-declaration character after the name. Use this character only in the declaration, not in the program itself. The Visual Basic type-declaration characters are listed in Figure 3-4.

Type-Declaration Character	Data Type Specified
%	Integer
&	Long
!	Single (real)
#	Double (real)
@	Currency (fixed-point)
$	String (character)

Figure 3-4.
The Visual Basic type-declaration characters.

Thus, the declaration *Const ONE& = 1* reserves 4 bytes of memory for a long constant, and the declaration *Const ONE# = 1* reserves 8 bytes and stores the value in a floating-point representation. In either case, you would use the name ONE (without the type-declaration character) in your program to refer to the value. You should get in the habit of defining constants for standard values; this practice will make your programs much easier to read.

> **Tip:** *Occasionally you might need to define a large constant—a value such as Avogadro's number, for instance. Avogadro's number, as I'm sure you remember, is 6.02×10^{23}. Fortunately, you don't have to type it in as 602000000000000000000000. Visual Basic allows you to enter single constants by specifying the fractional portion of the number (the mantissa) followed by the letter E followed by the exponent (6.02E23 in this case). For double constants, use the letter D instead of E (6.02D23).*

Rules for Names

When naming Visual Basic variables and constants, you must follow these rules:

- The first character of the name must be a letter.

- The subsequent characters in the name can be only letters, digits, or the underscore character (_).

- The name can contain no more than 40 characters.

- Keywords that have special meaning to Visual Basic, such as *Sub, Now,* and *End,* cannot be used as names. (If you are unsure whether a word is a Visual Basic keyword, press F1 to display the Help system and search for the topic *Reserved words.*)

These statements use illegal names:

```
Dim 1ceUponATime As Long        'Begins with a number
Const PRINT = 2                 'Print is a Visual Basic keyword
Dim This*is*it As Currency      'Asterisk character is not permitted
```

Comments

An apostrophe character (') prefaces a programmer's comments in Visual Basic code. The apostrophe, or *comment character,* allows you to insert remarks about your program anywhere in the code. Because Visual Basic ignores all characters to the right of the apostrophe, this text should contain only information or description that is useful to someone reading the program. When an apostrophe is the first character in a line, the entire line is a comment. Note that if your comment needs more than one line, you must precede each line with an apostrophe.

Here's what the *btnStart_Click* event procedure from the Stopwatch application in Chapter 1 might look like if you added comments:

```
Sub btnStart_Click ()
    'This procedure captures the time that the user clicked
    'on the Start button
    StartTime = Now                 'Store start time
    txtStart.Text = Format(StartTime, "hh:mm:ss")    'Display start time
    txtStop.Text = ""               'Clear stop time
    txtElapsed.Text = ""            'Clear elapsed time
    btnStop.Enabled = True          'Enable Stop button
    btnStart.Enabled = False        'Disable Start button
End Sub
```

The following statements are valid Visual Basic declarations:

```
Dim ThisIsALongVariableName As Integer
Dim RX7 As String
Const CM_PER_INCH = 2.54
```

Visual Basic pays no attention to the case of letters used in variable names; *HELLO*, *HeLLo*, and *hello* are identical variable names. After you define a variable name, Visual Basic will ensure that each reference to the variable conforms to the capitalization you used when you last entered the name. Programs are more readable when you use both uppercase and lowercase letters: Mixing case, for example, clarifies multiword variable names, and using all uppercase letters helps to identify constants.

Creating User-Defined Types

The data types that are built into Visual Basic are usually all you need for information that is easily broken down into individual text or numeric components, such as names, sizes, temperatures, and so on. But these data types can be inconvenient when you are working with information components that should be "clustered," or grouped together. Let's look at a specific example.

Suppose that your hobby is raising exotic animals and that you have acquired two Bavarian Tufted Forest weasels named Siegmund and Sieglinde. Eager to put your new programming skills to work, you decide to keep descriptive data about your pets in the computer, including data on the color, weight, length, and birthdate of the animals as well as the size and color of their tufts. (Long, silky tufts are the most valued characteristic of Bavarian Tufted Forest weasels.) You might begin by writing declarations such as these:

```
Dim Siegmund_Color As String
Dim Siegmund_Weight As Integer
Dim Siegmund_Length As Integer
Dim Siegmund_Birthdate As Double
Dim Siegmund_TuftColor As String
Dim Siegmund_TuftLength As Integer
```

And then you have to do it all over again for Sieglinde:

```
Dim Sieglinde_Color As String
Dim Sieglinde_Weight As Integer
Dim Sieglinde_Length As Integer
Dim Sieglinde_Birthdate As Double
Dim Sieglinde_TuftColor As String
Dim Sieglinde_TuftLength As Integer
```

It would be much easier to simply declare the relevant information once and be done with it. Visual Basic offers the perfect solution: creating your own data types.

A user-defined type is assembled from existing Visual Basic types: integers, strings, doubles, and so on. The Visual Basic keyword *Type* signals the beginning of a user-defined type declaration, as shown here:

```
Type BTFWeasel
    Color As String
    Weight As Integer
    Length As Integer
    Birthdate As Double
    TuftColor As String
    TuftLength As Integer
End Type
```

The type declaration consolidates all the information you believe to be important about your little furry friends. Note that you have not yet reserved any storage for the data; you have simply described to Visual Basic the structure or layout of the data. You can think of this declaration as a blueprint for the storage allocation. After you have defined the new type, you can create variables in the usual manner:

```
Dim Siegmund As BTFWeasel
Dim Sieglinde As BTFWeasel
```

These two statements create the variables *Siegmund* and *Sieglinde*—that is, storage is reserved and given the appropriate name. Each variable contains all the components of the data type you defined. In most programming languages, variables that contain multiple components are called *records,* and each separate component is called an *element* within the record. When you use the variable *Siegmund,* you refer to all the data (color, weight, birthdate, and so on) simultaneously. When you want to refer only to a single component, you can use the variable name followed by a period (.) and the component name. Thus, *Siegmund.Weight* is the integer data component that stores the weight value for the male, and *Sieglinde.Color* is the text string that describes the color of the female weasel's fur.

Practical Advantages

You should consider employing user-defined types whenever possible in your programs. Not only are they convenient, but they also make your programs easier to read and update. Consider the example of the weasel data. Your first attempt at creating variables involved 12 *Dim* statements, each defining an attribute of one of the weasels. To figure out what is going on, you must read all 12 statements to determine what attributes of Siegmund and Sieglinde are being declared. Even then, it's not clear whether other attributes are defined elsewhere, nor can you say with certainty that *Siegmund* and *Sieglinde* are related data items.

Contrast that confusion with the clarity of the user-defined type declaration. The attributes in the *Type* statement clearly belong to BTFWeasel. You can tell at a glance that the variables *Siegmund* and *Sieglinde* are both of the same type, and you can easily ascertain what specific information they contain. Furthermore, if you update the program later—deciding, for example, to add eye color to the collection of data you keep on the little critters—you can simply change the *Type* statement to update the definition for all the variables. Similarly, if your two weasels indulge in amorous behavior and present you with a baby weasel, you can add a variable for little Siegfried to the program with the single statement *Dim Siegfried As BTFWeasel.*

Déjà Vu

The way you access fields in user-defined types resembles the way you set the properties of the text box in the Stopwatch application (Chapter 1). In the Stopwatch program, you used the statement *txtElapsed.Text = Format(ElapsedTime,"hh:mm:ss")* to set the Text property of the txtElapsed display object.

Notice the similarity between the reference to *txtElapsed.Text* (which appears in the form *object.property*) in that statement and the references to variable components such as *Siegfried.Color* (which appear in the form *variable.element*). Each object is represented in memory; when you modify a property, you alter a component of that object. In some programming languages, *Siegmund* and *Sieglinde* would also be considered objects and their elements referred to as properties. Other common terminology describes a variable with many components as a *record* and refers to an individual element of the record as a *field*. This book uses the terms *field* and *element* interchangeably but reserves the word *property* to describe components of items that are specifically designated as objects by Visual Basic.

Determining Scope

Let's try an experiment:

1. Start Visual Basic, or choose the New Project command from the File menu to create a new project.

2. Create two command buttons on the form, one below the other. You can either double-click on the Command Button tool in the Toolbox or select the tool and draw the buttons on the form.

3. Select the first command button (Command1), and then select the Caption property from the Properties list in the Properties window. Set this button's caption to SetAndShow by typing this new caption in the Settings box. Then select the second command button and set its caption to Show, producing the results shown here:

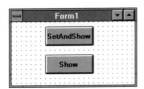

4. Double-click on the SetAndShow button to display the code window. In the code window, define the following *Click* procedure:

```
Sub Command1_Click ()
    Dim YourName As String
    YourName = InputBox("What is your name?")
    MsgBox "Your name is " + YourName
End Sub
```

Let's examine this set of instructions. The first line is the procedure declaration. The second line reserves storage for a string variable called *YourName*. The third line calls the *InputBox* function, a built-in function that displays a dialog box on the screen. The user types text in the dialog box, and the *InputBox* function returns the text as its value. The result is stored in the variable *YourName*. The fourth line of code uses the built-in procedure *MsgBox* to display a dialog box containing the text *Your name is*, followed by the value in *YourName*. The plus operator (+) *concatenates*, or "glues together," two strings; for example, the expression *"Hell" + "o, sailor"* is equivalent to the string *"Hello, sailor"*. Finally, the last line marks the end of the procedure.

5. Now select the Command2 button from the Object box in the code window, and enter the following code as its *Click* procedure:

```
Sub Command2_Click ()
    Dim YourName As String
    MsgBox "Hello, " + YourName
End Sub
```

This procedure will simply display the word *Hello* and the value of *YourName*. You can use the *MsgBox* procedure and the concatenation operator (+), just as you did in the previous procedure.

6. Close the code window, and press F5 to start this application.

7. Click on the SetAndShow button. Type a name in the input dialog box, and press Enter or click on the OK button. If you typed *Dorothy*, for example, the result should look like this:

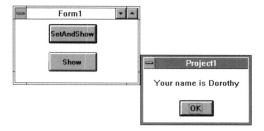

8. Click on OK to close the dialog box. Now click on the Show button. The dialog box displays the word *Hello*, but nothing else.

Why didn't Visual Basic preserve the value of the variable *YourName*? Why did this application behave differently than the Stopwatch application did in Chapter 1? There's a simple explanation: The Stopwatch program contained only one *Dim* statement, and it was not located inside a procedure. Let's try again, using the format that was successful in the Stopwatch application:

1. Press Alt-F4 to quit the application.

2. Double-click on the SetAndShow button in the form window to move to the code window, and delete the *Dim* statement from the *Click* procedure.

3. Select the Show button (Command2) from the Object box, and delete its *Dim* statement too.

4. Select (general) from the Object box. In this general declarations section, type the statement *Dim YourName As String*.

5. Close the code window and run the application again.

This time, the Show button is consistent with the SetAndShow button. You have just seen the effects of the scope of a variable.

Local and Module-Level Variables

The *scope* of a variable determines which procedures have access to the variable. The first time you ran the preceding example, you created two copies of the variable *YourName*, each of which was accessible only within its specific procedure. These are called *local variables*. The second time, you declared a single variable in the general declarations section of the form, making it a *module-level variable*. Variables declared this way are accessible to every procedure in the form. (The word *module* in this context essentially refers to a file; recall that all the code for a form is stored in a single file.) This difference between the two versions of the program is illustrated in Figure 3-5.

Constraining the scope of a variable is useful because it lets you reuse variable names. For example, if you add up a few numbers in one procedure, you can store the result in a local variable called *Sum*. If you write another procedure later that performs a similar but unrelated task, you can use the variable name *Sum* again without affecting the result of the other computation. Local scope allows each procedure to be a self-contained unit—that is, changes to other portions of the program do not interfere with the operation of a particular procedure.

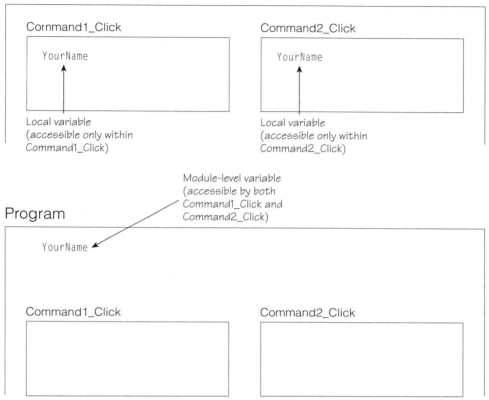

Figure 3-5.
Local variables versus module-level variables.

Global Variables

Module-level variables are visible only within one form. If you write a program with multiple forms, you will need some way of sharing information between the forms. Visual Basic therefore provides a third level of scope, *global variables*. Global variables are declared in code modules and are accessible from any part of the program. (We'll discuss code modules in the next section.) Figure 3-6 on the next page illustrates the three levels of variable scope.

Program

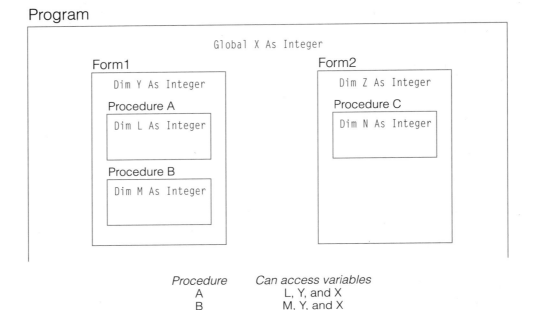

Procedure	Can access variables
A	L, Y, and X
B	M, Y, and X
C	N, Z, and X

Figure 3-6.
Global, module-level, and local variables.

Use the keyword *Global* instead of *Dim* to create global variables. The syntax is otherwise identical to that of the *Dim* statement:

Global *variable* [As *type*]

Scope rules also apply to constants. Constants declared with the *Const* statement are given local or module-level scope, depending on whether you define them in a procedure or in a module. To create global constants, place the declaration in the general declarations section of a module and use the *Global* keyword to begin the *Const* statement, as shown here:

```
Global Const LIGHTSPEED! = 186000
Global Const FIRST_PRESIDENT = "George Washington"
```

The exclamation point in the constant LIGHTSPEED tells Visual Basic to store the constant as a single-precision real number. Remember, however, that global variables and constants cannot be declared in a form.

The CONSTANT.TXT File

Visual Basic provides an extremely handy text file named CONSTANT.TXT. This file contains dozens of global constants that you might find useful. You can include all of these constants in your program automatically by following these steps:

1. Choose the New Module command from the File menu. In the module's code window, select the general declarations section.

2. Choose the Load Text command from the File menu.

3. Select the file CONSTANT.TXT from the Load Text dialog box and click on the Merge button.

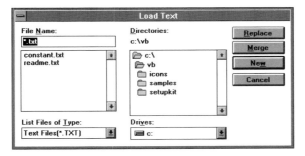

Warning: *Clicking on the Replace button in the Load Text dialog box will overwrite any declarations that currently appear in the general declarations section.*

To keep your program small, you can delete constants that you do not need. If you need only a few constants, you might find it easier to use Windows' Notepad application to open CONSTANT.TXT and simply copy and paste the constants you want from the file into your application.

Code Modules

As you've seen, the definition of a form and all its associated code are stored in a single file with the FRM extension. It is possible to create applications that have multiple forms and, consequently, multiple form files. You can also have application files that contain nothing but code. These *code modules,* whose files have the extension BAS, are created when you choose the New Module command from Visual Basic's File menu or click on the New Module button on the Toolbar.

Separate code modules are useful primarily for sharing code and for organizing your programs. Global declarations in a code module can be shared by the entire program. (Variable declarations in a form are accessible only within the form module.) When you are building large, complex programs, you might also find it helpful to put all the code related to a particular facet of the program in a separate module.

Default Declarations

You can declare a local variable without using a *Dim* statement: Simply begin using the variable name when you need it. You can use one of the type-declaration characters (%, &, !, #, or $) to specify the data type of the variable; if you do not, Visual Basic assigns the type variant by default. As an example, open a new project and place a single command button on the form. Define the *Click* event procedure for the command button as shown here:

```
Sub Command1_Click ()
    Answer$ = InputBox("Do you love me?")
    If Answer$ = "yes" Then
        MsgBox "He loves me"
    Else
        MsgBox "He loves me not"
    End If
End Sub
```

In this code fragment, the variable *Answer$* is not formally declared. The dollar sign indicates, however, that it is a string variable. By default, Visual Basic creates a variable with local scope.

Although default declarations are convenient, you would be wise to avoid them and instead fully declare every variable your program uses. Using default declarations can lead to errors in your programs. In the preceding example, for instance, you might declare a module-level variable named *Answer* as part of a later modification to the program. When you run the procedure, Visual Basic will assume that the variable *Answer* in the *Command1_Click* procedure refers to the module-level variable because an explicit local declaration is missing. Consequently, after this procedure is executed, any data stored in the module-level variable *Answer* is overwritten.

Default declarations always generate local variables. Module-level and global variables must be declared using the *Dim* statement or the *Global* statement in the general declarations portion of a code window. A *Dim* statement within a procedure creates a local variable.

Visual Basic can help you avoid default declarations. Choose the Environment command from the Options menu. In the Environment Options dialog box, set Require Variable Declarations to Yes, as shown in Figure 3-7.

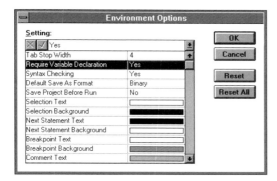

Figure 3-7.
The Environment Options dialog box.

Now each time you create a new file, Visual Basic adds the statement *Option Explicit* to the general declarations section of your code. (You can also enter this statement directly into the general declarations section if you want.) Then, if you attempt to run a program that contains an undeclared variable, Visual Basic highlights the variable name and displays the message *Variable not defined.*

Other Environment Options

The Environment Options dialog box lets you specify other settings, too. The Tab Stop Width, normally set to 4, can be altered to change the tab positioning in your code windows. Note, however, that Visual Basic does not insert actual ASCII tab characters into your code, but inserts spaces up to the next tab position.

The Syntax Checking option, when set to Yes, enables checking of each line of code as you enter it.

You can set the Default Save As Format to either Binary or Text. Binary is the default setting and is most efficient. In this mode, your forms and project files are saved in a representation that only Visual Basic can understand. Choose the Text setting if you want your application to be compatible with Visual Basic for MS-DOS or the Application Setup Wizard.

The Save Project Before Run option's default setting is No. If you set it to Yes, Visual Basic will automatically save the current version of your forms and project files before you run your application. This ensures that you don't lose any work in case of a system crash. You might want to leave this option disabled if you tend to make temporary experimental changes to your programs and don't want to save them.

The other options in the dialog box allow you to set the display colors for the text in code windows. By setting the colors, you can quickly recognize comments, variables, keywords, and so on, and distinguish the different components of your program.

4

Statements, Expressions, and Procedures

This chapter focuses your attention on simple Visual Basic statements. A *statement* in the Visual Basic language is the complete exposition of a command to the computer, the equivalent of a sentence in English. Within statements, you can create expressions by combining values and operators. This chapter describes the different kinds of operators and how to use them. It also provides a more detailed explanation of procedures, which you encountered earlier as you built your first application.

Assignment Statements

The simplest and probably the most common statement in a program is the *assignment* statement. It consists of a variable name, followed by the assignment operator (=), followed by some sort of expression. At its most basic, an *expression* consists of a simple constant value; it can, however, consist of a reference to another variable or to a mix of variables and constants on which certain operations are being performed. All of the following statements are legal assignment statements:

```
StartTime = Now
Explorer.Name = "Captain Spaulding"
BitCount = ByteCount * 8
Energy = Mass * LIGHTSPEED ^ 2
NetWorth = TotalAssets - TotalLiabilities
```

The assignment statement stores information. The value of an expression, which appears to the right of the assignment operator, is computed, and the result is stored in the variable to the left of the operator. The data type of the variable must be appropriate to the value of the computed expression. For example, a string constant or expression cannot be stored in an integer variable or in a double (floating-point) variable. If the data types are related but not exactly the same—for instance, you might want to store an integer value in a floating-point variable—Visual Basic converts the result of the expression to the variable's type. If you store the result of an expression in a variable of type variant, however, the type of the expression is preserved. Variant variables keep track of both type and value.

Unfortunately, the assignment operator is the same as the mathematical symbol used to represent equality (the equal sign, as in the equation *2 + 1 = 1 + 2*). Equality in the mathematical sense expresses a condition that is true. In the Visual Basic assignment statement, the symbol = is a command that places the result of the following expression in the preceding variable. It represents an action that the system is to perform rather than a statement of fact. The equation *2 + 1 = 1 + 2* is not a valid statement in Visual Basic because it lacks a variable to the left of the equal sign. If you attempt to enter that line as a complete statement, Visual Basic will report an error.

All of the program statements in the Stopwatch application that you created in Chapter 1 are assignment statements. In some statements, such as *btnStop.Enabled = True*, you assigned a simple constant value. In others, such as the statement *Elapsed-Time = EndTime − StartTime*, you used an expression. In statements such as *txt-Start.Text = Format(StartTime, "hh:mm:ss")*, you called a built-in function. The rest of this chapter explores Visual Basic's capabilities in these areas.

Expressions and Operators

As mentioned, an expression can be as simple as a single constant, although usually expressions represent computations to be performed. Commonly, an *operator* signals the type of computation. You are undoubtedly familiar with arithmetic operators, such as the plus sign (+), which indicates addition. The expression *2 + 1* tells Visual Basic to add the values 2 and 1. The 2 and the 1 are the *operands* of the addition operation. Besides the arithmetic operators, Visual Basic also provides a string concatenation operator, comparison operators, and logical operators (all of which are discussed later in this chapter).

By themselves, expressions are not valid statements because they are not complete. Simply entering the line *2 + 1* in your Visual Basic program, for example, causes an error. If a statement in the Visual Basic language is like a sentence, an expression is like a phrase. Expressions are usually allowed anywhere you can use a constant value.

Defining an expression is tricky. The best definition is actually self-referential. A partial definition might include these rules:

■ A constant value is an expression.

■ The combination of an expression followed by an operator followed by another expression is also an expression.

According to these rules, *3* is an expression, as is *1*; furthermore, *3 + 1* is also an expression. And it follows that *3 * 3 + 1* is an expression too, as is *3 * 3 + 1 + 1.* You can see where this is going: Expressions can be arbitrarily complex.

Expression Types

The type of an expression is determined by the type of the operands. For a constant value, the type of the expression is the same as the type of the constant. For an expression that contains an operation, Visual Basic uses the type of both operands to determine the type of the result. Naturally, if you add two integers, the result is an integer; if you add two double-precision values, the result is a double (real) type. If you mix different types—for instance, multiplying an integer by a single, as in the expression *2 * 7.5*—Visual Basic generally makes the result the type that has the widest range; in this case, it would be a single (real). To prevent possible ambiguity, however, you should not mix types in an expression.

To help avoid mixing types in an expression, you can use type-declaration characters with numeric constants. These characters force a constant to take on a specific type. For example, 100 would normally be an integer, but 100! is a single and 100@ is a currency value. (Visual Basic's type-declaration characters are listed in Chapter 3, Figure 3-4.)

> **Note:** *Visual Basic does not allow you to use type-declaration characters to truncate real constants to integer values. For example, you can't use 3.14% for the integer 3 (not that you would want to). But if you want to convert a floating-point variable to an integer, Visual Basic provides special conversion functions, which are documented in the Visual Basic reference manual.*

Expressions needn't be restricted to operators and constants. For example, the expression *17733.50 + (AdjustedIncome − 32450) * 23 / 100* would compute your 1990 federal income tax if you were married and in the 23 percent tax bracket. This expression includes a variable and a set of parentheses as well as operators and constants.

When expressions are more complex than two operands and a single operator, it is sometimes possible to evaluate the expression in more than one way. For instance, in the expression *2 + 6 / 2*, you might first add 2 and 6 to get 8 and then divide 8 by 2, with a result of 4. Or you could add 2 to the result of dividing 6 by 2 (which is 3), with a final result of 5. Parentheses are used to eliminate such ambiguity. The *subexpressions* contained in parentheses are always evaluated first. Writing the expression *2 + (6 / 2)* clearly indicates that the division operation should be performed first. Very complex expressions can contain multiple sets of parentheses. The innermost, or most deeply *nested,* expressions are evaluated first.

In the absence of overriding parentheses, Visual Basic uses a set of rules called *operator precedence* to determine which operation should be executed first. For example, because multiplication and division have higher precedence than addition and subtraction, Visual Basic always evaluates the expression *2 + 6 / 2* as if it were written *2 + (6 / 2)*. The next sections of this chapter describe the operators available in Visual Basic, grouped according to function and followed by a precedence table that illustrates how all the operators relate to one another.

Arithmetic Operators

The most familiar operators are those that carry out simple arithmetic operations. Figure 4-1 on the next page lists the arithmetic operators Visual Basic provides.

Operator	Operation
+	Addition
−	Subtraction
*	Multiplication
∧	Exponentiation
/	Floating-point division
\	Integer division
Mod	Modulus

Figure 4-1.
Arithmetic operators.

In the addition, subtraction, and multiplication operations, the results are numbers of the same type as the operands. (Mixed types are described in the preceding section.) In general, using integers or fixed-point numbers is faster than using real numbers, but unless you are performing many complicated calculations, you might not notice the difference.

Addition, subtraction, and multiplication all behave as you would expect. You must use the exponentiation operator because you can't superscript numbers in Visual Basic. And the three operators that relate to division are a bit more complicated.

Exponentiation

The exponentiation operator allows you to compute powers and roots. In mathematics, exponentiation is indicated by superscripts. For example, the value 2^8 is 2 to the eighth power, which is computed in Visual Basic by the expression *2 ∧ 8*. The square root of 2, which is 2 to the ½ power, can be computed using either the expression *2 ∧ (1 / 2)* or the expression *2 ∧ 0.5*. Figure 4-2 presents examples of exponentiation.

Expression	Result	Value Computed
10 ∧ 2	100	10 squared, or 10 * 10
10 ∧ 3	1000	10 cubed, or 10 * 10 * 10
10 ∧ −2	0.01	Inverse of 10^2, or $\frac{1}{100}$
25 ∧ 0.5	5	Square root of 25, or $25^{1/2}$
8 ∧ (1 / 3)	2	Cube root of 8, or $8^{1/3}$

Figure 4-2.
Examples of exponentiation.

Floating-point and integer division

The floating-point division operator (/) performs standard division, but it returns a floating-point number. Thus, the expression *3 / 2* evaluates to 1.5, as you might expect. Contrast this with the integer division operator (\), which returns an integer value. When this operator is used, the expression *3 \ 2* evaluates to 1. Just what we need, I hear you cry—an arithmetic function that returns the wrong answer.

Depends on your point of view, I guess. Imagine that you are a pickled-pepper packer who needs to know how many pickled peppers you can pack into a pint jar. As an expert in the field, you know that you can pack 150 pickled peppers into a gallon jar and that you never pack a partial pepper. A gallon jar is 8 times larger than a pint jar, so you can pack 150 \ 8—that is, 18—pickled peppers into each pint jar. You must use the integer division operator for the calculation, as shown in Figure 4-3, because you want to pack only whole peppers; performing the calculation with the floating-point division operator (150 / 8) would yield 18.75, which is not a reasonable value in this circumstance.

Because Visual Basic can convert between numeric data types, you might think that you could get the same result by simply assigning the result of a floating-point division to an integer variable, as shown in the code here:

```
Dim PintJar As Integer
PintJar = 150 / 8
```

In fact, after the assignment statement is executed, the value of *PintJar* will be 19 rather than 18. Visual Basic first computes the expression *150 / 8*, which yields 18.75. Because you want the value stored in an integer variable, Visual Basic *rounds* the floating-point number to the nearest integer, which in this case is 19. When you use the integer division operator, any fractional portion of the result is *truncated,* or dropped, rather than rounded. Figure 4-4 on the following page contrasts truncation and rounding.

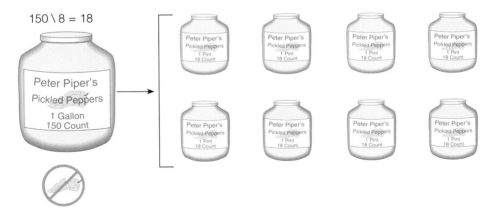

Figure 4-3.
Using the integer division operator.

Initial Value	Truncates To	Rounds To
24.1	24	24
24.5	24	24
24.50001	24	25
24.9999	24	25

Figure 4-4.
Truncation and rounding.

Modulus

The Mod operator, which is closely related to integer division, returns the remainder produced by dividing the first operand by the second. For example, if you divide 7 by 4, the result is 1 with a remainder of 3. Thus, the expression *7 Mod 4* evaluates to 3. Similarly, the expression *21 Mod 4* yields the result 1 (21 divided by 4 equals 5, with a remainder of 1).

To place this in the province of pickled-pepper packing once again, you now know that you can pack 18 pickled peppers into a pint jar. If you have 75 peppers to pack, the expression *75 \ 18* gives you the number of pint jars you can fill (4), and the expression *75 Mod 18* calculates the number of pickled peppers that will be left over (3), as illustrated in Figure 4-5.

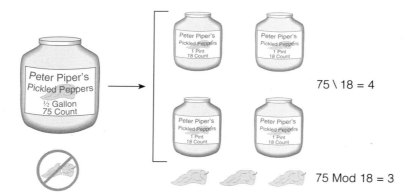

Figure 4-5.
Using integer division and the Mod operator.

Arithmetic operator precedence

Figure 4-6 indicates the precedence hierarchy for arithmetic operators. Exponentiation has the highest precedence; addition and subtraction operations are lowest in the hierarchy. Operators listed on the same line are equal in precedence.

Operator	Operation
^	Exponentiation
* /	Multiplication, Floating-point division
\	Integer division
Mod	Modulus (remainder)
+ −	Addition, Subtraction

Figure 4-6.
Arithmetic operators in order of precedence.

Figure 4-7 contains some sample Visual Basic expressions and the values that result when the expressions are computed. You can refer to the precedence hierarchy shown in Figure 4-6 to see how Visual Basic arrives at the result.

Expression	Result	Explanation
3 + 2 * 7	17	Multiplication has higher precedence
(3 + 2) * 7	35	Parentheses override precedence
1 + ((2 + 3) * 2) * 2	21	Nested parentheses evaluated first
14 / 5 * 2	5.6	Floating-point division and multiplication have equal precedence; operations performed from left to right
14 \ 5 * 2	1	Multiplication has higher precedence, and integer division truncates
27 ^ 1 / 3	9	Exponentiation has higher precedence
27 ^ (1 / 3)	3	Parentheses override precedence

Figure 4-7.
Using precedence rules to compute values.

The String Concatenation Operator

When the operands in an expression are strings, the plus sign (+) operator concatenates, or combines, the strings. You can use concatenation to "glue" two or more strings together to form one longer string. The result of concatenation is an entirely new string; none of the original operands are modified in any way. This program fragment uses concatenation to generate some lines from Lewis Carroll:

```
x$ = "bats"
y$ = "cats"
Debug.Print "Do " + x$ + " eat " + y$ + "?"    'Do bats eat cats?
Debug.Print "Do " + y$ + " eat " + x$ + "?"    'Do cats eat bats?
```

Interacting Directly with Visual Basic

Back in Chapter 1, you used the statement *Debug.Print* to write to the Debug window, which appears when your program is running. The Debug window is more than just a handy place to send messages, though; in this window you can interact directly with the interpreter.

Create a new project by choosing the New Project command from the File menu. Press F5 to start the "application." Although you have not written code or placed any objects on the form, Visual Basic will "run" the blank form. Now choose Break from the Run menu or click on the Toolbar's Break button. This command suspends the application, no matter what it was doing (not much in this case), and makes the Debug window the active window. Type the statement *Debug.Print "Hello"* in the Debug window, and press the Enter key. Visual Basic immediately processes and executes your command:

Because the Debug window is the active form at the time the interpreter executes your command, you don't have to include the name of the Debug object when you call the *Print* method; simply using *Print* is sufficient. In addition, Visual Basic allows you to abbreviate *Print* as *?* so that you can get results quickly, as shown here:

You can evaluate expressions and call functions in the Debug window. You can also call a procedure and, generally, execute almost any statement that you could code in a program. Popping into the Debug window is a quick and easy way to try out a line of code. When you are done, press F5 to continue normal execution of your application, or choose End from the Run menu to terminate the application.

Note that the operands must be strings. If you need to concatenate a number with a string for display purposes, you must use one of Visual Basic's built-in functions to convert the number to a string. The simplest such function is named *Str$*. In the expression *"The square root of 2 is " + Str$(2 ^ 0.5)*, for example, it converts the number in parentheses to a string.

You must remember to include blank spaces in your strings when necessary; otherwise, Visual Basic simply combines the strings you provide, without spaces.

Comparison Operators

The six comparison operators are listed in Figure 4-8. When two values are compared, the result of the operation is a Boolean value—that is, either True or False. (The word *Boolean* is derived from the name of the English mathematician George Boole.) Visual Basic provides built-in constants named True and False that stand for the integer values −1 and 0, respectively. The binary representation of 0 is a number with all its bits set to 0, and the representation of −1 is a binary number whose bits are all set to 1, which makes True the opposite of False.

Operator	Comparison
>	Greater than
<	Less than
>=	Greater than or equal to
<=	Less than or equal to
=	Equal to
<>	Not equal to

Figure 4-8.
Comparison operators.

Figure 4-9 on the next page evaluates and explains some typical comparison expressions. Comparison operators are also known as *relational operators* because they evaluate the relationship between the two operands. Although comparison operators have equal precedence among themselves, the precedence of any comparison operator is lower than that of any arithmetic operator.

You have probably noticed that the "equal to" operator uses the same symbol (=) as the assignment operator. This shouldn't be too confusing, however, because the assignment operator is valid in only one location: immediately following a variable in an assignment statement. In all other cases, the equal sign is a comparison, or relational, operator. For example, in the Visual Basic statement *Test = a = b*, the expression *a = b* is computed and yields either True or False. The resulting value is then assigned to the variable *Test*.

Expression	Result	Explanation
3 + 1 > 3	True	4 is greater than 3
"abc" <> "a" + "b" + "c"	False	After concatenation, both strings are equal ("abc")
"quid" <= "pro quo"	False	Strings are compared in alphabetic order, not by length
2.3 >= 1.1 * 2	True	2.3 is greater than 2.2
0 = (2 < 1)	True	2 < 1 is False, which is equal to 0

Figure 4-9.
Using comparison operators.

Logical Operators

The logical operators are sometimes called Boolean operators because they are derived from the algebra of mathematical logic, which was developed by George Boole. These operators have Boolean values as operands, and they return Boolean results. Figure 4-10 lists the logical operators in their order of precedence. (All of the logical operators have lower precedence than the comparison operators.)

Operator	Operation
Not	Logical not
And	Logical and
Or	Logical or
Xor	Exclusive or
Eqv	Logical equivalence
Imp	Logical implication

Figure 4-10.
Logical, or Boolean, operators in order of precedence.

The simplest logical operator is called Not. It precedes a single operand and returns its logical opposite—that is, it negates the operand. For example, the expression *Not False* yields the result True (the opposite of False); and the expression *Not (4 < 3)* evaluates to True because the expression *4 < 3* is False. The Not operator also has the highest precedence of all the Boolean operators.

The next operator in precedence order is And. It returns a result of True if (and only if) both its operands are True. If either operand is False, the And operator returns a result of False. It corresponds to the use of the word *and* in the English language, as expressed in the statement "I will be impressed only if he has a Ph.D. *and* if he is taller than 6 foot 2."

Expression	Result
False And False	False
False And True	False
True And False	False
True And True	True

The Or operator returns a result of True if either of its two operands is True or if both are True. Again, its Boolean meaning is similar to the use of the word in English—for example, "I will buy the cat if it costs less than $50 *or* if it is a Siamese."

Expression	Result
False Or False	False
False Or True	True
True Or False	True
True Or True	True

Although the operators Not, And, and Or are by far the most widely used, Visual Basic also provides three other operators: Xor, Eqv, and Imp. The Xor (exclusive or) operator returns a result of True if either of its operands is True but not if both are True. In other words, it works like the Or operator does, except for the case in which both values are True.

Expression	Result
False Xor False	False
False Xor True	True
True Xor False	True
True Xor True	False

The Eqv (equivalence) operator returns a result of True when its two operands have the same value.

Expression	Result
False Eqv False	True
False Eqv True	False
True Eqv False	False
True Eqv True	True

When you use the Imp (implication) operator, the result is False only when the first operand is True and the second operand is False. In all other cases, the result is True. The Imp operator is the only Boolean operator for which the order of the operands makes a difference in the result. Implication is sometimes used with the And operator, as illustrated in the famous syllogism "Socrates is a man *and* all men are mortal *implies* that Socrates is mortal."

Expression	Result
False Imp False	True
False Imp True	True
True Imp False	False
True Imp True	True

You can use more than one logical operator in an expression. Figure 4-11 provides a few examples; try evaluating each expression, and then check the results against the order of precedence shown in Figure 4-10.

Expression	Result	Explanation
Not False And True	True	Equivalent to (Not False) And True, based on precedence
True And False Xor False	False	Equivalent to (True And False) Xor False, based on precedence
True Eqv True Xor True	False	Equivalent to True Eqv (True Xor True), based on precedence

Figure 4-11.
Using multiple logical operators in an expression.

Precedence

Figure 4-12 lists the entire set of Visual Basic operators (except for the string concatenation operator), in order of precedence from highest to lowest. When you encounter a complex expression, you must determine which operator has the highest precedence and then evaluate that subexpression first. Next determine which operator has the second highest precedence, evaluate that subexpression, and so on until you calculate the final result.

Some operators, such as addition and subtraction or the entire set of comparison operators, have equal precedence. When you encounter operators with equal precedence, you evaluate the subexpressions from left to right.

For example, consider the following expression:

```
Temperature >= 451 And Flammable = True
```

Because the two comparison operators (>= and =) share the same level of precedence, Visual Basic evaluates them from left to right. Then Visual Basic performs the And operation. In this case, if *Temperature* is less than 451 or *Flammable* is False, Visual Basic determines that the value of the expression is False.

Operator	Operation
^	Exponentiation
* /	Multiplication, Floating-point division
\	Integer division
Mod	Modulus (remainder)
+ −	Addition, Subtraction
> < >= <= = <>	Comparison
Not	Logical not
And	Logical and
Or	Logical or
Xor	Exclusive or
Eqv	Logical equivalence
Imp	Logical implication

Figure 4-12.
Visual Basic operators in order of precedence.

Here's a more complex example:

```
Count * 2 < 15 Or Color = "Blue" And Count * 2 < 21
```

Working its way down the precedence table, Visual Basic first performs the two multiplication operations; then it evaluates the three comparisons from left to right. Next Visual Basic performs the And operation and, finally, the Or operation.

If that sounds like a good way to get lost, you're correct. Even if you don't want to override Visual Basic's default precedence, it's a good idea to add parentheses to help ensure that you and Visual Basic agree on the order of operations. Duplicating the way Visual Basic sees the example above makes it look like this:

```
((Count * 2) < 15) Or ((Color = "Blue") And ((Count * 2) < 21))
```

Common Mistakes

Nearly every programmer who is just starting out makes certain mistakes related to expressions. Let's take a look at some of the most frequently encountered problems so that you'll be able to avoid or at least identify them.

One such mistake is misusing the relational operators to test whether a variable is in a particular range. If you are working with the variable *Temperature*, for instance, you might want to see whether its value is greater than 32 degrees but less than 212 degrees. You can do this with the expression *Temperature > 32 And Temperature < 212*. You might have been tempted to use the expression *32 < Temperature < 212*, which looks fine mathematically but does not work correctly in Visual Basic. This shorter expression is syntactically correct but gives you the wrong answer. Why?

Begin by evaluating the two subexpressions from left to right. (The two operators are of equal precedence.) Because relational operators always return True or False, which are equivalent to the integers −1 and 0, the result of the subexpression *32 < Temperature* is either −1 or 0. Therefore, the second subexpression is either *−1 < 212* or *0 < 212*, both of which are True. As a result, the expression *32 < Temperature < 212* always returns a result of True, no matter what the value of the variable is. This process is shown graphically in Figure 4-13.

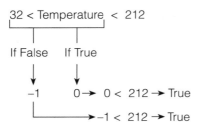

Figure 4-13.
An incorrect way to test for a range of values.

Another typical error is to write logical expressions with the same imprecision that is often found in spoken English. The expression in the previous example was carefully formulated to find a value that is "greater than 32 degrees but less than 212 degrees." If you were talking to a colleague, however, you might have stated the problem this way: "I want to know whether the temperature is greater than 32 degrees or less than 212 degrees." This formulation is less precise (and in fact inaccurate), but people are reasonably good at dealing with ambiguity, and your colleague probably would have understood what you meant. Phrasing the statement in that manner, however, might lead you to write the incorrect expression *Temperature > 32 Or Temperature < 212.*

Again, by examining this expression as Visual Basic deals with it, you can see the problem. The two relational expressions are evaluated first, and then a Boolean Or operation is performed. The subexpression *Temperature > 32* is True for all numbers greater than 32; the other relational subexpression, *Temperature < 212*, is True for all numbers less than 212. Now look at what happens when you join those subexpressions with the Or operator. If the variable has a value of 5 degrees, the first subexpression is False (5 > 32), and the second subexpression is True (5 < 212). The Or operation returns a result of True because one of the operands is True. Similarly, with a value of 900, the first subexpression is True and the second is False, causing the Or operation to produce a result of True. When *Temperature* has a value of 100, both subexpressions are True and the result is again True. By using the Or operator instead of the And operator, you have created another expression that always returns True. Figure 4-14 illustrates the problem.

Temperature > 32 Or Temperature < 212

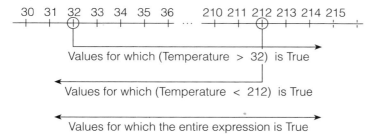

Figure 4-14.
Another incorrect way to test for a range of values.

A third common mistake is to think of an assignment statement as a mathematical condition rather than as the manipulation of data that occurs at one point in time. This problem is illustrated in the following code fragment:

```
A = 10
B = A / 2
A = 20
```

After these three statements are executed, *A* has the value 20 and *B* has the value 5. If you thought that *B* should have the value 10, you fell into the trap just mentioned. The second statement does not express a condition that is true for all time; rather, it is an expression that is evaluated once, with a specific value of the variable *A*. In this example, the statement is evaluated when *A* has the value 10. Later statements can alter the value of *A*, but *B* remains unchanged unless a different assignment statement is executed.

Let's look at one more common error. Up to this point, we've used only the values True and False in Boolean operations because that's what you'll encounter most frequently. Be aware, however, that because True and False are equivalent to the integers −1 and 0, Visual Basic will not generate an error message if you attempt to use And, Or, Imp, or any of the other logical operators with any integer operands, such as 6 or 237. Visual Basic actually performs the specified Boolean operation on each bit of the operands.

This can lead to strange errors. For example, let's say you want to know whether the variable *x* is equal to either 5 or 6. You might be tempted to code the statement as *Debug.Print x = 5 Or 6*. Visual Basic will perform the Or operation on the integers 5 and 6 one bit at a time, which yields the result 7. It then compares the value of *x* with 7, which is not exactly what you had in mind. Instead, you should code the statement as *Debug.Print (x = 5) Or (x = 6)*.

Procedures

Although you have already written a few procedures and probably have some understanding of what they are and how they work, it will be worth your while to formalize that understanding a bit. This section concentrates primarily on Visual Basic's built-in procedures; later, Chapter 7 focuses on designing and writing new procedures rather than simply using existing ones.

A procedure is a set of instructions that perform a particular service. You request the service by using the procedure's name. In Chapter 3, for example, you wrote a small program that used the procedure *MsgBox*. When that portion of your program executed, Visual Basic displayed in a dialog box the message you provided. When the dialog box closed, your program continued. Visual Basic provided the service of painting a dialog box around your message, creating an OK button, watching the mouse until the button was clicked, and removing the dialog box from the screen; all you had to do was supply the message.

Services provided by Visual Basic can be compared with those provided in everyday life. For example, if you have just purchased a painting by van Gogh and are worried that the check you wrote to Sotheby's is in danger of bouncing, you can call the bank and request a transfer. You provide the bank with the account numbers and the amount you want to transfer, and the bank performs the service without further action from you.

In other cases, a tangible object is returned by a service provider. For instance, you can visit the local pizza joint, give them your pizza order and a few dollars, and get a pizza in return. As you might remember, the Visual Basic procedures that return values are called functions. In the example program in Chapter 3, you called the function *InputBox*. You provided it with a prompt string to be displayed, and it displayed a dialog box and returned to you the text entered in the dialog box.

Visual Basic provides many useful built-in functions, some of which are described in Figure 4-15. You can use Visual Basic's online Help and the reference manual to explore these built-in functions in more depth.

Syntax for Procedures and Functions

To call a procedure or function, you must use its name. Beyond that, Visual Basic has specific additional rules about a statement's syntax—that is, about how the statement must be written and arranged in your code. (Although functions are also procedures, for simplicity this discussion of syntax will use the term *procedure* to refer to services that do not return a value and the term *function* to refer to services that do return a value.)

Function	Value Returned
Abs	Absolute value of a number
Asc	ASCII or ANSI code of a character
Chr$	Character corresponding to a given ASCII or ANSI code
Cos	Cosine of an angle
CurDir$	Current working directory name
Date$	Current date as a text string
Format	Date or number converted to a text string
InputBox	Text entered in a dialog box by a user
Len	Number of characters in a text string
Mid$	Selected portion of a text string
Now	Current time and date
Rnd	Random number
Sin	Sine of an angle
Sqr	Square root of a number
Str$	Number converted to a text string
Time$	Current time as a text string
Val	Numeric value of a given text string

Figure 4-15.
Some of Visual Basic's built-in functions.

To make use of, or call, a procedure, you write a Visual Basic statement in which the name of the procedure is the first item. A procedure call is a complete Visual Basic statement, and the procedure might not require any other information from you. If it does need further information, you must enter the values you want to send to the procedure, separated by commas. The values you pass on to a procedure (or a function) are called its *arguments*. In the case of the *MsgBox* procedure, you used a single argument, the text string to be displayed. The following statements are all examples of Visual Basic procedure calls:

```
MsgBox "Hello, sailor"
ChDir "\test\data"
Beep
SavePicture StarryNight, "vincent.bmp"
```

The syntax for calling a function is different. Because a function returns a value, it can be used anywhere an expression is valid. But expressions alone are not valid Visual Basic statements. Consequently, a function call is always found in the context of some other statement, most frequently an assignment statement.

When a function requires no arguments, you can simply use the function name as though it were the name of a variable, as in the statement *StartTime = Now*. The function *Now* requires no arguments and returns a time value. Visual Basic calls the function and assigns the returned value to the variable *StartTime*.

When a function requires one or more arguments, you must place a left parenthesis after the function name, enter the arguments separated by commas, and mark the end of the function call with a right parenthesis. The following expressions contain valid function calls (although they are not complete Visual Basic statements):

```
Sin(x) ^ 2              'Get the sine of x and square the result
Chr$(65)                'Return the ASCII character represented by 65
Format(Now, "hh:mm")    'Format the current time
```

Note that in the third example, the expression contains one function call inside another. The value of the function *Now* is passed as an argument to the *Format* function.

Methods

Procedures and functions have been a part of programming languages for many years. More recently, the designers of object-oriented programming languages have introduced special kinds of procedures and functions called *methods*. Although Visual Basic is not truly object-oriented, it includes methods for each of its objects, such as forms and command buttons. Methods operate in the same manner as procedures and functions, but they are components of specific objects, just as properties and field names are. To call a method, you use the object name and the method name, separated by a period—*Debug.Print*, for example.

This is a bit clumsier than simply using a procedure name, but it has the advantage of allowing more than one method to have the same name. In early versions of Basic, the PRINT procedure wrote a text string to the user's terminal. To write to the printer, the user had to call a different procedure, LPRINT. Both procedures operated in generally similar ways, but because of slight differences, they required two separate commands.

Visual Basic has no *Print* procedure. Instead, all the objects to which you can write have a method named *Print*. To write the string *"Hello"* to a form named MyForm, you would write the following code:

```
MyForm.Print "Hello"
```

To write to the printer, which is represented in Visual Basic by a special object named Printer, you would use this code:

```
Printer.Print "Hello"
```

The Debug window, which is represented by an object named Debug, also has a *Print* method. Because Visual Basic provides a *Print* method for each of these objects, you don't need several printing commands with different names. With fewer commands to learn, your work is a little easier.

Often, Visual Basic allows you to omit the object name when using a method. If you do this, Visual Basic directs the method to the object it believes you intended—usually the current form. If you had written the code *Print "Hello"* in the examples above, the output would have gone to the form that was active when the program was running. To avoid ambiguity, you can always use the full *object.method* naming convention.

Methods can act like procedures or like functions—that is, they can simply perform a service, as the *Print* method does, or they can return a value. Some methods—such as *Move*, which changes the location of an object—are implemented for nearly every object type. Others are more specialized. The *Print* method, for example, is implemented for only a few objects such as forms and the printer. The next chapter explores Visual Basic objects and their properties and methods.

5

Using Visual Basic's Forms and Tools

Visual Basic Objects

One of the great advantages of a graphical user interface is that the user can interact with a standardized set of objects, such as windows, buttons, and scroll bars. Applications that utilize these standard objects behave in standard ways, making applications easier to learn. Part of your job as a programmer is to select the style of interaction that is most appropriate to the situation and to write your programs in a way that the user finds intuitive.

In a GUI environment, the user interacts with the on-screen objects to initiate events—opening a window, clicking on an icon, choosing a menu item—and by doing so controls the application. Visual Basic translates a user-initiated event into programmatic activity by calling a procedure associated with that event. The code you provide for that event procedure implements an appropriate response to the user's interaction with the object.

A Note About This Chapter

This chapter describes most of the objects that are available to you as you build applications in Visual Basic, including forms and the objects created with various tools from the Toolbox. You've already encountered some of these objects in earlier chapters; here, however, we'll take a more in-depth look at some of the properties you can set and how they affect the objects, at the events that are generated when a user manipulates these objects in an application, and at some of the procedures and methods that can be used with each object. We'll also explore the process of designing and creating menus for your applications.

At the end of most sections in this chapter is a sample project that demonstrates how you can use the Visual Basic object that's been described. The instructions for the first two projects are detailed and explicit; for subsequent projects, however, the instructions are more general—simply telling you to "create a new project," for example, instead of explaining which commands to choose—on the assumption that you've gotten the hang of this by now.

Whether or not to save a sample application is generally your decision. In most cases, you probably don't need to. But if you know that you'll be using a specific tool or object in the near future, you might find it useful to save the associated project so that you can go back and reexamine it later.

You should also be aware that the lists of properties, events, procedures, and methods in this chapter are by no means exhaustive; rather, the aim is simply to provide you with enough tools to write useful programs. You might find the complete lists a little overwhelming at this point, but they are available in the Visual Basic online Help system and in the Visual Basic reference manual if you need further resources or information. Also, later chapters of this book will introduce some additional properties and procedures.

Note that many of the objects described here have identical properties or support similar events. In such cases, full descriptions of the properties, events, procedures, and so on are not repeated for every object. We'll begin by describing forms; you'll find the most extensive descriptions in that section.

A Note About Syntax

Many of the descriptions of procedures and methods include the syntax of the appropriate Visual Basic statements. In these syntax statements, items shown in *italics* indicate the type of information you should provide—for example, when you see the word *variable*, you should enter a variable name at that location in the statement. Items shown in roman (text) type indicate keywords or characters that you must enter as shown. Items enclosed in square brackets ([ ]) are optional—that is, the statement is valid even if these items are omitted. Items within braces ({ }) that are separated by a vertical bar (|) indicate a choice; you must select one of the items inside the braces. If a set of brackets or braces is followed by an ellipsis (. . .), the sequence inside the brackets or braces can be repeated. Here is an example:

The *noun* is [very] { big | small } [and { bold | timid | green }]...

Based on the syntax notation just described, you can use this example to build any of the following sentences:

The factory is very big.

The submarine is small and green.

The window is very small and bold and timid and green.

As you can see, correct syntax does not necessarily produce a meaningful statement; you'll find that it is all too easy to write programs that are syntactically correct but don't work properly. We'll tackle this problem in Chapter 8.

Forms

As you learned in Chapter 1, forms are the canvas on which you visually create your application. Each form corresponds to a window in the running application.

Properties

Many properties can affect the appearance and behavior of a form when it is displayed; only the most commonly used properties of forms are listed here. Except as noted, properties can be set either by using the Properties window as you design an application or by writing program code that sets properties as the program runs.

AutoRedraw The AutoRedraw property (discussed in detail in Chapter 10) governs how screen images are re-created. When you switch back to a Visual Basic form after working in another window that has covered the form, Visual Basic will automatically refresh or redraw any graphics on the form if the AutoRedraw property is set to True. When this property is set to False, Visual Basic must instead call an event procedure to carry out this task.

BackColor This property determines the color of the background. When you select BackColor from the Properties list in the Properties window, you will see the default setting &H80000005&, a hexadecimal (base 16) constant that defines a Visual Basic color. (These constants are contained in the CONSTANT.TXT file.) Chapter 10 provides more details about these color settings, but you don't need to know much about them to set the BackColor property: Simply click on the ellipsis button beside the Settings box in the Properties window, and Visual Basic will display a color palette as shown here:

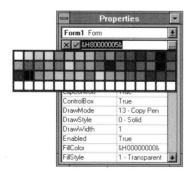

Choose a color from the palette by clicking on the appropriate square, or click on the X button beside the Settings box to close the palette.

BorderStyle You can set this property to one of four predefined settings. The BorderStyle property can be set only at design time. The setting does not affect the display of the form at design time, but it does change the window display at runtime as follows:

0 - None	The window has no border
1 - Fixed Single	The window has a fixed size (specified at design time) and a single-line border
2 - Sizable	The window is resizable and has a standard double-line border
3 - Fixed Double	The window has a fixed size (specified at design time) and a double-line border

Caption This property contains the text of the form window's title bar.

ControlBox This Boolean property should be set to True if you want a box for the Control menu to be displayed in the upper left corner of the window. You can modify this property only at design time. Setting the ControlBox property to True has no effect if you have set BorderStyle to 0 - None.

Enabled Every Visual Basic object has an Enabled property that can be set to True or False, activating or deactivating the object. For a form, this property is normally set to True, but you can set it to False to prevent any mouse or keyboard events from being sent to the form.

FontBold, FontItalic, FontStrikethru, FontUnderline You can set these Boolean properties to True if you want text that is printed to the form to appear in boldface type, in italics, with strikethroughs, or with an underline (or with any combination of these attributes). Only the characters printed after you change one or more of these properties are affected by the new setting.

FontName This property is set to the name of the font that will be used for printing to a form. If you change the font, any text already written to the form is not modified, but all subsequent printing is affected. For example, if you executed the following code, the letter *C* would print in the Courier New font, and all other characters would print in Times New Roman:

```
FontName = "Times New Roman"
Print "AB"
FontName = "Courier New"
Print "C"
FontName = "Times New Roman"
Print "DE"
```

FontSize This property allows you to specify a size (in points) for text printed to the form. (A *point* is a standard typographic unit for measuring the size of type; 1 point equals approximately $\frac{1}{72}$ inch.) The setting does not change the size of any text that has already been printed.

ForeColor This property defines the color of the foreground text or graphics. You set this property by choosing a color from a color palette, in the same way you set the BackColor property (more details in Chapter 10). All *Print* statements write text using the foreground color.

Height, Width These properties determine the height and the width of the form, measured in units called *twips*, or twentieths of a point. (A twip is equivalent to $\frac{1}{1440}$ inch.)

Icon You can set this property to the name of a file containing an icon. The icon will then represent the form when the form is minimized. To set this property at design time, select it from the Properties list in the Properties window, and then click on the ellipsis button that appears beside the Settings box. In the resulting dialog box, choose an icon file. If you want to set the property at runtime, you must use the *LoadPicture* function or assign the value of the Icon property of some other form.

MaxButton, MinButton You should set these Boolean properties to True if you want Maximize and Minimize buttons to be displayed in the upper right corner of the window. These two properties are ignored if you have set the BorderStyle property to 0 - None. Note that the Maximize and Minimize buttons do not disappear from the form at design time even if you set the MaxButton and MinButton properties to False; the effect of these settings is not visible in the window until runtime.

Name This property defines the name of the form in the program code. It cannot be changed at runtime.

Picture You can set this property to indicate that a bitmap picture is always displayed in the window. To set this property at design time, select it from the Properties list and click on the ellipsis button that appears beside the Settings box in the Properties window. In the resulting dialog box, choose a file containing the picture you want to display. To change this property at runtime, you must use the *LoadPicture* function.

Top, Left These properties control the location of the form on the screen by defining the location of the top of the window and the leftmost coordinate, measured by default in twips.

Visible The setting of this Boolean property indicates whether the form window is visible or not. Setting this property to False hides the form from view.

WindowState This property determines whether the window is displayed in its normal state (a setting of 0), in a minimized state as an icon (a setting of 1), or in a maximized state (a setting of 2).

Events

Click, DblClick, and Load are the most common events for a form to process. (The KeyPress event and the drag-and-drop process are introduced in Chapters 6 and 7.)

Click When the user clicks on the form, Visual Basic calls the *Form_Click* procedure. If the user clicks on an object that is contained in the form, the Click event is not passed to the form, even if the other object does not process the event.

DblClick This event is received if the user clicks twice in rapid succession at the same point on the form. This process actually triggers two events: a Click event for the first mouse button click, and a DblClick event for the second.

Load This event occurs automatically whenever a form is loaded—for example, when an application is started. A *Load* event procedure is handy for initializing properties and variables at the start of a program.

Procedures and Methods

The most interesting form methods are graphics methods. Because they are rather complex, an entire chapter (Chapter 10) is devoted to graphics later in this book. For now, we'll take a brief look at a few methods (and one function) to get you started.

Cls This method clears the form of all graphics and text. The complete syntax for the *Cls* method is as follows:

[*formName*].Cls

LoadPicture You can use this function to set the Picture property of a form. Here is the function's syntax:

LoadPicture([*fileName*])

The filename must be a string expression that identifies a file containing an icon, a Windows bitmap, or a Windows metafile. (These filenames typically have the extensions ICO, BMP, and WMF.) If you do not specify a filename, *LoadPicture* returns a blank picture.

Print This method writes text to the form. Use this syntax:

[*formName*].Print [[*expression*][{ ; ¦ , }]]...

Each expression is followed by a semicolon or a comma. If a semicolon is used, the output of the next expression follows immediately after the last character written. f a comma is used, the output position on the form is tabbed to the next column. (Columns are defined every 14 characters.) If the final expression in the *Print* statement ends with a semicolon or a comma, no carriage return is written to the form; otherwise, the output position is set to the next line. Here are some examples of using the *Print* method in the Debug window:

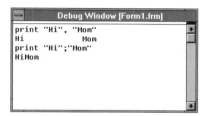

Strange as it might sound, the *Print* method is really a graphics method; you can find more information about it in Chapter 10.

The Smile Application

Now try constructing this sample project, which demonstrates some of the property settings, methods, and procedures associated with forms.

1. Start the Paintbrush application in Windows, draw a simple picture, and save it in a file on your hard disk. Here's an example, using a famous cultural icon from the 1970s:

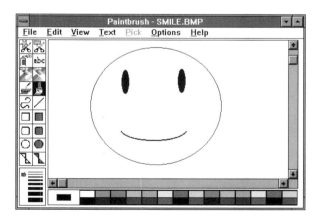

2. Return to Visual Basic, and create a new project by choosing the New Project command from the File menu.

3. In the Properties window, select the Picture property in the Properties list, and then click on the ellipsis button to the right of the Settings box. The Load Picture dialog box appears:

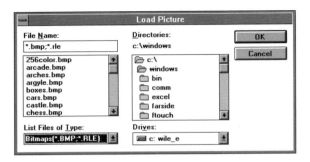

4. In the dialog box, specify the name of the graphics file you created in Paint-brush and click on the OK button. My version of the form now looks like this:

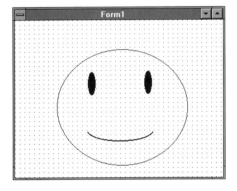

5. Select the FontBold property of the form in the Properties list, and set it to False in the Settings box.

6. Open the code window for Form1 by clicking on the View Code button in the Project window or by double-clicking on the form.

7. Select Form in the Object box at the top of the code window, and then select Click in the Procedure box. Enter the necessary code to create the *Form_Click* procedure, as shown here in color:

```
Sub Form_Click ()
    Form1.Print "Have a ";
    Form1.FontBold = True
    Form1.Print "nice";
    Form1.FontBold = False
    Form1.Print " day"
End Sub
```

8. Select DblClick in the Procedure box. Enter the line of code shown in color to create the *Form_DblClick* procedure:

```
Sub Form_DblClick ()
    Form1.Cls
End Sub
```

9. Now run the application by choosing the Start command from the Run menu, clicking on the Toolbar's Start button, or pressing F5. Click at various points on the form. The application should behave as shown here:

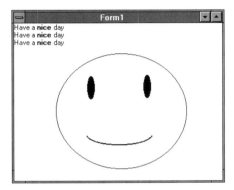

10. While the application is still running, try double-clicking on the form. This action causes your program to execute the *Form_DblClick* procedure. If you watch closely, you'll see that the program executes the *Form_Click* procedure once before the *Form_DblClick* procedure clears the form. Note also that the *Cls* method clears only the information that was added to the form, not the background picture.

The code written for this example is quite precise: It specifies using the *Print* method for Form1, and it explicitly modifies the FontBold property for Form1. Unfortunately, this precision can sometimes get you into trouble. To illustrate, quit the application (by pressing Alt-F4 or by clicking on the Toolbar's End button), and return to design mode. Now change the Name property of the form to Smile. When you try to run the program again, Visual Basic will display the error message shown in Figure 5-1 on the next page.

Visual Basic is complaining that it has no knowledge of an object named Form1. Indeed, your program contains no such object; the only form in your program is now called Smile.

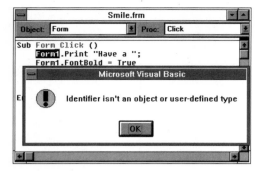

Figure 5-1.
A unidentified-object error message.

Although it's unlikely that you'll spend a lot of time renaming forms in your programs, you might want to incorporate a piece of one program into another at a later time. In that instance, you could run into this problem. Visual Basic offers a simple solution. Methods and properties have scope, just as variables do. If you use a method name or a property name without explicitly defining the object it belongs to, Visual Basic uses the current execution context to determine which object is affected. If you delete all the references to Form1, the code for the Smile application looks like this:

```
Sub Form_Click ()
    Print "Have a ";
    FontBold = True
    Print "nice";
    FontBold = False
    Print " day"
End Sub

Sub Form_DblClick ()
    Cls
End Sub
```

Because the *Form_Click* and *Form_DblClick* procedures always execute in the context of the form (regardless of the form's name), the *Print* and *Cls* methods and the FontBold property must be within the scope of the current form. Thus, you can easily use more general code (and you have less typing to do).

Picture Boxes and Images

The picture box and image controls both allow you to place graphics information in a specific location on a form. The Picture Box tool and the Image tool from the

Toolbox are shown in Figures 5-2 and 5-3. Picture boxes are the more flexible of the two controls, and they consequently require more memory and processing when you use them. Picture boxes are best suited for dynamic environments—for example, when you are drawing graphics directly to the screen while the program is running or animating an icon by moving it around on the screen. (Graphics methods, which allow you to draw lines and print text, are described in Chapter 10.) Image objects are best for static situations—that is, when the bitmap or icon that you have created and placed on the screen will not be modified.

Figure 5-2.
The Picture Box tool.

Figure 5-3.
The Image tool.

Properties

Picture boxes and image controls have the properties Enabled, Height, Left, Name, Picture, Top, Visible, and Width. Most of these properties behave exactly as described in the preceding section on forms, except that the coordinates for the Height, Left, Top, and Width properties are measured with respect to the location of the object within the form, not in absolute screen coordinates. (This is true for all the controls created from the Toolbox.) The Picture property can be set to display a bitmap or an icon: At design time, use the Properties window and the Load Picture dialog box (as we'll do in the sample project that follows); at runtime, you'll need to use the *LoadPicture* function.

Picture boxes, which behave almost like small forms within the main form, have the following properties that image controls do not: AutoRedraw, FontBold, FontItalic, FontName, FontSize, FontUnderline. These properties behave just as they do for forms. Image controls possess one property that picture boxes do not: the Stretch property. By default, Stretch is set to False, which causes the image control to resize itself to fit the picture it contains. If you set Stretch to True, the picture resizes to fit the control.

Picture boxes and image controls differ in another respect as well. A form's display is made up of three layers, as illustrated in Figure 5-4. All the information displayed directly on the form (by printing or drawing with the graphics methods, for example) appears on the bottom layer. Information from three graphical controls (the image, shape, and line controls) appears on the middle layer, and all other objects are displayed on the top layer. Consequently, text printed on a form could be hidden by an image, which in turn could be hidden by a picture box.

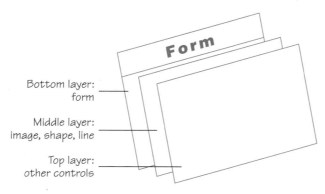

Bottom layer:
form

Middle layer:
image, shape, line

Top layer:
other controls

Figure 5-4.
The layers of a form's display.

Events

Like forms, both picture boxes and image controls can receive Click and DblClick events, which are among the simplest and most frequently encountered events.

Procedures and Methods

The *LoadPicture* function can be called to set the Picture property of a picture box or an image control. Picture boxes also support the *Cls* and *Print* methods as well as the graphics methods described in Chapter 10.

The Directions Palette

This sample project lets you use a series of images to create a palette of icons similar to the Visual Basic Toolbox. This program would work exactly the same way if you used picture boxes instead of image controls; remember, however, that picture boxes are less efficient when the display is static.

1. Create a new project in Visual Basic by choosing the New Project command from the File menu.

2. Set the properties of the form as shown here. (The notation [none] indicates that the setting should be an empty string.)

Property	Setting
BorderStyle	1 - Fixed Single
Caption	[none]
MaxButton	False
MinButton	False
Name	Directions

3. Click on the Image tool in the Toolbox, and drag the mouse pointer in the form to create a small image control in the upper left corner of the form:

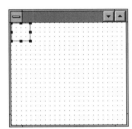

4. Create three more image controls of the same size, and arrange them in a 2 by 2 square. With the mouse, resize the boundaries of the form window to tightly fit the four image controls. Your form should now look like the one shown here:

5. Click on the image control in the upper left corner of the form (Image1) to select it. In the Properties window, select the Picture property for Image1 from the Properties list. Then click on the ellipsis button beside the Settings box to open the Load Picture dialog box (shown on page 78). In the dialog box, set the file type to display icon files (with the extension ICO). In the ARROWS subdirectory of the ICONS directory that comes with Visual Basic, you will find the file ARW02UP.ICO. When you choose that file, the icon it contains appears in the selected image control:

6. Double-click on the image, and define the following procedure in the code window:

```
Sub Image1_Click ()
    Debug.Print "Selected up"
End Sub
```

7. Repeat this same process for the other three image controls, loading the files ARW02DN.ICO, ARW02LT.ICO, and ARW02RT.ICO and defining three *Click* event procedures as follows:

```
Sub Image2_Click ()
    Debug.Print "Selected down"
End Sub

Sub Image3_Click ()
    Debug.Print "Selected left"
End Sub

Sub Image4_Click ()
    Debug.Print "Selected right"
End Sub
```

8. To visually separate the icons, you can place borders around them. Click on the image in the upper left corner to select it, and then hold down the Ctrl key while you click on the other three images to select all four at one time. In the Properties window, select the BorderStyle property from the Properties list, and set it to 1 - Fixed Single.

When you run this application (by pressing F5), your form will be a "Directions" palette. When you click on a few of the icons, you should see results like those shown in Figure 5-5.

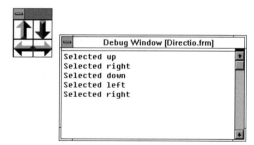

Figure 5-5.
Using the Directions palette.

By including code similar to this in a larger application, you could create a palette of icons that were appropriate to the program you were designing. The Visual Basic Toolbox, which is used during design mode, is an example of this kind of palette.

> *Tip:* *Visual Basic comes with a few hundred icons as well as with an icon editor program that lets you create your own. The icon editor itself was written in Visual Basic. You can start the icon editor by loading the project called ICONWRKS.MAK and running the application. The icon editor has its own online Help.*

Labels

A label provides an area in which you can present textual information that cannot be edited by the user. The content is set by modifying the Caption property of the label. You cannot print to or draw in a label. You create labels with the Label tool from the Visual Basic Toolbox, shown in Figure 5-6.

Figure 5-6.
The Label tool.

Properties

Labels have the properties FontBold, FontItalic, FontName, FontSize, FontUnderline, Height, Left, Name, Top, Visible, and Width, which operate in the standard manner. Some additional properties are described here:

Alignment This property determines how a label's caption is positioned. By default, the Alignment property is set to 0, which left-justifies the caption. You can also set Alignment to 1 - Right Justify or to 2 - Center.

AutoSize If this property is set to True, the label is automatically resized to fit the text specified by the Caption property. If AutoSize is set to False, the label will remain the size defined at design time; in that case, if the caption is too long, it will be clipped to fit.

BorderStyle This property can be set either to 0 (the default) for no border or to 1 for a single-line border.

Caption The Caption property contains the text that is displayed in the label's field, or screen area.

Enabled This property is normally set to True, but you can set it to False to gray the text and disable any mouse events.

Events

Label objects receive Click and DblClick events, just as picture boxes, image controls, and forms do.

Procedures and Methods

Label objects exist to display small blocks of text. Because the text is defined simply by setting the Caption property, none of the methods associated with labels are particularly useful or necessary for the beginner.

Modifying the Stopwatch Application

Let's make one more change to the Stopwatch program you created in Chapter 1. In this program, you used text boxes to display the output of the application. As you might remember, text boxes can be modified by the user. To illustrate this, load and run the Stopwatch program. After stopping the timer, select the text in the Starting Time box and type *xyz*—messes up the display, doesn't it? Of course, it's hard to imagine why a user would want to do something like this, but many a programmer has spent long lonely nights wondering just why users do the things they do. In any case, you can simply structure your application to avoid this problem by using labels rather than text boxes.

1. Stop the program and return to design mode. Delete the three text boxes by clicking on each one to select it and then pressing the Del key or choosing the Delete command from the Edit menu. In place of the three text boxes, draw three labels.

2. Set the BorderStyle property of each label to 1 - Fixed Single to create a single-line border. Delete any text that appears in the Settings box for the Caption property, leaving the Caption property setting empty for each label.

3. Set the Name property of the top label to lblStart. Then set the Name property of the middle label to lblStop and the Name property of the bottom label to lblElapsed.

4. You must also modify the code for the Start and Stop buttons. The previous version of the program displayed its results by setting the Text property of the text boxes. Labels, however, have a Caption property rather than a Text property. And, of course, you've replaced the text boxes themselves with labels. You need to edit the *Click* event procedures of the two buttons so that any references to the text boxes and the Text property are changed. Your new code should look like this:

```
Sub btnStart_Click ()
    StartTime = Now
    lblStart.Caption = Format(StartTime, "hh:mm:ss")
    lblStop.Caption = ""
    lblElapsed.Caption = ""
    btnStop.Enabled = True
    btnStart.Enabled = False
End Sub

Sub btnStop_Click ()
    EndTime = Now
    ElapsedTime = EndTime - StartTime
    lblStop.Caption = Format(EndTime, "hh:mm:ss")
    lblElapsed.Caption = Format(ElapsedTime, "hh:mm:ss")
    btnStop.Enabled = False
    btnStart.Enabled = True
End Sub
```

5. Run the application again to test your changes. The display should look exactly the same as it did when you ran the application in Chapter 1, but you can no longer select or modify any of the text on the screen.

Text Boxes

You have already worked with text boxes in earlier chapters, using the Text Box tool shown in Figure 5-7. Simply put, text boxes create a screen area in which the user can enter text.

Figure 5-7.
The Text Box tool.

Properties

Text boxes have the standard properties BorderStyle, Enabled, FontBold, FontItalic, FontName, FontSize, FontUnderline, Height, Left, Name, Top, Visible, and Width, plus the following:

MaxLength This property is usually set to 0 (the default), indicating that the text box will accept as many characters as the user types in. If you set MaxLength to a nonzero value, however, Visual Basic restricts the user input to the specified number of characters.

MultiLine Most often, you will want to set this property to False, which restricts user input to a single line of text. When the MultiLine property is set to True, the user can press the Enter key to place a carriage return in the text and continue text entry on the next line.

PasswordChar This property governs whether or not a text box is a password field. When a user types text in a password field, the characters that appear on the screen differ from the characters that are being typed. By default, this property is set to an empty string, which means that the user will see the characters he or she is entering. If the PasswordChar property is set to a character such as an asterisk (*), that character is displayed for every character the user types. Don't be confused: The actual contents of the text box are set to the text typed by the user; only the display is affected.

ScrollBars You can set this property to 0 (no scroll bars in the text box), 1 (a horizontal scroll bar only), 2 (a vertical scroll bar only), or 3 (both horizontal and vertical scroll bars).

SelLength This property contains the number of characters currently selected. Its value changes when the user selects text in the text box. You can also alter the selection programmatically by setting this property to an integer value in your code. If SelLength is 0, no characters are selected. This property and the SelStart and SelText properties are accessible only at runtime.

SelStart The setting of this property tells you where the current selection starts. A setting of 0 indicates that the selection (or insertion point) starts before the first character, a setting of 1 indicates that the selection starts before the second character, and so forth. You can modify this property programmatically as well.

SelText This property contains the text string that is currently selected. If no text is selected, the property contains an empty string. If you set SelText in your program code, you replace the selected text in the text box with the SelText setting. For example, if a text box called Text1 contains the line "Frankly, my deere, I don't give a damn" and the word *deere* is selected, you can correct the sentence by executing the statement *Text1.SelText = "dear"*. Note that this also changes the value of SelLength. Because the selection starts at the same position, however, SelStart is not affected.

Text The program reads this property to see what the user has entered. The program can also modify the Text property to change the text that is displayed.

Events

Text boxes do not support mouse events, but they can monitor every keystroke entered by the user. We'll take a look at some keyboard events later, in Chapter 7.

Change This event is signaled when the Text property of the text box is changed either by the user, who enters new information, or by the program, which can set a new value for the Text property. Note that if the user types the word *Hello*, the Change event is signaled five times, once for each letter typed.

LostFocus   This event is signaled when the user tabs to move away from the text box or uses the mouse to select some other object in the form. If you want to examine the contents of the Text property, it is usually more efficient to do so as part of the *LostFocus* event procedure rather than as part of the *Change* event procedure.

Procedures and Methods

The most useful method associated with text boxes is *SetFocus*, which places the cursor in a specific text box. When you create a form with multiple text boxes, you can use this method to direct the user's focus or attention to the most important box. The syntax is simple:

[*object*.]SetFocus

The NoteEdit Application

You've already used text boxes for simple, single-line text; now let's look at how the text box behaves in multiline mode, by implementing a small notepad that allows cutting, pasting, and simple editing.

Begin by opening a new project. Set the Caption and Name properties of the form to NoteEdit. Create a text box in the form, and set its properties as follows:

Property	Setting
MultiLine	True
Name	txtBox
ScrollBars	3 - Both
Text	[none]

Your NoteEdit form should now look like this:

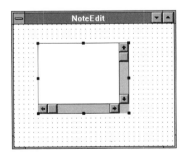

The text box will handle the text input and editing without any code-writing on your part. When you run the application, you can enter text, edit it, and cut, copy, and paste with the standard Windows shortcut keys Ctrl-X, Ctrl-C, and Ctrl-V.

To make the application look professional, you might want to make the text box fit entirely within the form window. To do this, edit the *Resize* procedure of the form as shown here:

```
Sub Form_Resize ()
    txtBox.Top = 0
    txtBox.Left = 0
    txtBox.Width = ScaleWidth
    txtBox.Height = ScaleHeight
End Sub
```

This procedure is executed every time the form is resized, including the first time the form is displayed. By setting the Top and Left properties of the text box to 0, you ensure that the upper left corner fits snugly against the top of the form, as shown in Figure 5-8. The Width and Height properties of the text box are set to match the ScaleWidth and ScaleHeight properties of the form (the full dimensions of the form's display area). Note that you could have written these two lines as *txtBox.Width = NoteEdit.ScaleWidth* and *txtBox.Height = NoteEdit.ScaleHeight*. Because the code is always executed in the context of the form, however, you don't need to use the form's name. Additionally, if you ever change the name of the form, you won't have to go back and edit the code.

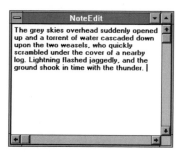

Figure 5-8.
Running the resized NoteEdit application.

Command Buttons, Check Boxes, and Option Buttons

These three Visual Basic objects are quite similar from a programmer's point of view. To the user, however, they differ visually, and they serve different purposes. Command buttons usually cause an action to occur (that is, a command to be executed) when they are clicked, whereas check boxes and option buttons indicate status and allow the user to change the status. The user clicks on a check box to select or deselect a certain feature; when an X appears in the check box, the feature is selected, or turned on. Each check box operates independently. In contrast, option buttons appear in sets and allow the user to choose one option from a set of options. When one option button is turned on, the others are turned off. (Option buttons are sometimes referred to as *radio buttons*.)

The tools from the Toolbox that are used to create these three kinds of Visual Basic objects are shown in Figures 5-9, 5-10, and 5-11.

Figure 5-9.
The Command Button tool.

Figure 5-10.
The Check Box tool.

Figure 5-11.
The Option Button tool.

Properties

Command buttons, check boxes, and option buttons have these properties, among others: Caption, Enabled, FontBold, FontItalic, FontName, FontSize, FontUnderline, Height, Left, Name, Top, Visible, and Width. In addition, you'll find the following properties useful:

Cancel This property is supported only by command buttons. When a command button's Cancel property is set to True, pressing the Esc key has the same effect as clicking on the button (like a Cancel button in a dialog box, for example). Only one command button in a form can have its Cancel property set to True.

Default The Default property is supported only by command buttons. When this property is set to True, pressing the Enter key has the same effect as clicking on the button (like an OK button in a dialog box). Only one command button in a form can have its Default property set to True.

Value This property indicates the status of a check box or an option button. An option button's Value property can be set to either True or False; when it is set to True, the button is "on"—that is, the center of the button is highlighted. A check box's Value property can be set to 0, 1, or 2: A setting of 0 indicates that the box is not checked; a setting of 1 indicates that the box is checked; and a setting of 2 indicates that the check box is grayed.

Events

All three of these objects receive the Click event, although you are likely to use a *Click* event procedure only for command buttons. Option buttons and check boxes automatically display their state when you click on them; generally, no programming is necessary.

Procedures and Methods

You cannot print to or draw on command buttons, check boxes, or option buttons. None of the other methods discussed thus far apply to these three kinds of objects.

The Game Application

This project presents the kind of "face" you might see on a video game. Begin by opening a new project. Create three command buttons, four option buttons, and two check boxes, arranging them in this fashion:

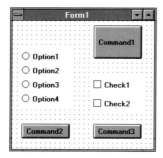

Set the properties of the objects as shown in Figure 5-12. After you've set the properties, your form should resemble the one shown in Figure 5-13.

Object	Property	Setting
Option1	Caption	1 Player
	Value	True
Option2	Caption	2 Players
Option3	Caption	3 Players
Option4	Caption	4 Players
Check1	Caption	Sound
Check2	Caption	Bonus Points
Command1	Caption	Coin Return
Command2	Caption	Start
	Default	True
Command3	Cancel	True
	Caption	Quit

Figure 5-12.
Property settings for the Game application.

Figure 5-13.
The Game interface.

Finally, edit the *Click* procedures for the Command2 and Command3 buttons to include this code:

```
Sub Command2_Click ()
    MsgBox "Game over"
End Sub

Sub Command3_Click ()
    End
End Sub
```

Run the program a few times to see how it behaves. Try pressing the Enter and Esc keys to see which commands they execute.

If you want to display in the Debug window the status of the option buttons and check boxes, you can change the *Click* procedure for Command2 as shown here:

```
Sub Command2_Click ()
    Debug.Print Option1.Value
    Debug.Print Option2.Value
    Debug.Print Option3.Value
    Debug.Print Option4.Value
    Debug.Print Check1.Value
    Debug.Print Check2.Value
End Sub
```

Frames

Frames exist to partition groups of other objects on the screen. In the case of option buttons, frames also affect the behavior of the buttons, as the sample project will demonstrate. For other objects, frames provide a visual separation as well as an overall enable/disable feature. To place a frame on a form, use the Frame tool from the Visual Basic Toolbox, shown in Figure 5-14.

Figure 5-14.
The Frame tool.

Properties

The Name property of the frame is used to identify it in your program code, and the Caption property defines the text that is visible as part of the frame. Frames also have the Enabled, FontBold, FontItalic, FontName, FontSize, FontUnderline, Height, Left, Top, Visible, and Width properties.

The familiar Enabled property behaves somewhat differently for frames. This property is usually set to True; when it is set to False, the frame's caption text is grayed, and all of the objects within the frame are disabled, including text boxes, button controls, and other objects.

Events

Frames do not respond to mouse events or user input.

Procedures and Methods

You cannot print to or draw in frames, nor can you associate them with graphics.

Modifying the Game Application

Because frames aren't terribly interesting by themselves, let's simply modify the Game project from the previous section, rather than creating a new application.

1. In the form window of the Game application, delete the option buttons labeled 3 Players and 4 Players. In their place, draw a frame like the one shown here:

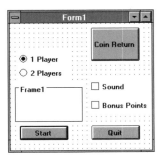

2. Place two new option buttons inside the frame. Note that you must draw them inside the frame; in this case, you cannot double-click on the Option Button tool to create the buttons and then drag them into the frame.

3. Set the Caption property of the frame to Mode.

4. Set the Value property of the Option3 button to True.

5. Set the Caption property of the Option3 button to Beginner and the Caption property of the Option4 button to Advanced.

The result should look like the interface shown in Figure 5-15. When you run the program, notice that the option buttons inside the frame operate independently of the ones outside it.

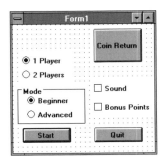

Figure 5-15.
The redesigned Game interface.

List Boxes

List boxes allow you to give the user a choice of options. The list box displays the options that are available, and the user selects an item, or list entry, by clicking on it. Visual Basic will add scroll bars to the list box if the entire list is too long to be displayed at one time. To work correctly, a list box must be at least three lines high. If you want to add a list box to a form, use the List Box tool from the Toolbox, shown in Figure 5-16. (Drop-down list boxes, such as the Settings box that appears in the Visual Basic Properties window, are a variant of combo boxes, which are discussed in the next section.)

Figure 5-16.
The List Box tool.

The contents of a list box cannot be defined at design time. Instead, your program must use the *AddItem* method to enter items in the list box. It's usually best to initialize a list box in the *Load* event procedure of the form containing the list box.

Properties

The usual properties are supported by list boxes: Enabled, FontBold, FontItalic, FontName, FontSize, FontUnderline, Height, Left, Name, Top, Visible, and Width. Special properties of list boxes include the following:

Columns When this property is set to 0 (its default), all the list items are displayed in a single column. If the property is set to 1 or more, the list items are arranged in a multicolumn layout; the value of the property setting indicates how many columns are visible at a given time. Horizontal scroll bars are added to the list box when necessary.

List This property, which cannot be modified at design time, holds the array of all values stored in the list box. (Arrays are discussed in Chapter 6.) You can access individual items in the list box using this syntax:

object.List(*index*)

ListCount The ListCount property, which cannot be modified directly, contains the number of items in the list box.

ListIndex   The setting of this property indicates the number of the most recently selected list item. The index value of the first item in the list box is 0, the index value of the next item is 1, and so on. If no item is selected, ListIndex is set to −1. If you set the ListIndex property programmatically, the highlight in the list changes to reflect the setting. You can determine the text of the selected item by reading the Text property.

MultiSelect   This property controls how many items in the list box can be selected. If this property is set to 0 - None, the user can select only one item at a time (that is, no multiple selection is allowed). If the setting is 1 - Simple, the user can select more than one item. When MultiSelect is set to 2 - Extended, the user can select a range of items by clicking on the first item, holding down the Shift key, and clicking on the last item in the range. The user can also hold down the Ctrl key and click on items to select or deselect each item individually. Note that even when multiple items are selected, the ListIndex and Text properties indicate only the most recent selection. You must examine each element of the Selected property to determine which items are selected.

Selected   The Selected property is an array with an element set to True or False for each item in the list box. A setting of True indicates that the item is selected; a setting of False indicates that the item is not selected. To check the status of a given item, specify the index of the item using the following syntax:

object.Selected(*index*)

Sorted   If you want Visual Basic to maintain the list items sorted in alphabetic order, you should set this property to True. When it is set to False (the default), the list items are displayed in the order in which they were added.

Text   This property, which cannot be modified directly, contains the text of the most recently selected list item.

Events

List boxes receive both Click and DblClick events. Typically, you would not code a *Click* procedure because the user might first select one item and then decide to select a different item. Instead, your program would likely read the Text property when the user clicks on a command button or when a DblClick event occurs.

Procedures and Methods

The most commonly used methods for list boxes include the *AddItem, Clear,* and *RemoveItem* methods. All three of these methods allow you to modify the list box's contents at runtime.

AddItem This method allows you to insert a line of text into the list box. You specify the text to insert and, optionally, the index of the inserted item. If you don't specify an index, Visual Basic inserts the item after all the existing items. If the Sorted property is set to True, do not specify an index value; Visual Basic inserts the item in alphabetic order. Here is the syntax for the *AddItem* method:

object.AddItem *text* [, *index*]

Clear This method removes all items from the list box. The syntax for the *Clear* method is quite simple:

object.Clear

RemoveItem The *RemoveItem* method allows you to remove a line of text from the list box. You must specify the index of the item you want to remove, using the following syntax:

object.RemoveItem *index*

The Cheese Application

This sample project will transfer items between two list boxes. The items in one box will be sorted in alphabetic order; items in the other box will appear in the order in which they are added.

Begin by creating a new project. On the form, draw two list boxes, as shown in Figure 5-17, and set the Sorted property of the list box on the right (List2) to True. The rest of the application is created with the code shown in Figure 5-18. The *Form_Load* procedure initializes the list box. The *List1_DblClick* and the *List2_DblClick* procedures are nearly identical, except that they transfer list items in opposite directions.

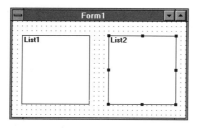

Figure 5-17.
The form design for the Cheese application.

```
Sub Form_Load ()
    List1.AddItem "Gouda"
    List1.AddItem "Camembert"
    List1.AddItem "Cheddar"
    List1.AddItem "Venezuelan Beaver Cheese"
    List1.AddItem "Wensleydale"
    List1.AddItem "Edam"
    List1.AddItem "Brie"
End Sub

Sub List1_DblClick ()
    List2.AddItem List1.Text
    List1.RemoveItem List1.ListIndex
End Sub

Sub List2_DblClick ()
    List1.AddItem List2.Text
    List2.RemoveItem List2.ListIndex
End Sub
```

Figure 5-18.
Program code for the Cheese application.

When you double-click on an item in one of the list boxes, the item is removed from that box and added to the other box. List box List2 will continue to sort its entries in alphabetic order, whereas List1 will maintain its entries in the order in which they are added.

Combo Boxes

Combo boxes are created with the Combo Box tool from the Toolbox, shown in Figure 5-19. The combo box is so named because it can combine a text box and a list box in a single control. Unlike a list box, however, it does not support multiple columns. You can specify any one of three types of behavior for a combo box by setting its Style property.

Figure 5-19.
The Combo Box tool.

Properties

In addition to the usual properties, combo boxes have two properties of interest, the Style property and the Text property.

Style The Style property, which determines the type of combo box and how it behaves, can be set to 0, 1, or 2.

When Style is set to 2, the combo box becomes a drop-down list box. Initially, only a single item of the list is visible; but when the user clicks on the down-arrow button beside the box, the complete list drops down, displaying all the items and allowing the user to select one, just as in a list box. The Object box in the Visual Basic Properties window is a familiar example.

A Style setting of 1 creates what is referred to as a simple combo box: an edit area in which the user can enter text, with a standard list box directly below it. The list does not drop down; it is always displayed. The user can either select an item from the list or enter text in the edit area.

Setting the Style property to 0 creates a drop-down combo box, which looks like a drop-down list box but also allows the user to enter text or select from the drop-down list. The Settings box in the Visual Basic Properties window often functions as a drop-down combo box.

Text This property can contain the text of an item selected from the list or text entered directly in the edit area by the user.

Events

How a combo box responds to events depends on its style of operation—that is, on how the Style property is set. For example, a DblClick event is received only if the Style property is set to 1 (a simple combo box). In the other two styles, only the Click event is received. The two styles that allow text entry receive the Change event when the user types in the edit area of the combo box. In general, you will simply want your program to read the Text property of the combo box after the user has made a selection.

Procedures and Methods

The *AddItem, Clear,* and *RemoveItem* methods that were described for list boxes are also implemented for combo boxes and are used in the same way.

The Flight Application

This project includes all three combo box styles side by side so that you can experiment with them. The application simulates a dialog box that queries the user about personal preferences for an upcoming airline flight.

1. Create a new project. Place three labels and two command buttons on the form, setting the Caption property of each object to match the captions that are shown here:

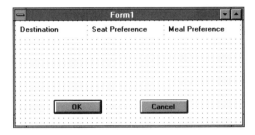

2. Set the Default property of the OK button to True and the Cancel property of the Cancel button to True.

3. Beneath the Destination label, draw a combo box and set its Style property to 1 and its Name property to cboDest. Make it large enough to display four or five lines of text in the list box portion.

4. Create another combo box below the Seat Preference label, setting the box's Style property to 2 and its Name property to cboSeat.

5. Create one more combo box below the Meal Preference label. Set the box's Name property to cboMeal and its Style property to 0. Your form should look like the one shown here:

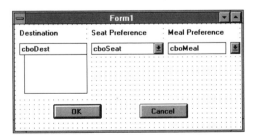

6. You will need to write two procedures, one to report the results of the user's actions when the user clicks on the OK command button, and one to initialize the combo boxes. The latter will be part of the *Form_Load* procedure. These procedures are shown in Figure 5-20.

```
Sub Command1_Click ()
    Debug.Print cboDest.Text
    Debug.Print cboSeat.Text
    Debug.Print cboMeal.Text
    End
End Sub

Sub Command2_Click ()
    End
End Sub

Sub Form_Load ()
    cboDest.Text = ""
    cboDest.AddItem "Paris"
    cboDest.AddItem "Moscow"
    cboDest.AddItem "New York"
    cboDest.AddItem "Cairo"
    cboDest.AddItem "Melbourne"
    cboDest.AddItem "Rio de Janeiro"
    cboDest.AddItem "Tokyo"

    cboSeat.AddItem "Aisle"
    cboSeat.AddItem "Window"
    cboSeat.AddItem "Center"
    cboSeat.ListIndex = 1

    cboMeal.AddItem "Chicken"
    cboMeal.AddItem "Lasagne"
    cboMeal.AddItem "Vegetarian"
    cboMeal.AddItem "Kosher"
    cboMeal.Text = "No preference"
End Sub
```

Figure 5-20.
Program code for the Flight application.

When you execute the application, note which combo boxes allow you to type in entries. Also note that the appearance of each type of combo box, as shown in Figure 5-21, gives you a cue as to how to continue.

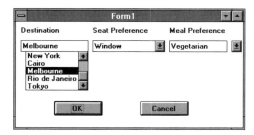

Figure 5-21.
Running the Flight application.

Horizontal and Vertical Scroll Bars

Horizontal and vertical scroll bars (shown in Figure 5-22) behave alike except for their direction. These objects simply report the position of the scroll box in the scroll bar; you have control over the range of the scroll bar and the increments by which the scroll box can be advanced. For example, if you were using a scroll bar to represent the throttle of an automobile, it might range from 0 to 100 in increments of 5. A volume control might range from 0 to 10 in increments of 1.

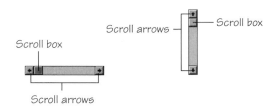

Figure 5-22.
Horizontal and vertical scroll bars.

To create these objects, use the Horizontal Scroll Bar tool (shown in Figure 5-23) or the Vertical Scroll Bar tool (shown in Figure 5-24 on the next page) from the Visual Basic Toolbox.

Figure 5-23.
The Horizontal Scroll Bar tool.

Figure 5-24.
The Vertical Scroll Bar tool.

Properties

The standard properties supported by scroll bars include Enabled, Height, Left, Name, Top, Visible, and Width. Special properties of both horizontal and vertical scroll bars include LargeChange, Max, Min, SmallChange, and Value.

LargeChange The setting of this property represents the increment added to or subtracted from the number contained in the Value property when the user clicks inside the scroll bar.

Max This property can be set to a number in the range −32,768 through 32,767. When the scroll box is at its rightmost or bottom position, the Value property is set to this number.

Min This property can be set to a number in the range −32,768 through 32,767. When the scroll box is at its leftmost or top position, the Value property is set to this number.

SmallChange The setting of this property represents the increment added to or subtracted from the number contained in the Value property when the user clicks on one of the scroll arrows at either end of the scroll bar.

Value This property contains the number representing the current position of the scroll box within the scroll bar. If you set this property programmatically, Visual Basic moves the scroll box to the appropriate location. Setting the Value property outside the range defined by the Max and Min property settings produces an error message.

Events

The primary events associated with a scroll bar are the Scroll and Change events. The Scroll event is repeatedly triggered while the scroll box is being dragged within the scroll bar. The Change event is signaled after the scroll box's position has been modified. Use the Scroll event to track dynamic changes in the scroll bar, and use the Change event to get the scroll bar's final value.

Procedures and Methods

None of the commonly used procedures or methods discussed previously apply to scroll bars.

The Scroll Bar Application

This project will simply provide you with some visual feedback about how a scroll bar works.

1. Create a new project. On the empty form, place a label field and a horizontal scroll bar, as shown here:

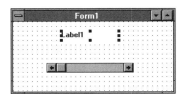

2. Set the BorderStyle property of the label to 1 - Fixed Single, and set the Caption property to an empty string. Set the properties of the horizontal scroll bar as follows:

Property	Setting
LargeChange	10
Max	100
Min	0
SmallChange	2

3. Double-click on the scroll bar to bring up the code window, and enter this procedure to handle the Change event:

```
Sub HScroll1_Change ()
    Label1.Caption = Str$(HScroll1.Value)
End Sub
```

Because the label's Caption property accepts only string values, you must use the *Str$* function to convert the value of *HScroll1.Value* to a string.

4. Enter the following procedure to deal with the Scroll event:

```
Sub HScroll1_Scroll ()
    Label1.Caption = "Moving to" + Str$(HScroll1.Value)
End Sub
```

Now start the application. When you click in the gray area of the scroll bar, the value displayed in the label changes in units of 10. When you click on a scroll arrow at either end of the scroll bar, the value changes in units of 2.

By dragging the scroll box with your mouse, you can adjust the value in units other than 2 or 10. The value displayed in Figure 5-25, for example, could have been produced either by clicking on the scroll arrows or by dragging the scroll box. Notice that the procedure for the Scroll event updates the label caption as you drag the scroll box. Choose Break from the Run menu or click on the Toolbar's Break button, and then enter the statement *HScroll1.Value = 17* in the Debug window. Observe that the position of the scroll box changes when the value changes. Now enter the statement *HScroll1.Max = 500*. The scroll box position changes again, maintaining the appropriate position relative to the Min and Max settings.

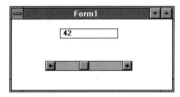

Figure 5-25.
Running the Scroll Bar application.

Timers

Timers, which are created with the Timer tool shown in Figure 5-26, are objects that can cause events to be triggered at regular intervals. You program a timer by setting its Interval property to the number of milliseconds ($\frac{1}{1000}$ second) that should elapse between timer events.

Figure 5-26.
The Timer tool.

A timer is limited by the capabilities of your system hardware. Most personal computers support a timer resolution of no more than 18 events per second, or approximately $\frac{56}{1000}$ second between events. In practical terms, this resolution means that values less than 56 are not particularly useful—in other words, interval values that differ by 5, 10, or even 20 are likely to produce the same result. This limitation does not mean that you should be sloppy in your calculations—future hardware, after all, will probably have better support for timers—but it does mean that you should not rely on timers to be fantastically accurate.

In addition, some timer events can simply get lost in the shuffle. Suppose that your program receives a timer event once a second but that part of the program involves an extremely complicated calculation that takes 10 seconds to perform. When that calculation is finished, you might expect that 10 timer events would be stacked up somehow, as if they had gotten in a slow lane at the grocery checkout counter. In fact, however, only 1 timer event will occur immediately after the calculation. Before generating a timer event, the system always checks to see whether an earlier timer event is already pending; if it is, no new timer events are generated.

You are no doubt wondering about the utility of timers, given all these restrictions. They can in fact be quite useful, albeit not as a source of precision timing. You can think of a timer event as a "kick in the pants" for your application. At regular intervals, a timer can nudge your program, saying, in effect, "Hey, it's time to check up on things."

Properties

The Name and Enabled properties are standard for timers. The most important property of timer objects is the Interval property. This property is set to the number of milliseconds between timer events, with values ranging from 0 through 65,535, theoretically generating events at rates that range from 1000 events a second to less than 1 event every minute. A 0 interval is equivalent to disabling the timer. If you want to generate an event n times per second, use the formula $1000 / n$ to find the setting for the Interval property. For example, if you want a timer event to occur every half second (two times per second), the calculation $1000 / 2$ indicates an Interval setting of 500.

Events

The Timer event is generated at regular intervals when the timer is enabled.

Procedures and Methods

No procedures or methods operate on timer objects.

The Metronome Application

This project—which creates a metronome, using a timer and a scroll bar—demonstrates what happens when you try to use a timer object as an extremely accurate timekeeper. Metronomes typically operate in a range from about 40 beats per minute for slow music to 200 beats per minute for very fast music. A setting of 40 beats per minute is ⅔ beat per second, or 1 beat every 1500 milliseconds. At the other end of the scale, 200 beats per minute is 3⅓ beats per second, or 1 beat every 300 milliseconds. Thus, the values 300 and 1500 can serve as maximum and minimum points for a scroll bar in your application. (Note that the higher the value, the slower the beat; therefore 1500 is the minimum value, not the maximum.)

1. Create a new project, and add a horizontal scroll bar to the form. Then create a timer object by double-clicking on the Timer tool in the Toolbox. You do not need to draw or resize a timer object; it shows up on the form at design time, but it will be invisible when the program is running.

2. Place a label below the left end of the scroll bar, and set its Caption property to Slow. Below the right end of the scroll bar, create a label with the caption Fast. Here is what you should see on your screen:

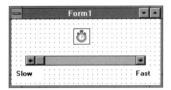

3. Set the Interval property of the timer object to 1000.

4. Set the properties of the horizontal scroll bar as follows:

Property	Setting
LargeChange	100
Max	300
Min	1500
SmallChange	25
Value	1000

5. You need to add two lines of program code for this application, one line in the scroll bar's *Change* procedure, and the other line in the *Timer* procedure of the timer object. The *Change* procedure keeps the timer object in sync with the scroll bar, and the *Timer* procedure generates the metronome's tick (or, in this case, its beep):

```
Sub HScroll1_Change ()
    Timer1.Interval = HScroll.Value
End Sub

Sub Timer1_Timer ()
    Beep
End Sub
```

When you start the application, the metronome will tick at 1 beat per second. Moving the scroll box will alter the speed of the ticking. Try moving the window around on the screen or running another application in the background. When nothing else is going on, the timer is fairly accurate, but you can see how some of the timer events get lost when the computer shifts its attention to some other task.

Lines and Shapes

To enhance the appearance of the forms in your applications, you can add simple lines and solid-shape graphics using the Toolbox's Line tool and Shape tool, which are shown in Figures 5-27 and 5-28. Objects created with these tools appear in the same graphics layer as image objects.

Figure 5-27.
The Line tool.

Figure 5-28.
The Shape tool.

The line and shape controls (as well as the image control) are useful primarily for providing visual backgrounds for your form. The Line tool creates simple, straight line segments. You can alter the size, color, and pattern of the lines by modifying their properties. The Shape tool always creates a rectangle on the screen, but by setting the object's Shape property, you can create circles, ovals, and rounded rectangles. In addition, you can set the colors and fill patterns of the shapes.

Properties

Both of these objects have the usual Name and Visible properties. Shape objects also have the standard Height, Left, Top, and Width properties. Line objects have positional properties X1, Y1 and X2, Y2, which are the coordinates of the two endpoints of the line. Other properties determine how the objects appear on the screen.

BorderColor This property determines the color of the object's outline (or, in the case of line objects, the color of the line). You set the BorderColor property by choosing a color from a palette, just as you set the BackColor and ForeColor properties of a form.

BorderStyle The BorderStyle property controls how the line or the outline of the shape is drawn. You can use any one of these seven settings:

0 - Transparent

1 - Solid

2 - Dash

3 - Dot

4 - Dash-Dot

5 - Dash-Dot-Dot

6 - Inside Solid

BorderWidth This property allows you to specify the width of the line or the outline of the shape. If you set BorderWidth to a value other than 1, you cannot use any of the dashed or dotted BorderStyle values.

Shape objects also have the FillColor and FillStyle properties:

FillColor Analogous to the BorderColor property, FillColor lets you define the interior color of a shape. You set this property in the same way you set the Border-Color property, by using a color palette.

FillStyle The FillStyle property setting determines the interior pattern of a shape object:

0 - Solid

1 - Transparent

2 - Horizontal Line

3 - Vertical Line

4 - Upward Diagonal

5 - Downward Diagonal

6 - Cross

7 - Diagonal Cross

Events

Line objects and shape objects do not receive any events.

Procedures and Methods

None of the methods covered in this chapter apply to lines or shapes.

The Layer Project

This sample project is not a complete application; instead, it simply lets you experiment with display objects so that you will become more comfortable with the tools.

1. Create a new project. On the form, place a picture box, a command button, a shape, a line, and an image control, as shown here:

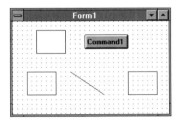

2. Select the Picture property of Picture1 in the Properties window. Click on the ellipsis button beside the Settings box to display the Load Picture dialog box. In the dialog box, set the file type to display filenames with the ICO extension. In the MISC subdirectory of the ICONS directory that comes with Visual Basic, you'll find the icon file FACE01.ICO. Choose this file to load the icon in the picture box. In a similar fashion, set the Picture property of Image1 to load the icon FACE02.ICO in the image control.

3. Set the FillStyle property of Shape1 to 0 - Solid and the FillColor property to red. (Click on the ellipsis button beside the Settings box and select red from the palette.) Set the BorderWidth of Line1 to 4. The form should now look like this:

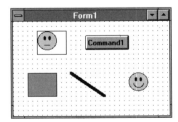

4. Move the shape toward the center of the form, and then move the other objects over the shape so that they overlap somewhat, as shown here:

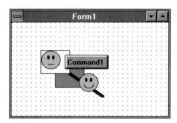

Notice that in each layer of the display the most recently created object appears on top of the previously created objects. (The picture box and the command button reside on the top layer, and the shape, the line, and the image are on the middle layer.)

The order in which certain objects overlay other objects is called the *Z-order*, and it can be altered. Click on Line1 to select it, and choose the Bring To Front command from Visual Basic's Edit menu. The line, which already appeared over the shape, now also appears over the image. Note, however, that when you move the line around on the screen, it will not cover the picture box or the command button. The Bring To Front and Send To Back commands operate only within a layer; middle-layer objects will always appear behind top-layer objects. You can use these two commands on all controls, which allows you to adjust the Z-order within each layer. Try using Send To Back after selecting the command button.

Drive List Boxes, Directory List Boxes, and File List Boxes

The three tools from Visual Basic's Toolbox shown in Figures 5-29, 5-30, and 5-31 allow you to build customized dialog boxes that interface with the file system. Each file system control manages a separate component of the system: A drive list box appears as a drop-down list box containing the names of all the disk drives on the system; a directory list box displays all the subdirectories in the current directory; and a file list box displays some or all of the files in the current directory.

Most of the time you will not use the drive list box or directory list box individually. Instead, when the user is selecting a file to open or save, you will provide access to all the file system components at once. In this case you can use the common dialog control, which neatly packages the File Open and File Save As functions.

On occasion, however, you might need a dialog box with components beyond those provided in the standard File Open and File Save As dialog boxes. For example, Microsoft Word for Windows has additional buttons for File Sharing and Options in the Save As dialog box. In such cases you might use the Drive List Box, Directory List Box, and File List Box tools. (See Chapter 9 for a sample application.)

Figure 5-29.
The Drive List Box tool.

Figure 5-30.
The Directory List Box tool.

Figure 5-31.
The File List Box tool.

Properties

The three file system controls have many of the usual properties: Enabled, FontBold, FontItalic, FontName, FontSize, Height, Left, Name, Top, Visible, and Width. In addition, the following properties are important:

Drive This property, which applies only to drive list boxes, contains the name of the currently selected drive.

FileName Only file list boxes have the FileName property, which contains the currently selected filename in a file list box.

List, ListIndex These properties are supported only by file list boxes and are identical to the List and ListIndex properties of list boxes.

Path In directory and file list boxes, this property contains the current path. The Path property doesn't apply to drive list boxes.

Pattern This property of file list boxes contains a string that determines which files will be displayed. It supports the use of the * and ? wildcard characters in filenames. For example, setting the Pattern property to *.DAT would display all the files that have the filename extension DAT.

Events

Directory and file list boxes respond to the Click event, although drive list boxes do not. The DblClick event is received only by file list boxes. Two other events are important to the file system controls:

Change This event is recognized only by drive and directory list boxes. It is triggered whenever the user or the program changes the selection in the list box.

PathChange This event applies only to file list boxes. It occurs whenever the path changes, either because the user double-clicked on a directory folder or because the program changed the FileName or Path property. This allows your program to update the contents of a matching directory list box.

Procedures and Methods

None of the procedures or methods discussed thus far are applicable to the file system controls.

Other Visual Basic Tools

The Visual Basic Toolbox also includes a few other tools, which are described briefly here. These tools and the objects they create are covered later in this book because they require a good deal of programming effort and some fairly advanced techniques. See Chapters 11 and 12 for more information about these advanced tools.

Grids

The Grid tool, pictured in Figure 5-32, lets you create a grid control. A grid is a two-dimensional block of cells that resembles the rows and columns of a spreadsheet. You can use a grid control to implement spreadsheet-like functions in Visual Basic. A project that uses a grid must include the file GRID.VBX in its project file. See Chapter 11, "Databases and Grids," for more detailed information about the Grid tool.

Figure 5-32.
The Grid tool.

Data

The Data tool, shown in Figure 5-33, lets you create a data control through which you can provide access to specific data in a database. The data control has a number of properties that define the connection between your Visual Basic application and the database you plan to access. Before you use the Data tool in Visual Basic, you'll need to enable file sharing. See Chapter 11, "Databases and Grids," for more detailed information about the Data tool.

Figure 5-33.
The Data tool.

OLE 2.0

Microsoft OLE (object linking and embedding) technology allows you to create in one application an object that contains data from an unrelated application. For example, a chart from a graphing program or a detailed drawing from a CAD (computer-aided design) program could be placed in your Visual Basic program. Rather than simply taking a snapshot of the graph or drawing, OLE maintains a link to the original application so that if you change the original data, the copy in the Visual Basic application is automatically updated.

The OLE tool from Visual Basic's Toolbox, shown in Figure 5-34, lets you add object linking and embedding capabilities to a Visual Basic program. Chapter 12 discusses OLE in detail.

Figure 5-34.
The OLE tool.

The AUTOLOAD.MAK File

As you've noticed, Visual Basic automatically includes the GRID.VBX file, the CMDIALOG.VBX file, and the MSOLE2.VBX file in every project you create. Unless you are using a grid, a common dialog box, or an OLE control, however, you can delete these files from your project file. To prevent Visual Basic from automatically including them in your projects, choose the Open Project command from the File menu and open the AUTOLOAD.MAK file from the Open Project dialog box.

Each time you create a new project, Visual Basic copies the contents of the AUTOLOAD.MAK file into the new project. If you delete the GRID.VBX file and the MSOLE2.VBX file from AUTOLOAD.MAK (choose Remove File from the File menu), they will no longer appear in your new projects. Leave CMDIALOG.VBX in the AUTOLOAD.MAK file for the time being. In fact, the Grid tool and the OLE tool will disappear from the Toolbox. You can, however, include these files and tools on a project-by-project basis by using the Add File command from the File menu.

Common Dialog Boxes

To give the user a standard interface for common operations in Windows-based applications, Microsoft created a set of common dialog boxes for standard Windows functions. The code for these functions was first shipped with Windows 3.1 but can be used with Windows 3.0 if the file COMMDLG.DLL is added to the SYSTEM directory. Visual Basic provides access to these functions via the Common Dialog tool. Using the Common Dialog tool ensures that your application will conform to the standard look and feel of the supported operations.

Like the Timer tool, the Common Dialog tool, shown in Figure 5-35, is invisible at runtime. When you place the icon on one of your forms, however, you can invoke any one of the five standard functions supported by the tool. These are the standard Windows dialog boxes for Open, Save As, Color, Font, and Printer. In addition, the Common Dialog tool can invoke the Windows Help system. You must load the file COMMDLG.VBX into your Project Window to access the Common Dialog tool.

Figure 5-35.
The Common Dialog tool.

Execution of the selected function begins when you set the Action property of the common dialog control. Your Visual Basic statements are suspended until the user dismisses the dialog box. You can then examine the properties of the control to determine what action occured. There are no events or methods associated with a common dialog control. You specify its operation by setting property values and then assigning a value to the Action property.

In addition to the Action property, the CancelError property is used by all the Common Dialog functions. CancelError defaults to False, but if it is set to True, Visual Basic will signal an error if the user chooses the Cancel button in the dialog box. If you plan to set CancelError to True, you should use Visual Basic's error-handling features, which are described in Chapter 8.

The following paragraphs describe the functions of the Common Dialog tool. Because there are so many, a complete example program has not been provided, but a program fragment illustrating a typical use of the control is shown.

Open

The Open dialog box, shown in Figure 5-36, is invoked when the value 1 is assigned to the Action property. You can set any of the following properties to control the appearance of the dialog box. Note that this dialog box does not actually open a file; it simply allows the user to select the filename.

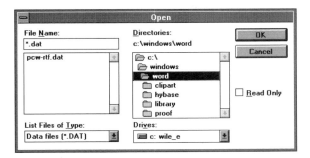

Figure 5-36.
The Open dialog box.

Properties

DialogTitle   This property can be set to any string. The string is displayed in the title bar of the dialog box. By default, the title is "Open."

FileName   This property is used to set the initial name in the File Name text box of the dialog box. After the dialog box is dismissed, this property can be read to determine the name of the selected file.

Filter   The Filter property can be set to restrict the filenames that appear in the file list box. The Filter property must be a text string with one or more pairs of components. The component pairs are made up of a description and a wildcard character, separated by the pipe symbol (|). Multiple pairs are also separated by the pipe symbol. For example, the following string specifies three component pairs:

```
"Documents (*.DOC)|*.DOC|Text Files (*.TXT)|*.txt|All Files|*.*"
```

The first filter limits the file list to files with the extension DOC, the second filter is for files with the TXT extension, and the third filter allows any file to be selected. Note that there are no spaces before or after the pipe characters.

FilterIndex   This property is set to an integer indicating which of the filter component pairs will be the default filter. In the example above, 1, 2, or 3 would be a legal value for FilterIndex.

Flags   The Flag property can be set to a combination of one or more values that control special features of the dialog box. The legal flag values are listed in the file CONSTANT.TXT and are described in Visual Basic's online Help. An example is the flag OFN_FILEMUSTEXIST, which forces the user to select an existing file.

Example

This program fragment displays an Open dialog box. It forces the user to choose a file that already exists and applies a default filter for data files (*.DAT). It assumes the common dialog object is named *Dlog*.

```
Dlog.FileName = ""
Dlog.Filter = "Data Files (*.DAT)¦*.DAT¦All Files (*.*)¦*.*"
Dlog.FilterIndex = 1                        'Start with *.DAT filter
Dlog.Flags = OFN_FILEMUSTEXIST Or OFN_PATHMUSTEXIST
Dlog.Action = 1                             'Display the dialog box
If Dlog.FileName = "" Then MsgBox "No file selected."
```

Save As

The Save As dialog box, shown in Figure 5-37, is invoked when the value 2 is assigned to the Action property. The properties for Save As are identical to those described above for Open, except that the default value for the DialogTitle property is Save As.

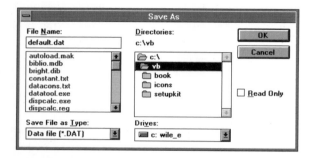

Figure 5-37.
The Save As dialog box.

Properties
DefaultExt This property can be set to a string of 1 to 3 characters, which is used as the default extension if a filename is specified without an extension.

Example
This program fragment displays a Save As dialog box. It assumes the common dialog object is named *Dlog*. In this example, the CancelError property is set to True; otherwise it would be impossible to tell if a filename has been selected or not. Note that this code does not actually save any file; it simply allows the user to select the filename.

```
Dlog.CancelError = True
Dlog.DefaultExt = "DAT"                  'Append .DAT by default
Dlog.FileName = "DEFAULT.DAT"            'Start with this filename
Dlog.Filter = "Data Files (*.DAT)¦*.DAT¦All files (*.*)¦*.*"
Dlog.FilterIndex = 1                     'Start with .DAT filter
Dlog.Flags = OFN_OVERWRITEPROMPT Or OFN_PATHMUSTEXIST
Dlog.Action = 2                          'Display the dialog box
MsgBox "Writing to file " + Dlog.FileName
```

Color

The Color dialog box, shown in Figure 5-38, is invoked when the value 3 is assigned to the Action property. You can set any of the following properties to control the appearance of the dialog box.

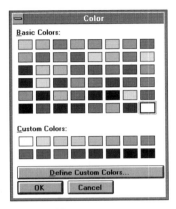

Figure 5-38.
The Color dialog box.

Properties

Color This property is used to set the initial color. After the dialog box is dismissed, this property can be read to determine the color selected by the user.

Flags This property must be set to CC_RGBINIT to set or read the Color property.

Example

This program fragment displays a dialog box for color selection. It assumes the common dialog object is named *Dlog* and uses the selected color to set the current form's background.

```
Dlog.Color = BackColor          'Current color
Dlog.Flags = CC_RGBINIT
Dlog.Action = 3                 'Display dialog
BackColor = Dlog.Color          'New color or same if canceled
```

Font

The Font dialog box, shown in Figure 5-39, is invoked when the value 4 is assigned to the Action property. You can set any of the following properties to control the appearance of the dialog box.

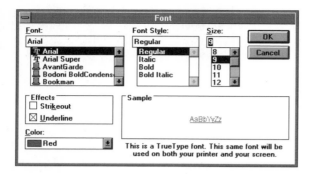

Figure 5-39.
The Font dialog box.

Properties

Color This property allows the font color to be set or read. (It is active only if the Flags property includes the CF_EFFECTS flag).

Flags This property can be set to modify the behavior of the dialog box. It must, however, include one of these values: CF_PRINTERFONTS, CF_SCREENFONTS, or CF_BOTH. They determine which fonts are to be listed in the dialog box (printer fonts only, screen fonts only, or both sets).

FontBold, FontItalic, FontStrikethru, FontUnderline These are Boolean properties that can be set or read to determine style information for the font. The Flags setting must include CC_EFFECTS to enable setting of styles.

FontName This property can be set to initialize the default font and read to determine the user's font selection.

FontSize This property can be set or read and determines the point size of the font.

Example

This subroutine allows the font attributes of a text control to be changed. The control is passed as a parameter. It assumes the common dialog object is named *Dlog*.

```
Sub SetTextProps (TxtCntl As Control)
    Dlog.Color = TxtCntl.ForeColor              'Get current settings
    Dlog.FontBold = TxtCntl.FontBold
    Dlog.FontItalic = TxtCntl.FontItalic
    Dlog.FontStrikethru = TxtCntl.FontStrikethru
    Dlog.FontUnderline = TxtCntl.FontUnderline
    Dlog.FontName = TxtCntl.FontName
    Dlog.FontSize = TxtCntl.FontSize
```

(continued)

```
        Dlog.Flags = CF_EFFECTS Or CF_FORCEFONTEXIST Or CF_BOTH
        Dlog.Action = 4                        'Display dialog
        TxtCntl.ForeColor = Dlog.Color         'Set selected values
        TxtCntl.FontBold = Dlog.FontBold
        TxtCntl.FontItalic = Dlog.FontItalic
        TxtCntl.FontStrikethru = Dlog.FontStrikethru
        TxtCntl.FontUnderline = Dlog.FontUnderline
        TxtCntl.FontName = Dlog.FontName
        TxtCntl.FontSize = Dlog.FontSize
    End Sub
```

Print

The Print dialog box, shown in Figure 5-40, is invoked when the value 5 is assigned to the Action property. You can set any of the following properties to control the appearance of the dialog box.

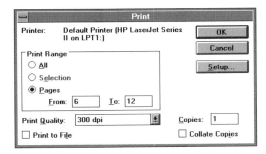

Figure 5-40.
The Print dialog box.

Properties

Copies This integer property specifies the number of copies to be printed.

Flags This property handles special features of the dialog box. You can refer to the CONSTANT.TXT file and the Visual Basic manual for more information.

Example

This program fragment displays a dialog box for printing. It assumes the common dialog object is named *Dlog*. Note that invoking the Print dialog box does not actually start the printing process. You must write to the printer object in Visual Basic. The dialog box simply allows the user to select certain print options.

```
    FirstPage = 1
    LastPage = 57
    Dlog.CancelError = True          'Abort if dialog canceled
```

(continued)

continued

```
Dlog.Copies = 1                    'Default setting
Dlog.Min = FirstPage
Dlog.Max = LastPage
Dlog.Flags = PD_USEDEVMODECOPIES Or
 PD_NOSELECTION                    'Allow more than one copy
Dlog.Action = 5                    'Display dialog box
PrintAll = Dlog.Flags And PD_ALLPAGES
If Not PrintAll Then
    FirstPage = Dlog.FromPage
    LastPage = Dlog.ToPage
End If
```

Invoke Help

The Windows Help application, shown in Figure 5-41, is invoked when the value 6 is assigned to the Action property. You can set any of the following properties to control the appearance of the dialog box.

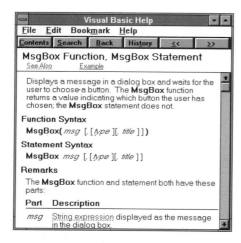

Figure 5-41.
The Help application.

Properties

HelpCommand This property specifies the kind of Help you want to invoke. Typically, you will use the constant HELP_KEY, indicating Help for a specific keyword. The definition of HELP_KEY is listed in CONSTANT.TXT.

HelpFile This property specifies the Help filename.

HelpKey This property specifies the keyword that should be used for the initial Help screen.

Example

This program fragment invokes Windows Help for the *MsgBox* function.

```
Dlog.HelpCommand = HELP_KEY
Dlog.HelpFile = "VB.HLP"
Dlog.HelpKey = "MsgBox"
Dlog.Action = 6        'Invoke Help
```

Menus

Although you have now created several small applications, you might feel that none of them look like "real applications." Why not? For starters, none of them have menu bars. You can remedy this situation, however, because Visual Basic makes it easy to create menus. Menus operate in an event-oriented manner, much like the objects we've discussed.

To create a menu for an application, you must use Visual Basic's Menu Design window, shown in Figure 5-42. Create a new project, and open this window by choosing the Menu Design command from the Window menu or by clicking on the Menu Design Window button on Visual Basic's Toolbar.

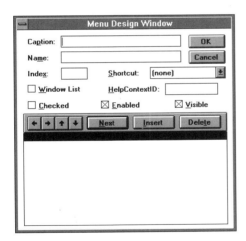

Figure 5-42.
Visual Basic's Menu Design window.

You build your application's menu bar by creating a hierarchy of items in the Menu Design window. For each menu item, you must define a Caption property and a Name property. The caption is the text that will appear in the menu bar or on the drop-down menu. The name of the menu item identifies it in your program's code. A name is required because each menu item will have a *Click* procedure.

Suppose that your computer includes hardware that will show television images inside a window. The menus for the application that controls the hardware might resemble a TV remote control. Here is a possible layout for the menu structure, with three levels in its hierarchy:

File

    On

    Off

    Exit

Channel

    Select...

    Up

    Down

Sound

    Mute

    Preset

        Soft

        Moderate

        Loud

    Louder

    Softer

Note that an ellipsis (...) appears after the Select menu item to indicate to the user that this selection will produce a dialog box.

Let's implement the menu portion of this application. Before you move to the Menu Design window, however, you need to refine your menu list a bit further.

In most Windows-based applications, you can use the keyboard to choose items from a menu without using the mouse. These keyboard shortcuts are called *access keys* and are usually based on pressing the Alt key and typing the characters that are underlined on the menu. For example, in Visual Basic, you can type Alt, F, S to choose the File menu's Save command. In the Menu Design window, you can specify the access key for a menu item by placing an ampersand (&) in front of the character that is to be underlined on the application's menu. (The ampersand is not displayed on the menu.)

Always use the first character of a menu item's caption as the access key unless a conflict exists. In our sample application, for example, both On and Off begin with the letter *O*, so you will need to choose another character for one of them. (One other exception involves using the *x* in Exit rather than the *E*; using the keyboard sequence Alt, F, X for exiting an application has become a de facto standard.)

Here are the menu entries for the sample application, with the access key characters specified:

&File

    &On

    Of&f

    E&xit

&Channel

    &Select…

    &Up

    &Down

&Sound

    &Mute

    &Preset

      &Soft

      &Moderate

      &Loud

    &Louder

    &Softer

In addition to a caption and an access key, each menu item needs a name. Although it might seem logical to use the same word as both name and caption, it is frequently impossible to do so. For example, *Exit* is a Visual Basic keyword and can be used as a caption but not as an object name in code.

It's best to use a standard naming scheme that lets you immediately recognize each item. Clear names are important because each menu item has a *Click* procedure; when you are working on code, it's easy to lose track of which menu item you are working with. For the sample project here, try using the prefix mnu for all object names; that will identify the objects as menus, as opposed to, say, command buttons or scroll bars.

For menu items in the first level of the hierarchy, follow the mnu prefix with the caption: mnuFile, for example. For items in the second level, use mnu followed by a three-letter abbreviation that indicates the first-level item to which the second-level item is subordinate, followed by the second-level item's caption: mnuFilOn, for instance, or mnuChaSelect. Likewise, for items in the third level, include two three-letter abbreviations that indicate the "parent" items. Here are suggested names for this application:

mnuFile

mnuFilOn

mnuFilOff

mnuFilExit

mnuChannel

mnuChaSelect

mnuChaUp

mnuChaDown

mnuSound

mnuSouMute

mnuSouPreset

mnuSouPreSoft

mnuSouPreModerate

mnuSouPreLoud

mnuSouLouder

mnuSouSofter

Now you're ready to move to the Menu Design window to create the menu for this application.

1. Click in the Caption text box of the Menu Design window, and type *&File*. Then press the Tab key to move to the Name text box. Type *mnuFile* in this text box, and press the Enter key. The caption (but not the name) will appear in the list box at the bottom of the window.

2. Click on the right-arrow button above the list box. Four dots will appear in the line below &File, indicating that the next items to be inserted are at the second level of the menu hierarchy.

3. Return to the Caption text box, and type *&On*. Tab to the Name text box, type *mnuFilOn*, and press Enter. Move back to the Caption text box, and type *Of&f*; then tab to the Name text box, type *mnuFilOff*, and press Enter. Use the same procedure for the caption E&xit and the name mnuFilExit. Your Menu Design window should now look like this:

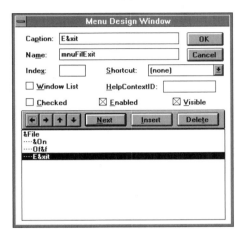

4. Click on the left-arrow button to return the hierarchy to the first level. Now enter the rest of the captions and names from your list. To enter items at the third level of the menu hierarchy, first click twice on the right-arrow button. If you make a mistake in placing an item in the hierarchy, you can select the item's name in the list box and click on the left-arrow or right-arrow button to adjust its level. The up-arrow and down-arrow buttons move the name to a different position in the list.

5. When you have completed entering the menu items, click on the OK button.

The menu bar now appears on the application's main form. You can view the menu items by clicking on a name on the menu bar. That menu will drop down, displaying the entries it contains, as shown in Figure 5-43 on the next page.

If you click on a menu entry in the form, Visual Basic opens a code window for the corresponding *Click* procedure. In this window, you write the code for the operation that will take place when the user selects the menu item. For example, click on the Exit item of the File menu to open the code window for the event procedure *mnuFilExit_Click*. The Visual Basic command used to terminate an application is End, so the procedure for the Exit item should look like this:

```
Sub mnuFilExit_Click ()
    End
End Sub
```

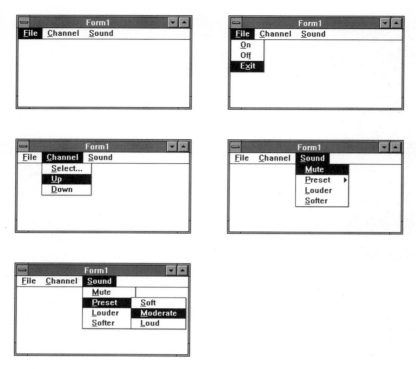

Figure 5-43.
A form with a menu bar and drop-down menus.

Experiment with the application by putting *Debug.Print* statements in various menu procedures and then running the application again. As you select different menu items, keep an eye on the Debug window for confirmation that the menu procedures are being executed.

Additional Menu Design Options

The Menu Design window also offers a number of other interesting options. For example, if you enter the hyphen (-) as a caption, Visual Basic places a separator bar in the menu, which visually sets off groups of related menu items. (You must also assign a name to the hyphen entry, even though it will not be used in your program.)

You can also assign shortcut keys to menu items. Open the Menu Design window again, and select E&xit. Then click on the down-arrow button beside the Shortcut box. You can assign any of the keystrokes listed in the drop-down list to the Exit menu item.

The Checked, Enabled, and Visible check boxes in the Menu Design window correspond to properties of a selected menu item. Each property can be set to True (as indicated by an X in the check box) or False (an empty check box). Setting the Checked property to True places a checkmark on the menu beside the menu item, indicating that the option is active. (You can see such a checkmark next to the Tool Bar item on Visual Basic's View menu.) The Enabled property is set to True by default; if you set this property to False, the menu item is grayed and cannot be selected from the menu. If you set the Visible property to False, the menu item will not appear on the menu at all.

Figure 5-44 shows what the Sound menu of your TV remote-control application might look like if you added two separator bars to the first level, set the Checked property of the mnuSouPreLoud menu item to True, added a new item named Really Loud, and—in deference to your neighbors—set its Enabled property to False.

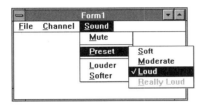

Figure 5-44.
A menu with separator bars, a checkmark, and a disabled option.

The Checked, Enabled, and Visible settings in the Menu Design window indicate the property settings at startup. You can change any of these settings in your program's code with statements of the following form:

   object.property = {True ¦ False}

The other options that appear in the Menu Design window—Window List, Index, and HelpContextID—are advanced features that are beyond the scope of this book. You can find information about these features in your Visual Basic reference manual.

Popup Menus

Although menus are typically invoked from the menu bar, sometimes you might want to display a menu from a control. This type of menu is called a *popup menu* because it is not normally visible but "pops up" when you click on a control. You can set up any menu to be invoked as a popup by using the PopupMenu method.

For example, you could associate the Sound menu shown in Figure 5-45 on the next page with a picture of a volume control knob. Use the Picture tool to create a picture box on the screen, and then use the Shape tool to draw a circular control knob inside the picture box. (The shape will initially be a rectangle. To create a circle, set the Shape property to 3 - Circle.) Enter the following code for the MouseDown event in the picture box.

```
Sub Picture1_MouseDown (Button As Integer, Shift As Integer,
 X As Single, Y As Single)
    PopupMenu mnuSound
End Sub
```

Whenever the user presses the mouse button inside the area of the Picture box, the Sound menu is invoked, as Figure 5-45 shows.

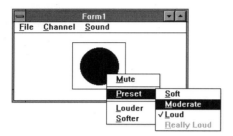

Figure 5-45.
A popup menu.

Note that in this example the Sound menu is available both as a popup and through the menu bar. If you want a menu to be visible only as a popup, you must set its Visible property to False in the Menu Design window. The Visible property of a top-level item applies only to items in the menu bar and is ignored by the PopupMenu method.

6

Program Control

The small programs you have written so far have been extremely simple: They execute sequential statements, perform fairly straightforward tasks, and, in general, are relatively uncomplicated. This chapter introduces concepts that help to give you additional control over how a program executes, allowing you to write code that can deal with various circumstances and choices, with necessary repetition, and with a wider range of data.

Making Choices

The programs you wrote in earlier chapters consisted entirely of commands and expressions, the equivalent of imperative statements in English. But no one, not even the most exalted dictator-for-life, can get by with only the ability to give commands. In real life, people must make choices. Visual Basic's primary tool for dealing with choices is the *If* statement.

The *If* Statement

Imagine that you are teaching a friend how to obey traffic rules. In particular, what should you do when you encounter a Yield sign? You might explain a Yield sign like this: "Slow to 15 miles per hour. If no one is coming, continue on your way; otherwise, stop and let the car pass." You could also restate those instructions in a simplistic form of Basic:

```
Speed = 15                'Approach Yield sign
If Cars_Coming = 0 Then   'No one is coming
    Speed = 25            'Resume previous speed
Else                      'Someone is coming
    Speed = 0             'Stop
End If
```

The classic form of the *If* statement specifies a choice between two options. The words "Two roads diverged" express the visual image quite well, although the poet

Robert Frost was not contemplating a computer program. Indeed, Frost was concerned that only one of the roads could be traveled, whereas a programmer must be concerned with both paths.

As a programmer, you must give directions to the computer. Because you cannot always know exactly what conditions the program will encounter at each moment when it is running, you need to include instructions for handling various cases. In the example of the Yield sign, you don't know whether or not your friend will encounter traffic, so you provide the correct instructions for both possibilities. In your program code, you provide what is known as *conditional branching,* using the *If* statement.

Here is the syntax for the *If* statement in Visual Basic:

```
If Boolean expression Then
    [statement]...
[Else
    [statement]...]
End If
```

The keyword *If* is followed by a Boolean expression, which (as you will recall from Chapter 4) is an expression that evaluates to either True or False. Here is another example of mapping the binary world into experience: True or False, left fork or right fork, *If* or *Else.* If the Boolean expression is True, all the statements following the word *Then* and continuing up to the keyword *Else* are executed. (The ellipsis in the syntax description indicates that more than one statement can follow.) The program then skips the next statements and continues execution after the *End If* keywords. If the Boolean expression is False, the program statements immediately following the word *Then* are skipped. When the *Else* portion of the statement is encountered, the program continues with the statements following *Else.* The two possible execution paths are shown here:

```
If True Then                          If False Then
    'These statements                     'These statements
    'are executed                         'are skipped
Else                                  Else
    'These statements                     'These statements
    'are skipped                          'are executed
End If                                End If
    'Execution continues here             'Execution continues here
```

The *If* statement is a *compound* statement—that is, it is evaluated as a single unit, although it can contain many other statements inside it. Many programmers indent these other statements, to make it easier to see that they are contained inside the *If* statement. Notice how difficult it is to read our earlier example when it is not indented:

```
Speed = 15                          Speed = 15
If Cars_Coming = 0 Then             If Cars_Coming = 0 Then
    Speed = 25                      Speed = 25
Else                                Else
    Speed = 0                       Speed = 0
End If                              End If
```

If you examine the syntax definition for the *If* statement, you can see that the *Else* portion of the statement is optional. This allows you to avoid unnecessary programming in case no statements need to be placed in the *Else* clause. Thus, these two code fragments are equivalent:

```
If Count = "Dracula" Then           If Count = "Dracula" Then
    Print "Aieeeeeee!"                  Print "Aieeeeeee!"
Else                                End If
End If
```

Multiple Choices

The *If* statement allows your program to handle a choice between two options. But how can your program handle a choice among many items? Actually, the *If* statement is all you need to handle a multiple-choice situation.

As an example, consider the problem of identifying one of the Three Stooges. Obviously, you have three possibilities from which to choose. In this case, hairstyle makes a good distinguishing characteristic. You can construct a simple test, as shown in Figure 6-1.

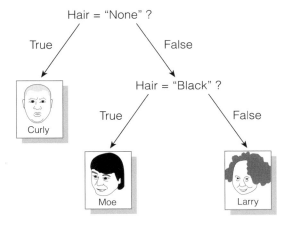

Figure 6-1.
Identifying a Stooge.

Using the *If* statement to make a one-of-many selection can remind you of the parlor game Twenty Questions, in which one person thinks of an item in some predetermined category and the other players attempt to guess the item by asking questions that can be answered only by a "Yes" or a "No." With each answer, specific items or categories are eliminated, and the game moves on in a certain direction.

The Visual Basic code designed to implement the Three Stooges test in Figure 6-1 is shown here; the second *If* statement is a nested statement, which is contained completely inside the first:

```
If Hair = "None" Then
    Stooge = "Curly"
Else
    If Hair = "Black" Then
        Stooge = "Moe"
    Else
        Stooge = "Larry"
    End If
End If
```

When you need more than two or three *If* tests, the nesting of *If* statements can be cumbersome. Visual Basic supports a variant of the *Else* clause called *ElseIf*, which combines an *Else* clause with the functionality of another *If* statement. Here is a version of the preceding code that has been recast using *ElseIf*; beside it is the complete syntax for Visual Basic's *If* statement:

```
If Hair = "None" Then            If Boolean expression Then
    Stooge = "Curly"                 [statement]...
ElseIf Hair = "Black" Then       [ElseIf Boolean expression Then
    Stooge = "Moe"                   [statement]...]
Else                             [Else
    Stooge = "Larry"                 [statement]...]
End If                           End If
```

As indicated in the syntax statement, the *ElseIf* clause can be repeated many times, which eliminates the need for writing multiple nested *If* statements.

The Slots Application

To explore the *If* statement further, let's build a simulation of a slot machine. With a command button as a "lever," the Slots program will display three icons at random for each "pull." If the icons match, the user wins. The program will even keep track of the player's winnings.

Visual Basic includes some icons suitable for gaming: You can use the heart, club, diamond, and spade icons named, respectively, MISC34, MISC35, MISC36, and MISC37. The program will pick one of these icons at random for each of three display slots. Each play costs the player $1.00. If all three icons match, the player wins $10.00. If all three are diamonds, the player wins $25.00.

Think It Through

Review your assumptions closely when programming with the *If* statement. You must be careful not to accidentally include unwanted options or, conversely, to exclude options that should be included. Don't be too quick to assume that your first attempt at writing an *Else* clause covers the only possible alternatives.

The code you wrote to identify one of the Three Stooges, for example, assumes that if Curly and Moe are eliminated, the only remaining possibility is Larry. But, as students of cinema know, there are actually other possibilities, such as Shemp or Curly-Joe. (For those unacquainted with these matchless examples of cinematic art, the trio of Moe Howard, Larry Fine, and Curly Howard made most of the Three Stooges films. After Curly suffered a stroke, however, some later films were made with different actors playing the third Stooge.)

For a similar example of this kind of error, imagine testing the color of an item. If the item is not red and not white, you might assume that it is therefore blue. This works if you know that all your items are elements of the U.S. flag; otherwise, however, your test might not be valid.

To design the display, create a new project. At the top of the form, add three image controls, which will contain the slot machine's display. Below the image controls, place a command button that will serve as the slot machine's "lever." To the left, add a label field to display the player's winnings; to the right, create another command button that will let the player quit the game. Finally, to hold the four icons that will be used, add four more image controls at the bottom of the form. Your form should look like the one shown in Figure 6-2.

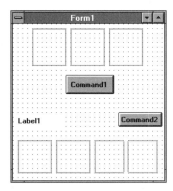

Figure 6-2.
The initial form design for the Slots application.

To set up the four lower image controls, begin by selecting the leftmost one and set-ting its Name property to imgHearts. Then set its Picture property by selecting Pic-ture in the Properties list and clicking on the ellipsis button beside the Settings box. In the Load Picture dialog box, choose the file MISC34.ICO from the appropriate icon directory (\VB\ICONS\MISC if you installed Visual Basic using the default directo-ries). Repeat this process for the other three image controls, naming them imgClubs, imgDiamonds, and imgSpades and setting their Picture properties to load the files MISC35.ICO, MISC36.ICO, and MISC37.ICO, in that order.

Next set the properties of all the display elements as shown in Figure 6-3. Your form should now resemble Figure 6-4.

Object	Property	Setting
Form1	BorderStyle	3 - Fixed Double
	Caption	Slots
	Name	Slots
Image1	BorderStyle	1 - Fixed Single
	Name	imgSlot1
	Stretch	True
Image2	BorderStyle	1 - Fixed Single
	Name	imgSlot2
	Stretch	True
Image3	BorderStyle	1 - Fixed Single
	Name	imgSlot3
	Stretch	True
Command1	Caption	Spin
	Name	btnSpin
Label1	BorderStyle	1 - Fixed Single
	Caption	[none]
	Name	lblTotal
Command2	Caption	Quit
	Name	btnQuit

Figure 6-3.
Property settings for the Slots application.

To begin working on the code for the program, double-click on the form to open a code window. Enter the following lines of code in the general declarations section:

```
Const CLUB% = 1, HEART% = 2, DIAMOND% = 3, SPADE% = 4
Dim Winnings As Currency
```

The integers 1 through 4 will map randomly selected numbers to the appropriate icons. The constant declarations allow you to use the names CLUB, HEART,

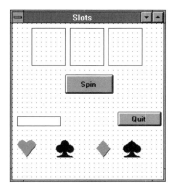

Figure 6-4.
The completed form design for the Slots application.

DIAMOND, and SPADE in the program, making it easier to read and understand. The form-level variable *Winnings*, which is also declared here, is used to keep track of the player's winnings.

Now select Form from the Object box in the code window, and set the Procedure box to Load. Add these lines of code, which will be run when the form is first loaded (that is, at the start of the program):

```
Sub Form_Load ()
    Randomize
    Winnings = 0
End Sub
```

The Randomize command tells Visual Basic to "scramble" the numbers produced by its random-number generator; without this statement, the series of plays would be the same each time the program is run. Because the player has not yet begun to play, you must set the *Winnings* variable to 0.

Here is the code for the Quit button:

```
Sub btnQuit_Click ()
    End
End Sub
```

The procedure for the Spin button is presented in Figure 6-5 on the following page. The local variables *P1*, *P2*, and *P3* will each hold a random number that will be used to select the icons that will appear in the top three image controls (imgSlot1, imgSlot2, and imgSlot3). The *Payoff* variable will hold the player's winnings for one play (one "spin" of the slot machine).

```
Sub btnSpin_Click ()
    Dim P1 As Integer, P2 As Integer, P3 As Integer
    Dim Payoff As Currency

    'Pay to play
    Winnings = Winnings - 1

    'Generate random results
    P1 = Int(4 * Rnd + 1)
    P2 = Int(4 * Rnd + 1)
    P3 = Int(4 * Rnd + 1)

    'Display icon 1
    If P1 = HEART Then
        imgSlot1.Picture = imgHearts.Picture
    ElseIf P1 = CLUB Then
        imgSlot1.Picture = imgClubs.Picture
    ElseIf P1 = DIAMOND Then
        imgSlot1.Picture = imgDiamonds.Picture
    ElseIf P1 = SPADE Then
        imgSlot1.Picture = imgSpades.Picture
    End If

    'Display icon 2
    If P2 = HEART Then
        imgSlot2.Picture = imgHearts.Picture
    ElseIf P2 = CLUB Then
        imgSlot2.Picture = imgClubs.Picture
    ElseIf P2 = DIAMOND Then
        imgSlot2.Picture = imgDiamonds.Picture
    ElseIf P2 = SPADE Then
        imgSlot2.Picture = imgSpades.Picture
    End If

    'Display icon 3
    If P3 = HEART Then
        imgSlot3.Picture = imgHearts.Picture
    ElseIf P3 = CLUB Then
        imgSlot3.Picture = imgClubs.Picture
    ElseIf P3 = DIAMOND Then
        imgSlot3.Picture = imgDiamonds.Picture
    ElseIf P3 = SPADE Then
        imgSlot3.Picture = imgSpades.Picture
    End If
```

Figure 6-5.   *(continued)*

The btnSpin_Click *procedure for the Slots application.*

Figure 6-5. *continued*

```
    'Check to see whether player has won
    If P1 = P2 And P2 = P3 Then
        If P1 = DIAMOND Then
            Payoff = 25
            MsgBox "You win BIG!!!"
        Else
            Payoff = 10
            MsgBox "You WIN!"
        End If
    Else
        Payoff = 0
        Beep
    End If

    'Compute and display total winnings
    Winnings = Winnings + Payoff
    lblTotal.Caption = Format(Winnings, "$0.00")
End Sub
```

The program first decrements the player's winnings by $1.00, the cost of one spin. Next it generates three random numbers. The formula *Int(n * Rnd + 1)* uses the Visual Basic built-in function *Rnd* to return a random integer in the range 1 through *n*.

The program then examines the random number *P1* and sets the Picture property of imgSlot1 accordingly by copying the picture from one of the predefined icons at the bottom of the form. This process is repeated for imgSlot2 and imgSlot3.

Once the slot machine's display has been set, the program checks for a winning combination. If all three random numbers are equal, the player wins. Additionally, the program checks to see whether the winning combination consists of three diamonds. The *Payoff* variable is then set to either 10 or 25, according to the particular combination. If the player did not win, the *Payoff* variable is set to 0.

Finally the program adds any payoff to the player's winnings and displays the total stake in the label. The Visual Basic *Format* function ensures that the amount is displayed in dollars and cents.

When you close the code window, you're ready to run the application. Before you do this, however, resize the form to hide the four predefined icons, as shown in Figure 6-6 on the following page. They'll still be part of the application, but they'll no longer appear in the user interface.

Feeling lucky? Press F5 to try your hand at the slots. When you finish playing, you might want to save this program so that you can return to it later.

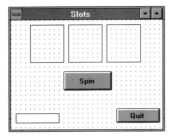

Figure 6-6.
The resized form for the Slots application.

Getting Repetitious

The ability to execute assignment statements and make choices using the *If* statement theoretically gives you the tools to write any program. Then again, many tasks are easier in theory than in practice. Consider the problem of printing the entire range of numbers from 1 through 1000. The obvious solution—writing a program consisting of 1000 *Print* statements (*Print 1, Print 2, Print 3*, and so forth)—would be more than tedious. Fortunately, Visual Basic provides a better way.

The Visual Basic *Do* statement can repetitively process a set of statements. Here is the simplest syntax for this statement:

```
Do
    [statement]...
Loop
```

The *Do* keyword marks the beginning of a compound statement, which includes all the statements up through the *Loop* keyword. The statements are executed in order until the *Loop* keyword is reached; at that point, execution begins again at the top of the block with the *Do* statement.

The set of statements that repeat is called a *loop.* When a program is repeatedly executing those statements, it is said to be *looping.* (One might infer that programs with many loops are *loopy,* but this terminology is usually applied only to programmers who have been working too hard.) The loop gets its name from the circular diagram of the program flow, as shown in Figure 6-7.

The loop shown in Figure 6-7 is an *infinite* loop—that is, Visual Basic will execute the compound statement forever. Usually, of course, you want the program to stop looping at some point and move on. Visual Basic allows you to accomplish this in several ways.

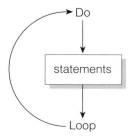

Figure 6-7.
A diagram of a Do *loop.*

You can append a *While* clause to either the *Do* statement or the *Loop* statement. The example of printing numbers from 1 through 1000 is handled easily with a *Do While* loop, as shown here:

```
Counter = 1
Do While Counter <= 1000
    Print Counter
    Counter = Counter + 1
Loop
```

The variable *Counter* is set to 1. Then a *Do While* statement, which executes "while" *Counter* is less than or equal to 1000 and terminates when *Counter* exceeds 1000, surrounds a *Print* statement and an assignment statement. When the loop ends, execution continues with the program statements following the *Loop* keyword.

The *While* keyword must be followed by a *condition* in the form of a Boolean expression. If the expression is False, the statements following it, through the keyword *Loop,* are skipped, and execution continues with the statements that follow the *Loop* statement. In this example, *Counter* is checked at the top of every loop, including the first one. (If *Counter* had been initialized to 50,000, none of the statements inside the loop would have been executed.)

Note that unless the statement *Counter = Counter + 1* is included, the Boolean expression will always be True (because *Counter* remains 1), and the loop will execute forever. Inadvertently creating infinite loops is a common error, even among experienced programmers. Remember that in Visual Basic you can always press Ctrl-Break to interrupt a running program and stop an infinite loop.

The *While* keyword can be associated with the *Loop* statement rather than the *Do* statement for a slightly different effect, as shown in this code:

```
Do
    Password = InputBox("Enter secret word")
Loop While Password <> "Groucho"
```

Placing the *While* clause at the end of the loop guarantees that the statements inside the loop will execute at least once, because the test for termination comes after the *Loop* keyword. In the example, a dialog box prompting the user to enter the "secret word" is displayed repeatedly until the user enters the correct word.

Finally, to make your programs more readable, you can use the keyword *Until* in place of *While*. Using *Until* inverts the logic of the condition. Contrast the two previous examples using *While* with restated code using *Until*:

Examples with *While*	Examples with *Until*
| ```
Counter = 1
Do While Counter <= 1000
    Print Counter
    Counter = Counter + 1
Loop


Do
    Password = InputBox("Enter
      secret word")
Loop While Password <> "Groucho"
``` | ```
Counter = 1
Do Until Counter > 1000
    Print Counter
    Counter = Counter + 1
Loop


Do
    Password = InputBox("Enter
      secret word")
Loop Until Password = "Groucho"
``` |

Here is the complete syntax for the Visual Basic *Do* statement:

Test at top of loop	Test at end of loop

Do { While ¦ Until } *expression*
    [*statement*]...
Loop
	Do
	    [*statement*]...
	Loop { While ¦ Until } *expression*

The Banker Application

Let's use your newly acquired knowledge to write a program that will serve as a private banker for some specific information: When the user enters in a combo box the amounts of all the checks written during a certain period, the program will tell the user the average amount spent per check. To find the average, the program adds all the individual values and divides by the number of checks—a perfect job for a *Do While* loop.

Create a new project in Visual Basic. The Banker interface requires a combo box to hold all the values of the checks, a command button to compute the average, and a label to display the average. Design a form containing these three objects, and set the properties of the objects as described in Figure 6-8. Your form should look like the one shown in Figure 6-9.

Object	Property	Setting
Form1	Caption	Banker
	Name	Banker
Command1	Caption	Average
	Name	btnAvg
Label1	BorderStyle	1 - Fixed Single
	Caption	[none]
	Name	lblAvg
Combo1	Name	cboInput
	Style	1 - Simple Combo
	Text	[none]

Figure 6-8.
Property settings for the Banker application.

Figure 6-9.
The form design for the Banker application.

Now you need to modify the combo box a bit. Usually a combo box provides a list of choices for the user. In this case, you'll use it to build a list of user entries: Every time the user enters a value in the text portion of the combo box, the program adds the value to the items in the list portion. To do this, you need to use an event procedure that was not discussed in Chapter 5, one that is based on the KeyPress event.

The KeyPress event takes place each time the user presses a key. Double-click on the combo box, and select KeyPress from the Procedure box in the code window. The procedure definition will look like this:

```
Sub cboInput_KeyPress (KeyAscii As Integer)

End Sub
```

A variable named *KeyAscii* is defined inside the parentheses. This variable is a parameter. *Parameters* are like local variables, except that they are initialized by the calling procedure rather than by the procedure containing the declaration. (Parameters in procedures are explained more fully in Chapter 7.) For the moment, you simply need to know that the event procedure *KeyPress* comes with a predeclared variable called *KeyAscii*. When the procedure begins to execute, the value of *KeyAscii* is the ASCII code for the character the user has just typed. For example, if the user types the letter *A*, the value of *KeyAscii* is 65. Typing *a* generates a value of 97; typing *3* generates a value of 51.

The code in the *KeyPress* procedure can modify the *KeyAscii* variable. If it does, Visual Basic enters the modified character in the combo box instead of the character the user typed. Try experimenting with this feature for a moment. Define the *KeyPress* procedure as follows:

```
Sub cboInput_KeyPress (KeyAscii As Integer)
    If KeyAscii = 83 Or KeyAscii = 84 Then
        KeyAscii = 42
    End If
End Sub
```

Press F5 to start the application, and type *TESTING* in the text portion of the combo box. The letters S and T are replaced by asterisks. (The ASCII code for an asterisk is 42.) Quit the application and edit the *KeyPress* code again, as shown here:

```
Sub cboInput_KeyPress (KeyAscii As Integer)
    If KeyAscii = 13 Then              'If key is Enter key
        cboInput.AddItem cboInput.Text 'Insert user's new text
        cboInput.Text = ""             'Clear text portion
        KeyAscii = 0                   'Discard keystroke
    End If
End Sub
```

This procedure is set up to detect the Enter key (ASCII code 13). If the key the user presses is not the Enter key, Visual Basic simply inserts the character the user typed in the text portion of the combo box. When the program detects the Enter key, however, this procedure takes the text portion of the combo box and inserts it as a new item in the list portion. It then erases the entry in the text portion and sets *KeyAscii* to 0. Because 0 is the ASCII code for the null character, Visual Basic simply ignores this character.

Computing the average

After the user has entered all the values, he or she can click on the Average button to have the program compute the average amount. Double-click on the Average command button now, and enter the following code:

```
Sub btnAvg_Click ()
    Dim Current As Integer, Total As Single

    Total = 0                                       'Sum of all checks
    Current = 0                                     'Current check
    Do While Current < cboInput.ListCount
        Total = Total + Val(cboInput.List(Current)) 'Compute sum
        Current = Current + 1                       'Next check
    Loop
    lblAvg.Caption = Str$(Total / cboInput.ListCount) 'Display avg as text
End Sub
```

The *Dim* statement defines two local variables: *Current*, which identifies by item number the check value the program is currently working with; and *Total*, which holds the sum of all the values. *Total* is then initialized to 0 and the *Current* item set to 0. (Items in a list box or a combo box are identified as item 0, item 1, and so on.)

The *Do While* statement directs Visual Basic to continue processing as long as the number of the current item is less than the total number of items. (You can't expect the program to find item 21 if only 7 items have been entered.) The next statement contains the expression *cboInput.List(Current)*, which specifies the list item. Because items in a list box or a combo box are always stored as text, Visual Basic's *Val* function is used to convert the text digits to a numeric value. Similarly, the *Str$* function later converts the computed average to a text string before the program writes it to the label's caption.

Now you can run the Banker program. Type a series of check values in the text portion of the combo box, pressing Enter after each amount. When you have entered the entire list, click on the Average button. Your results should be similar to those shown in Figure 6-10.

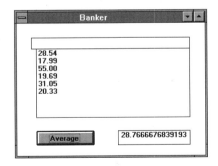

Figure 6-10.
Running the Banker application.

Loops That Count

The *For* statement is a specialized statement in Visual Basic that handles looping with a steadily increasing or decreasing count. It has the following syntax:

For *variable* = *firstValue* To *lastValue* [Step *increment*]
    [*statement*]...
Next *variable*

The *For* statement creates a loop in which the counter variable is initialized to *firstValue* and is then incremented by *increment* each time the program executes the loop, until the value of the variable reaches *lastValue*. If you omit the *Step* clause, the increment is assumed to be 1. The value of *firstValue* should be less than the value of *lastValue* unless the increment is negative; in that case, the value of *firstValue* should be greater than the value of *lastValue*.

A *For* loop can be written as a *While* statement, but the *For* loop is more common because it is simpler. The syntax of the equivalent *While* loops is shown here:

Positive increment	Negative increment
variable = *firstValue*	*variable* = *firstValue*
Do While *variable* <= *lastValue*	Do While *variable* >= *lastValue*
[*statement*]...	[*statement*]...
variable = *variable* + *increment*	*variable* = *variable* − *increment*
Loop	Loop

Note that the *To* expression in the *For* loop is equivalent to a less than or equal to comparison in the *While* loop when the increment is positive and equivalent to a greater than or equal to comparison when the increment is negative. This implies that the final value of *variable* might not always be equal to *lastValue*. As an example, look at this loop and its output:

```
For Count = 1 To 10 Step 4
    Print Count
Next Count
```

Output

```
1
5
9
```

If you choose, you can rewrite the Banker program code using a *For* loop. Compare your changes with this version (which shows the changed lines in purple):

```
Sub btnAvg_Click ()
    Dim Current As Integer, Total As Single

    Total = 0                                        'Sum of all checks
    For Current = 0 To cboInput.ListCount - 1
        Total = Total + Val(cboInput.List(Current))  'Compute sum
    Next Current
    lblAvg.Caption = Str$(Total / cboInput.ListCount) 'Display avg as text
End Sub
```

When you wrote your version of the code, did you set the ending value of the *For* loop to *cboInput.ListCount − 1*? This change is important, but it is easy to overlook. Remember that Visual Basic numbers the items in the combo box beginning with 0—that is, three items are numbered 0, 1, and 2. The original version of the code used a loop with a less than comparison, but a *For* loop uses a less than or equal to comparison.

These subtle differences can cause errors in which the loop executes one too many or one too few times. Even experienced programmers make these mistakes, so be sure to test your programs carefully. For instance, when I first created the Banker program, I ran it with the test values 1, 2, 3, and 4. Because I knew that the average of these values is 2.5, I could verify that the code was working correctly. When your program produces no result at all, you immediately know that it contains an error. When your program does produce a result, however, it is all too tempting to assume that the result must be correct.

Expect the Unexpected

Even when a program produces correct results some of the time, it might not do so all the time. Such is the case with the Banker program. The Banker program will fail if the user clicks on the Average button without entering any data in the combo box. You might believe that no one would do such a thing. But part of your job as a programmer is to understand that anything that can be done probably will be done. And you must try to anticipate such events as best you can.

In the Banker program, the *Do While* loop (or the *For* loop, if you made the change) correctly refuses to add any values to the total if the combo box is empty. The problem arises in computing the average. Because the program finds no items in the combo box, the expression *Total / cboInput.ListCount* causes division by zero. In this instance, Visual Basic provides some error handling by displaying a dialog box that says *Division by zero*, but this is not much comfort to the user. And some systems (such as MS-DOS) simply terminate a program that tries to divide by zero. Clearly, it is better for you as a programmer to anticipate this error than to rely on the system to handle it in some (possibly unpleasant) fashion.

You can amend the Banker program in a couple of possible ways. One is to insert the following code at the beginning of the *btnAvg_Click* procedure:

```
If cboInput.ListCount = 0 Then
    Exit Sub
End If
```

This code causes the program to simply ignore the mouse click when the click is inappropriate, by leaving the procedure without further processing. It will appear that the Average button is not responding, which might, of course, confuse the user. If you are concerned about that possibility, you might choose to display a dialog box, as the code shown here does:

```
If cboInput.ListCount = 0 Then
    MsgBox "No entries to average"
    Exit Sub
End If
```

Using Arrays

In the Banker program, you used the variable *cboInput.List,* which is an array. *Array variables* can contain multiple values. That might sound a little like the user-defined types introduced in Chapter 3, but the two are not the same. A record variable contains a fixed number of component elements, each with a separate name and data type. In an array, every element has the same type, and the individual elements are numbered rather than named. To refer to a field in a record, you use both the variable name and the field name, as in *Sieglinde.Color.* To refer to an element of an array, you use the array variable name followed by the number of the element in parentheses—*cboInput.List(3),* for example. The number that specifies an array element is called an *index.* Index values are always integers. Visual Basic stores array values in index order beginning (by default) with element 0. Figure 6-11 contrasts memory storage for simple variables and records (user-defined types) with memory storage for arrays.

Reserving Memory for Arrays

Visual Basic allows you to create arrays of any data type, including user-defined types. The Banker program used an array of strings (*cboInput.List*) that was a predefined property of the combo box. If you want to create an array, you must use a variable declaration to reserve memory for it. Like other variables, arrays are declared with the *Dim* statement. Here is the syntax for a standard array declaration:

{ Dim | Global } *name*(*maxSize*) [As *type*]

Figure 6-11.
Memory allocation for simple variables, records, and arrays.

The value in parentheses (*maxSize*) is called the *dimension* of the array; it tells Visual Basic how much memory to allocate for the array. The declaration creates an array with indexes that begin at 0 and continue through *maxSize*. For example, the statement *Dim X(3) As Integer*, declaring an array with a *maxSize* value of 3, actually creates an array with four elements: *X(0)*, *X(1)*, *X(2)*, and *X(3)*. The *maxSize* value must be an integer type, which means that no array can have an index that is larger than 32,767.

Experimenting with Arrays

Arrays are incredibly useful, allowing you to write programs that are more general and less dependent on specific data. To demonstrate, consider our friends from Chapter 3, the Bavarian Tufted Forest weasels.

To evaluate your prowess as a weasel breeder, you might decide to compute the average length of your weasels and compare it against the national average for weasels (9 inches). The expression that will compute this average value is *(Siegmund.Length + Sieglinde.Length + Siegfried.Length) / 3*. Of course, any program that incorporates this expression is valid only for those specific weasels. Every time your weasel population changes, you must change your program. What you need is a more general way of storing information.

Instead of storing the vital statistics of each weasel in a separately named variable, you can alter the type description to contain the weasel's name. The new data type, BTFWeasel, is shown on the following page.

```
Type BTFWeasel
    Name As String
    Color As String
    Weight As Integer
    Length As Integer
    Birthdate As Double
    TuftColor As String
    TuftLength As Integer
End Type
```

You can now store all the information about the weasels collectively in the single array variable *Weasels*. You can declare the variable *Weasels* with the statement *Dim Weasels(20) As BTFWeasel*. Because the array will hold information about several weasels (21, to be exact), you also need to declare another variable that holds the number of weasels you currently have: Use the statement *Dim WeaselPopulation As Integer*.

After you declare the variables, you can store data about the weasels in much the same way you did when you were using separate variables. The statements that follow show how some of these values might be initialized:

```
WeaselPopulation = 3
Weasels(0).Name = "Siegmund"
Weasels(0).TuftColor = "brown"
Weasels(0).Weight = 18
    ⋮
Weasels(1).Name = "Sieglinde"
Weasels(1).Weight = 14
    ⋮
Weasels(2).Name = "Siegfried"
Weasels(2).Length = 8
```

Now, assuming that all the information about the weasels has been stored, you can write a program that computes the average length of your weasels, no matter how many you have. Not surprisingly, it looks like the code used in the Banker program:

```
Dim Current As Integer, Total As Integer, AvgLength As Single

Total = 0
For Current = 0 To WeaselPopulation - 1
    Total = Total + Weasels(Current).Length
Next Current
AvgLength = Total / WeaselPopulation
```

This code will continue to be useful as the weasel population changes. The key to successful programming is to examine a problem to see whether it can be generalized and then write a program to solve the general case, rather than writing a program that solves a single problem but must be constantly modified as the problem changes.

Using Loops with Arrays

As the sample programs in this chapter have no doubt suggested to you, arrays and loops fit together like a hand in a glove. Operations such as adding sums, computing averages, and finding minima and maxima all lend themselves nicely to array processing. All of these operations need to examine the entire array. Other operations, such as searching, do not.

Consider the array of weasels. Now that the vital statistics are stored anonymously, you can't use a named variable such as *Siegmund* to extract the data for a given weasel. Instead, you must search the array until you find a weasel whose Name element is set to *Siegmund*. For example, if you want to print out Siegmund's weight, the most straightforward approach might look like this:

```
Dim W As Integer, Match As Integer

Match = -1                                  'No match yet
For W = 0 To WeaselPopulation - 1           'Walk through array
    If Weasels(W).Name = "Siegmund" Then    'If Siegmund is found
        Match = W                           'Save the index in Match
    End If
Next W                                      'Continue the search
Print Weasels(Match).Weight
```

Unfortunately, this program will examine every element of the array, even if Siegmund is the first weasel in the array. This problem isn't serious with a small weasel population, but the search could consume quite a bit of time if you had thousands of weasels.

You need to alter the condition of the loop so that it ends when the match is found. You could write this loop in either of two ways. The first method is to reformulate the loop itself into a *Do While* statement in which the loop condition tests both for reaching the end of the array and for a match:

```
Dim W As Integer, Match As Integer

Match = -1                                  'No match yet
W = 0
'Loop while more to process and no match
Do While (W <= WeaselPopulation - 1) And Match = -1
    If Weasels(W).Name = "Siegmund" Then    'If Siegmund is found
        Match = W                           'Save the index in Match
    End If
    W = W + 1                               'Next index
Loop                                        'Continue the search
Print Weasels(Match).Weight
```

By converting the *For* loop to *Do While*, you can define a more precise test condition. This loop will end when *W* maxes out or when the *Match* variable is set (which happens only when Siegmund has been found).

The alternative method is to keep the *For* loop, breaking out of it when the match is found. Visual Basic provides the *Exit* statement for that purpose:

```
Dim W As Integer, Match As Integer

Match = -1                                  'No match yet
For W = 0 To WeaselPopulation - 1           'Walk through array
    If Weasels(W).Name = "Siegmund" Then    'If Siegmund is found
        Match = W                           'Save the index in Match
        Exit For                            'Break out of the loop
    End If
Next W                                       'Continue the search
Print Weasels(Match).Weight
```

When the *Exit* statement is encountered, the flow of control immediately transfers to the statement after *Next W*.

Both programming methods are acceptable solutions. The first has the advantage of explicitly stating the termination conditions in the loop, making the code easier to understand. The second method is slightly more efficient because the loop does not have to process the additional test of the *Match* variable each time through the loop; when a match is found, the loop terminates. The *Exit* statement that ends the loop is buried inside the body of the loop, however, and could easily be missed by someone reading the code. My personal preference is to go with the more efficient and slightly less messy *For* loop.

All three versions of this code contain a common problem: the *Print* statement. The code assumes that a match has been found, even though this might not be the case. A corrected version would replace the *Print* statement with the following code:

```
If Match = -1 Then
    MsgBox "No match found"
Else
    Print Weasels(Match).Weight
End If
```

Determining Array Size at Runtime

When you write a *Dim* statement to declare an array, you effectively predetermine the size of the array. Perhaps you know exactly how large the array should be, or perhaps you know its maximum value. (For instance, you might know only too well that it would be too much work to keep more than 21 weasels.) In such cases, a fixed array size works well. A problem arises, however, when the array size is unknown. Suppose, for example, that you want to sell your weasel-tracking program to weasel breeders everywhere. How can you dimension the array?

You could simply pick some arbitrary large number and hope that it will be big enough. You'll find two problems with this approach, however. One, it wastes memory; the *Dim* statement reserves memory for the full array size, whether or not it is used. Two, you are taking a risk by simply relying on good luck. If you sell your program to a breeder with more weasels than the program can accommodate, the program will fail, and you'll have an unhappy customer.

To solve this problem, Visual Basic provides the *ReDim* statement, which redimensions an array. *ReDim* is not a declaration; rather, it is a command that can be executed many times during the course of a program. To use *ReDim*, you must remove the *maxSize* dimension from your original array declaration. Omitting *maxSize* tells Visual Basic to create a *dynamic* array (one whose size can change) rather than a fixed-size array. Examine this program fragment, which does nothing except illustrate how *ReDim* works:

```
Dim Test() As Integer              'In declarations section

'In some event procedure
For Size = 10 To 50 Step 10
    ReDim Test(Size) As Integer    'Resize test array
Next Size
```

Because the original declaration of the array *Test* has no *maxSize* component, Visual Basic recognizes it as a dynamic array. At some point, the *For* loop is executed. The first time through the loop, *Test* is dimensioned as an 11-element array (with elements numbered 0 through 10). The next time through the loop, *Test* is redimensioned as a 21-element array. When the loop is completed, *Test* is dimensioned as a 51-element array. Here is the syntax for the *ReDim* statement:

ReDim [Preserve] *variable*(*maxSize*) [As *type*]

This syntax resembles that of the *Dim* statement except that the *Preserve* keyword can be included and that the *maxSize* value can be any integer expression. When *ReDim* is used without *Preserve*, any existing copy of the array is discarded, and a completely new array is created. If you use *ReDim* with *Preserve*, values in the old array are preserved in the new array. If the new array's dimension is smaller than the old array's dimension, however, values with indexes greater than the new dimension cannot be preserved.

Using Control Arrays

In addition to arrays of data values, Visual Basic also allows you to define arrays of control objects, which are useful when you have several controls that perform essentially the same action. Control arrays share the same event procedures. If you have an array of three command buttons, for example, the same *Click* procedure is called no matter which button is clicked.

Visual Basic lets you differentiate among the items in a control array by passing an index value to the procedure. Let's look at how this works. On an empty form, create two new command buttons. Set the Name property of both buttons to btnTest. When you attempt to set the Name property of the second button, Visual Basic presents a dialog box that asks whether you intend to create a control array:

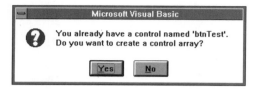

Click on Yes in the dialog box. Now open the code window by double-clicking on either command button. You will see that an *Index* parameter has been added to each event procedure, as in the example shown here:

```
Sub btnTest_Click (Index As Integer)

End Sub
```

This event procedure is called if either button is clicked; the Index property of the button is passed as an integer parameter to indicate which button was clicked.

When you create a control array, Visual Basic assigns an index value to each object. Using the Properties window, examine the Index property for the two command buttons you created:

The first button has an index value of 0, and the second has an index value of 1. To give the buttons special index values, you can change the Index property at design time. This property cannot be changed while the program is running.

You refer to an element of a control array by specifying the array name, followed by the index value in parentheses. For example, this *Click* procedure sets the captions of the command buttons in your form to the time they were last clicked:

```
Sub btnTest_Click (Index As Integer)
    btnTest(Index).Caption = Format(Now, "hh:mm:ss")
End Sub
```

Control arrays are especially useful with option buttons. You can define all of the option buttons within a single frame as a control array and then use the Index property or the Caption property in an assignment statement. For example, you could use this *Click* procedure with the control array of option buttons shown in Figure 6-12:

```
Sub optColor_Click (Index As Integer)
    MyWeasel.Color = optColor(Index).Caption
End Sub
```

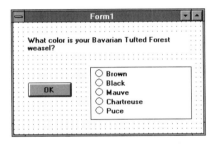

Figure 6-12.
A control array of option buttons.

A handy shortcut for creating a control array is to create the first control object and set its properties. Then you can copy the control and paste it as many times as necessary to create additional controls that are the same size and whose property settings are the same.

7

Using Procedures and Functions

Most of the procedures you have written in earlier chapters have been event procedures—that is, they were specially designed to respond to specific events initiated by the user or the system. As you might remember, however, not all procedures are event procedures. This chapter shows you how to write and use general procedures (including both sub procedures and function procedures) that carry out a particular task when they are explicitly called by the program code (rather than being triggered by an event). It also explores the use of parameters, which allow the program to pass specific values to the procedures and functions it calls. Even Visual Basic objects can be passed as parameters, as you'll see. Finally, this chapter takes a look at some advanced event procedures, such as those that let you track mouse movement and implement drag-and-drop features.

General Procedures

The first applications you wrote had a linear flow of control: After one statement was executed, the next sequential statement ran. In the previous chapter, you began to work with conditional branching (*If* statements) and loops that modify the order in which statements are executed. Figure 7-1 on the following page diagrams these three kinds of flow.

Like loops, procedures allow your program to execute a set of statements more than once. Instead of repeatedly executing a set of statements, however, procedures allow you to collect statements into a group that can be executed whenever you want. A Visual Basic event procedure, for example, executes when the user performs an action; a *general procedure* executes when it is called by the application's code.

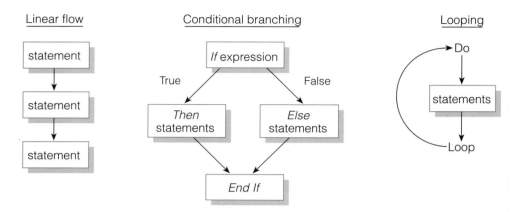

Figure 7-1.
Flow of control in programs.

Consider a program that mimics the actions of a small child traveling in an automobile. This code illustrates a behavior known as whining:

```
Answer = InputBox("Are we there yet?")
If Answer = "No" Then
    MsgBox "I'm bored"
End If
```

In a program that simulated a child's behavior, you might expect to duplicate those lines any number of times. Instead of coding multiple copies of the statements, you can collect the statements in a procedure and execute them simply by using the name of the procedure. Add a procedure declaration and give it a descriptive name:

```
Sub Whine ()
    Dim Answer As String

    Answer = InputBox("Are we there yet?")
    If Answer = "No" Then
        MsgBox "I'm bored"
    End If
End Sub
```

Given the procedure you have just written, the following two program fragments are equivalent:

```
Whine                           Answer = InputBox("Are we there yet?")
MsgBox "I hate this"            If Answer = "No" Then
Whine                                MsgBox "I'm bored"
                               End If
                               MsgBox "I hate this"
                               Answer = InputBox("Are we there yet?")
                               If Answer = "No" Then
                                    MsgBox "I'm bored"
                               End If
```

Flow of Control

Procedures obviously affect the flow of control. When Visual Basic encounters a procedure name, it "remembers" the current location in the program and then moves on to execute the named procedure. When it completes the named procedure, it returns to the original location in the program and continues execution from there. This process is referred to as a *procedure call* because the program *calls* the named procedure. Because Visual Basic can keep track of hundreds of levels of calls, a procedure called by a program can itself contain a procedure call, and so on, as shown in Figure 7-2.

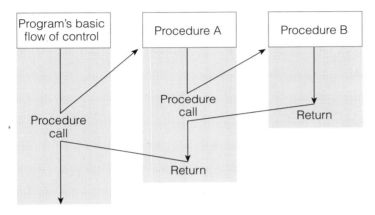

Figure 7-2.
Procedure calls.

Parameters

Assume that you are writing a program that needs, at some point, to print the integers 1 through 10. At another point, the same program needs to print the integers 1 through 17. The code for those two routines is contrasted here:

First routine	**Second routine**
``` For Count = 1 To 10 Print Count Next Count ```	``` For Count = 1 To 17 Print Count Next Count ```

Because the routines are quite similar, it would be fairly simple to generalize—that is, to make the same code serve both purposes. The only difference between the two is the ending value in the *For* loop, which you could replace with a variable. Then you could use a single procedure, calling it after setting the variable to the proper value, as shown on the next page. (Assume that the statement *Dim EndCount As Integer* appears in the general declarations section of the program.)

First call	Second call	Procedure

EndCount = 10
PrintLoop
	EndCount = 17
	PrintLoop
		Sub PrintLoop ()
		    Dim Count As Integer
		
		    For Count = 1 To EndCount
		        Print Count
		    Next Count
		End Sub

As you can see, the combination of variables and procedure calls allows you to solve general-case problems easily and provides you with excellent programming tools. Some practical problems arise with the implementation shown here, however. In particular, you must declare global or module-level variables for communication between the main program and the procedure it calls; and you must keep track of the names, using different variable names for each procedure to avoid having one procedure call the other and overwrite its own variable.

Visual Basic solves these problems by allowing all procedures to have parameters, variables that are local to a procedure but are initialized by the code that calls the procedure. The calling routine initializes these variables by specifying a set of values after the procedure name. Here is the syntax for such a procedure call:

>   name [value [, value]…]

Note that commas separate the arguments. The calling routine does not need to know the names of the parameters because the arguments are assigned, in order, to the parameters declared in the procedure.

In the procedure declaration, parameters are declared inside the parentheses following the procedure name. Visual Basic allows procedures to have more than one parameter. Here is the syntax for a procedure declaration that includes parameters:

>   Sub name ([parameter [As type][, parameter [As type]]…])
>   End Sub

Take a look at the previous example redone with parameters:

First call	Second call	Procedure

PrintLoop 10	PrintLoop 17	Sub PrintLoop (EndCount As Integer)
		    Dim Count As Integer
		
		    For Count = 1 To EndCount
		        Print Count
		    Next Count
		End Sub

To illustrate multiple parameters, you could change the *PrintLoop* procedure to accept both a starting value and an ending value, as shown here:

First call	Second call	Procedure
PrintLoop 1, 10	PrintLoop 1, 17	Sub PrintLoop (StartCount As Integer, EndCount As Integer) Dim Count As Integer

```
Sub PrintLoop (StartCount As
    Integer, EndCount As Integer)
    Dim Count As Integer

    For Count =
      StartCount To EndCount
          Print Count
    Next Count
End Sub
```

Function Procedures

From the preceding examples, you might have noticed that the lines of communication run only one way in a general procedure call—that is, the calling routine passes values to the procedure, which performs some action but does not return any information to the calling routine. You can, however, use a special kind of procedure called a *function procedure* (or simply a *function*) that returns a value to the caller, much as Visual Basic's built-in functions do.

When you declare a function, you must declare the type of value it returns as well as any parameters it requires, as this syntax definition shows:

Function *name* ([*parameter* [As *type*][, *parameter* [As *type*]]...]) [As *type*]
   [*statements*]
   name = *expression*
   [*statements*]
End Function

You can see two differences that distinguish a function procedure from a sub procedure. A function procedure is bracketed by *Function* and *End Function* statements, whereas a sub procedure requires *Sub* and *End Sub*. And, as the syntax definition shows, somewhere within the body of the function you must assign a value (*expression*) to the name of the function. This is the value that will be returned to the calling routine. For example, this function returns the larger of two integers:

```
Function MaxInt (X As Integer, Y As Integer) As Integer
    If X > Y Then
        MaxInt = X
    Else
        MaxInt = Y
    End If
End Function
```

The syntax for calling a function procedure is slightly different from the syntax used to call a sub procedure. Because a function returns a value, it can be called anywhere an expression is valid. The function's parameters are therefore enclosed in parentheses to separate them from other parts of the expression. Here are some statements calling the *MaxInt* function:

```
Print MaxInt(7, 14)
TwiceAsBig = MaxInt(3, 4) * 2
If MaxInt(FirstGuess, SecondGuess) > 20 Then
```

When you call a function that needs no parameters, you simply use the function's name, as if it were a variable. Visual Basic's built-in function *Now* (which returns the current time and date) is an example of a function that does not require parameters.

Writing Procedures

The discussion that follows uses the term *procedure* to refer to the general idea of a callable routine. When necessary, the term *function procedure* (or simply *function*) or the term *sub procedure* is specified for clarity.

> *Note: Although Visual Basic allows user-defined procedures and functions, it does not allow user-defined methods; only the built-in methods are available.*

To create a callable procedure in Visual Basic, you must open a code window. From the View menu, choose the New Procedure command. In the New Procedure dialog box, type the name of the new procedure, choose either Sub or Function by clicking on one of the option buttons, and click on the OK button. Visual Basic then creates a new item in the Procedure box of the code window and supplies the appropriate *End* statement for your procedure. You can now add any parameter declarations that your procedure needs.

Let's write a sample program called Temperature Conversion, which performs a simple temperature conversion between Celsius and Fahrenheit. Open a new project, and place a vertical scroll bar, six labels, and two text boxes on the form, arranging them as shown in Figure 7-3. Set the properties of the objects to the settings listed in Figure 7-4.

The program will allow the user to adjust the scroll bar to any temperature setting between the points labeled −40 and 212 on the Fahrenheit scale or the corresponding temperatures (−40 and 100) on the Celsius scale. The application will then display the temperature value for the chosen setting in both Fahrenheit and Celsius. Note that the Min property setting for the scroll bar is greater than the Max setting. Setting the properties in this way forces the scroll bar to use the largest number at the top of its range rather than using the smallest at the top, which it typically does when the Min setting is less than the Max setting.

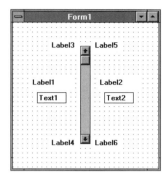

Figure 7-3.
The initial form design for the Temperature Conversion application.

Object	Property	Setting
Form1	BorderStyle	3 - Fixed Double
	Caption	Temperature Conversion
	Name	Temp
VScroll1	LargeChange	10
	Max	−40
	Min	100
	Name	vscThermometer
	SmallChange	1
Label1	Alignment	2 - Center
	Caption	Fahrenheit
Label2	Alignment	2 - Center
	Caption	Celsius
Label3	Alignment	1 - Right Justify
	Caption	212
Label4	Alignment	1 - Right Justify
	Caption	−40
Label5	Alignment	0 - Left Justify
	Caption	100
Label6	Alignment	0 - Left Justify
	Caption	−40
Text1	Name	txtDegreesF
	Text	[none]
Text2	Name	txtDegreesC
	Text	[none]

Figure 7-4.
Property settings for the Temperature Conversion application.

For simplicity, the program always "thinks" in degrees Celsius and performs a conversion to get the Fahrenheit temperature. First you must write the function that returns a Fahrenheit temperature when the program supplies it with a Celsius temperature. Begin by opening the form's code window. From the View menu, choose the New Procedure command. In the dialog box, type *CToF*, choose the Function option button, and click on OK. Then edit the new function as follows (being sure to add the parameter and type declarations to the *Function* statement):

```
Function CToF (TempC As Integer) As Integer
    CToF = CInt(TempC * 9 / 5 + 32)
End Function
```

The *CToF* function uses the standard metric conversion formula. Accepting a Celsius temperature as a parameter, it returns the equivalent temperature measured on the Fahrenheit scale. To simplify output and the use of scroll bars, all the values are restricted to integers. (The *CInt* function converts a floating-point value to an integer by rounding.)

Now you can write the code that reads the scroll bar's value and displays the temperature values. Enter the following sub procedure below the function:

```
Sub DisplayTemps ()
    Dim TempC As Integer

    TempC = CInt(vscThermometer.Value)
    txtDegreesC.Text = Str$(TempC)
    txtDegreesF.Text = Str$(CToF(TempC))
End Sub
```

After you enter the first line (the *Sub* statement), note that Visual Basic adds the procedure name to the Procedure box and adds the *End Sub* statement to the code you are writing. As you can see, you can create a new procedure either by choosing the New Procedure command from the View menu or by entering the new procedure's *Sub* or *Function* statement anywhere in the code window.

The code for the *DisplayTemps* procedure reads the scroll bar's value, *vscThermometer.Value*, and stores it in the variable *TempC*. This value is displayed in the text box txtDegreesC. Then the txtDegreesF text box is set to the result generated by the conversion function *CToF*.

Finally, choose vscThermometer (the scroll bar) from the Object box in the code window, and edit its *Change* and *Scroll* event procedures as shown here:

```
Sub vscThermometer_Change ()
    DisplayTemps
End Sub

Sub vscThermometer_Scroll ()
    DisplayTemps
End Sub
```

Now each time the user changes the scroll bar, the *DisplayTemps* procedure will do its job. Run the application to see whether it works the way you expected. The result should resemble the example shown in Figure 7-5.

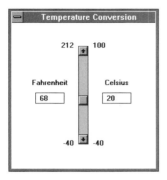

Figure 7-5.
Running the Temperature Conversion application.

Thinking Ahead

It might seem as though you did some unnecessary work in writing the code for the Temperature Conversion application. After all, because each procedure is used only once, why not do all the computations in-line and centralize all the code in the scroll bar's *Change* event procedure? The resulting program code would look something like this:

```
Sub vscThermometer_Change ()
    Dim TempC As Integer

    TempC = CInt(vscThermometer.Value)
    txtDegreesC.Text = Str$(TempC)
    txtDegreesF.Text = Str$(CInt(TempC * 9 / 5 + 32))
End Sub
```

In fact, this program is perfectly acceptable, and it works just as well as the first version. But the original Temperature Conversion program is preferable for the following reasons:

- It replaces formulas with named functions in the main program. Names add clarity and help to explain what is happening in the program.

- It contains general routines that can be used again. Copying the *CToF* function to another program would be trivial.

- Its procedures are component parts that can be easily manipulated if you decide to alter the program.

As an illustration, consider an enhancement of the program. In the current version, you must use the scroll bar to set a particular temperature. But it might be helpful to allow the user to enter a temperature value directly and then have the program compute the required conversion. By using the building blocks you've already created, you can make this task relatively simple. If you had written the program as a single chunk, such a change might require duplicating or rewriting code.

Generalizing

The best tools are ones that can be used for more than one job. Often you can easily convert a few lines of specific code that are useful only in one context to a general routine. Consider the code you wrote in Chapter 6 to search for a particular weasel by name; a full version appears in Figure 7-6. Figure 7-7 presents a version that uses a general procedure derived from the original code. This second version provides a routine that will find any weasel by name and that is likely to be useful many times in the program.

```
Dim W As Integer, Match As Integer

Match = -1
For W = 0 To WeaselPopulation - 1
    If Weasels(W).Name = "Siegmund" Then
        Match = W
        Exit For
    End If
Next W
If Match = -1 Then
    MsgBox "No match found"
Else
    Print Weasels(Match).Weight
End If
```

Figure 7-6.
Program code that searches for one weasel by name.

```
Function FindWeasel(ItsName As String) As Integer
    Dim W As Integer, Match As Integer

    Match = -1
    For W = 0 To WeaselPopulation - 1
        If Weasels(W).Name = ItsName Then
            Match = W
            Exit For
        End If
```

Figure 7-7.   *(continued)*
Program code containing a general procedure that can search for any weasel.

Figure 7-7. *continued*

```
    Next W
    FindWeasel = Match
End Function

W = FindWeasel("Siegmund")
If W = -1 Then
    MsgBox "No match found"
Else
    Print Weasels(W).Weight
End If
```

Recycling Code

Today you are writing programs to keep track of Bavarian Tufted Forest weasels. Tomorrow it might be Mugwumps. And when you're writing your program for the Mugwumps, it's handy to be able to say, "Oh, I wrote something just like that two weeks ago." If you write general-purpose routines, you can simply retrieve the code from the old program and use it in the new one. The code has already been debugged, you have less work to do, and your project is completed quickly. What more could you ask for?

Although it's fine to reuse code you developed yourself, it is usually unethical (and often illegal) to directly copy code someone else has written. You are, however, free to copy code from the sample programs shipped with Visual Basic; Microsoft has granted permission to copy the code. (The permission statement appears at the top of the main module in each application.)

How Parameters Work

So far, you've used parameters simply to pass arguments to procedures. But parameters are actually much more flexible than this. Let's take a look at the two mechanisms that are available in Visual Basic for passing parameters.

Passing by Reference

When I first introduced parameters, I described them as though they were local variables. In truth, that is not always the case. Consider the *Increment* sub procedure, which adds 1 to the value of parameter X:

```
Sub Increment (X As Integer)
    X = X + 1
End Sub
```

If X were a true local variable, this procedure would be useless. The parameter value from the calling routine would be assigned to X, and the procedure would increment the value and then terminate, effectively destroying the local variable. In fact, X is a *reference* to the original value in the calling routine, and any changes to X modify the original value. If the code shown here called the *Increment* procedure, the value 4 would be printed:

```
Dim A As Integer
A = 3
Increment A
Print A
```

Because parameter X is a reference, no memory is allocated for storing the value. Instead, Visual Basic simply stores the information that X is a reference. Using the reference allows Visual Basic to operate very efficiently. This efficiency is not apparent for integer variables, but consider the *Aside* procedure, which prints its string parameter enclosed in parentheses:

```
Sub Aside (Str As String)
    Print "(";
    Print Str;
    Print ")"
End Sub
```

If parameters were true local variables, Visual Basic would have to allocate space for each string passed to it and copy the string for every call. Because strings can be thousands of characters long, it is much less work to simply create a reference to the original string.

Passing by Value

You can also make parameters work the other way—that is, just like local variables. If you begin the parameter declaration with the keyword *ByVal*, Visual Basic allocates local storage for the parameter and copies the value of the matching argument into the parameter. Here is an example of such a declaration:

```
Sub Increment (ByVal X As Integer)
    X = X + 1
End Sub
```

Passing by reference is generally more efficient, but passing by value gives you a local variable, which you will sometimes need in your programs. For example, let's look at a function that computes x to the y power, or x^y. This computation uses repeated multiplication (x^3, for instance, equals $x * x * x$). For the sake of simplicity, the function will ignore negative exponents. The parameter Y specifies the number of multiplications that need to be performed. The value of Y is decremented after each multiplication, and the computation is completed when Y reaches 0.

```
Function Power (X As Single, ByVal Y As Integer) As Single
    Dim Result As Single

    Result = 1
    Do While Y > 0
        Result = Result * X
        Y = Y - 1
    Loop
    Power = Result
End Function
```

Because you want to modify *Y* locally but don't want to change the value of the variable that was passed, you must declare *Y* with the *ByVal* keyword. Examine the following code fragment, which calls the *Power* function:

```
'Approximate e^n using Taylor series
Result = 1
For Approx = 1 To 10
    Result = Result + Power(N, Approx) / Factorial(Approx)
Next Approx
```

The programmer expects this routine to loop 10 times while performing its computation. If, however, the *Power* function it is calling did not use the *ByVal* keyword, this routine would go into an infinite loop. After the routine called *Power* for the first time, *Approx* would be reset to 0 (because the local variable *Y* would be a reference to *Approx*). The *Factorial* function would be called with the wrong value, and then the *For* statement would increment *Approx* to 1 and continue through the loop again. Because *Power* would continue setting *Approx* to 0, the *For* loop would never stop.

A good rule of thumb is that any parameter declaration for an integer, long, or single type should be a *ByVal* declaration (that is, the parameter should be passed as a value) unless the calling routine explicitly expects the procedure to modify the value that is passed. Conversely, strings and arrays should be passed by reference for the sake of efficiency. User-defined data types (such as BTFWeasel) and controls can be passed only by reference in Visual Basic.

For the other data types (double, currency, and variant), the decision is not quite as simple. Good programming practice dictates that you pass these parameters by value because you will be less likely to inadvertently misuse a parameter variable. But it is more efficient to pass these parameters by reference.

My advice is to stick with good engineering principles first: Pass all variables (except strings, arrays, and user-defined types) by value initially. After you have completed your program and have it running correctly, you can investigate ways to speed it up. Then, if your program operates incorrectly after you remove some of the *ByVal* keywords, you will also know where to look for problems.

Passing Array Parameters

You can declare an array parameter just as you do any other parameter, except that you omit the array size from the declaration. For example, this function computes the average of any array of double-precision values:

```
Function AvgD (Darray() As Double, ByVal Dcount As Integer) As Double
    Dim Total As Double, Ix As Integer

    Total = 0
    For Ix = 0 To Dcount - 1
        Total = Total + Darray(Ix)
    Next Ix
    If Dcount = 0 Then
        AvgD = 0
    Else
        AvgD = Total / Dcount
    End If
End Function
```

The parameter *Darray* is declared as an array of type double, but its size is undeclared. This code is another example of a generalized solution. Because the array size is undeclared, this same function can be called with arguments that are arrays of any size (as long as the elements in the array are type double).

To pass an array as an argument to a procedure, simply use the name of the array variable followed by a set of empty parentheses. This code fragment shows how the procedure *AvgD* might be used:

```
Dim MyData(100) As Double, ItemsRead As Integer
ItemsRead = LoadData(MyData(), 100)
Print "The average data value is"; AvgD(MyData(), ItemsRead)
```

MyData is declared as an array with a dimension of 100. The *LoadData* procedure (not shown here) is called, and *MyData* is passed as a parameter, along with the maximum size of the array. Presumably, the *LoadData* routine fills in as much of the array as possible. Next the program prints out the average. The call to *AvgD* passes the array and the number of elements that were filled by *LoadData*.

You can, of course, also pass individual array elements when appropriate. Simply index the array to specify the element you want to pass, as in this line of code:

```
Print "The square root of item three is"; sqr(MyData(3))
```

You can modify the Banker application from Chapter 6 to use a function, as shown in Figure 7-8. Each time you click on the Average button, the program redimensions the dynamic array *ValueList* to match the number of items in the list box. Because the list box contains an array of strings rather than numbers, each element must be converted as it is copied into *ValueList*. The program then passes the entire array to the *AvgD* function.

```
Dim ValueList() As Double

Function AvgD (Darray() As Double, ByVal Dcount As Integer) As Double
    Dim Total As Double, Ix As Integer

    Total = 0                           'Sum of all items
    For Ix = 0 To Dcount - 1
        Total = Total + Darray(Ix)      'Compute sum
    Next Ix
    If Dcount = 0 Then
        AvgD = 0
    Else
        AvgD = Total / Dcount           'Compute and return avg
    End If
End Function

Sub btnAvg_Click ()
    Dim I As Integer

    ReDim ValueList(cboInput.ListCount - 1)
    For I = 0 To cboInput.ListCount - 1
        ValueList(I) = Val(cboInput.List(I))
    Next I
    lblAvg.Caption = Str$(AvgD(ValueList(), cboInput.ListCount))
End Sub
```

Figure 7-8.
A modification of the Banker application.

This modified program is a bit longer than the original application. But you have created a new tool—the function *AvgD*—that you can use over and over. For example, to extend the Banker program to handle more than one account, you can call the *AvgD* function for each account rather than writing a separate loop for each one. If you need to write a program that computes average rainfall, you can load the Banker program, copy the *AvgD* function, and paste it into your new program.

Local Allocation

You are already familiar with local variables from the discussion of scope in Chapter 3. Now that you are working with parameters, which are similar to local variables, it's useful to look at the way Visual Basic manages the memory used by local variables.

When you start a program, Visual Basic knows how many global variables exist and allocates memory for them. But it does not know how many local variables exist or even whether each procedure in the program will be called. Local variables and parameters are created when the procedure in which they are contained is called, and they are destroyed when the procedure ends. If the procedure is called again, the variables are re-created. This process not only delays the allocation of memory until it is needed but also allows memory to be reused for variables belonging to different procedures. Modern computers perform this temporary allocation and deallocation very efficiently.

Sometimes, however, you might not want to lose the value stored in a local variable when the procedure containing the variable ends. You could declare a module-level or a global variable, but this solution is undesirable if the variable is used by only one procedure.

Visual Basic provides the *Static* keyword to handle the problem. If you use *Static* in place of *Dim* inside a procedure, the variables so declared will have local scope, visible only to that procedure; but they will be permanent, just as if they were declared at the module level. Visual Basic initializes all *Static* variables to 0, which makes them useful for situations such as the following:

```
Sub Command1_Click ()
    Static Counter As Integer
    Counter = Counter + 1
    MsgBox "This button has been pressed" + Str$(Counter) + "times."
End Sub
```

Open a new form, add a single command button, and try out this program. Then change the *Static* keyword to *Dim* to demonstrate that the program doesn't work with a purely local variable.

Objects as Parameters

The procedures you have written so far have passed numeric values, arrays, and strings as parameters. Visual Basic also allows you to pass controls and forms. The syntax is similar: Simply use the keyword *Control* or *Form* in place of *String, Integer,* and so on in the procedure declaration.

This feature enhances your ability to write general-purpose code. For example, suppose that you are writing an application with a number of buttons on the screen. At various points in the application, you want to draw attention to a particular button by italicizing its caption text and setting its background color to red. The following sub procedure does just that:

```
Sub Attention (Btn As Control)
    Btn.FontItalic = True
    Btn.BackColor = RED      'RED is defined in CONSTANT.TXT
End Sub
```

You pass an object as a parameter by using the object's name. You could pass a button named btnNext to this procedure with the statement *Attention btnNext.*

In a similar manner, you can declare a parameter to be a form. You can set or examine the form's properties and call its methods. You can pass the form by name, or you can use the built-in variable *Me,* which is the currently active form.

The Evade Application

Let's build a program called Evade that plays a practical joke on the user. It will deliver an error message, as if it has failed during startup. The user will see a dialog box with two command buttons, Cancel and Retry. What happens when the user clicks on one of these buttons is a bit unusual, however. The button will "run away" to some random point on the form, and the user will never be able to cancel the program by simply clicking on the buttons. This application illustrates how you can pass objects as parameters and how you can use the *Move* method—a method that can be implemented for most Visual Basic controls.

Each command button should have the same behavior. To a certain extent, you can ensure this by calling a common procedure. But one of the actions of the procedure will be to move the button to a new location. This action means calling the button's *Move* method, which requires that you pass the button as a parameter.

Create a new project, and arrange two label fields, two command buttons, and an image control on the form as shown in Figure 7-9. Figure 7-10 lists the necessary property settings.

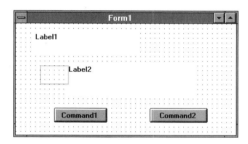

Figure 7-9.
The initial form design for the Evade application.

Object	Property	Setting
Form1	Caption	Error
	Name	Evade
Label1	Caption	Initialization Failure:
	FontSize	12
Label2	Caption	Memory error in RAM chip - third from the right
Image1	Picture	TRFFC14.ICO
Command1	Caption	Cancel
Command2	Caption	Retry

Figure 7-10.
Property settings for the Evade application.

Figure 7-11 contains the program code for the Evade application, and Figure 7-12 demonstrates how the application might look when the user runs it.

```
Function RandInt (InMin As Integer, InMax As Integer) As Integer
    RandInt = Int(InMax - InMin + 1) * Rnd + InMin
End Function

Sub Jump (Ctl As Control)
    Dim Horiz As Integer, Vert As Integer

    Horiz = RandInt(0, Width - Ctl.Width)
    Vert = RandInt(0, Height - Ctl.Height - 375)
    Ctl.Move Horiz, Vert
End Sub

Sub Command1_Click ()
    Jump Command1
End Sub

Sub Command2_Click ()
    Jump Command2
End Sub
```

Figure 7-11.
Program code for the Evade application.

Figure 7-12.
Running the Evade application.

The *Jump* procedure used in this application can adjust the location not only of command buttons but also of nearly any kind of control that is passed as a parameter, because most controls possess a *Move* method. Sometimes, however, you might want to perform special kinds of processing that are specific to a certain kind of object. Visual Basic provides the *If TypeOf* statement to determine control parameter types. It operates in the same fashion as a conventional *If* statement; only the syntax of the first line is different:

```
If TypeOf object Is objectType Then
```

If you wanted the *Jump* procedure to distinguish option buttons from the other types of controls, the first line of the *If TypeOf* statement would look like this:

```
If TypeOf Ctl Is OptionButton Then
```

Advanced Event Procedures

This section examines some Visual Basic event procedures that are more complicated than simple *Click* and *DblClick* procedures. These techniques allow you to build applications with more sophisticated mouse and keyboard handling and to implement a graphical technique called drag and drop.

Mouse Events

Our previous examples paid attention to the mouse only when it was used to click on an object. All you had to do then was simply code a *Click* or *DblClick* event procedure. But certain types of applications will need to track mouse activities much more closely.

A drawing or painting program, for example, needs to know the location of the mouse when you are dragging a graphic or creating a new image. A game might use the location of the mouse to control some aspect of play. Visual Basic does not contain a mouse object, however. Instead, a MouseMove event is triggered whenever the mouse's location changes. Most often, mouse events are associated with forms and picture boxes, but they can be used with other objects as well. For purposes of illustration, this section concentrates on working with forms.

Each form has these three procedure templates:

```
Sub Form_MouseDown (Button As Integer, Shift As Integer,
  X As Single, Y As Single)

Sub Form_MouseUp (Button As Integer, Shift As Integer,
  X As Single, Y As Single)

Sub Form_MouseMove (Button As Integer, Shift As Integer,
  X As Single, Y As Single)
```

Visual Basic calls these procedures when the user interacts with the mouse. The MouseDown event occurs whenever a mouse button is pressed. The MouseUp event is signaled when a mouse button is released. The MouseMove event occurs when the location of the mouse changes. Figure 7-13 on the following page describes the parameters that are passed to these event procedures.

Parameter	Description
Button	This parameter holds a value indicating which mouse button has been pressed. It is created by combining the appropriate constants via an Or operation: LEFT_BUTTON, RIGHT_BUTTON, MIDDLE_BUTTON.
Shift	This parameter represents the status of the Shift, Ctrl, and Alt keys using the constants SHIFT_MASK, CTRL_MASK, and ALT_MASK. A bit is set if the indicated key is being held down.
X, Y	These values correspond to the current mouse location, using the coordinate system specified by the scaling properties.

Figure 7-13.
Parameters of mouse event procedures.

The best way to illustrate these events is by writing a simple application. The code for the Line Drawing application, shown in Figure 7-14, is based on the Scribble program in the Visual Basic documentation. This application uses the *Line* method, a graphical method for drawing to a form. (We'll discuss the *Line* method in more detail in Chapter 10.)

```
'From CONSTANT.TXT
Const LEFT_BUTTON = 1, SHIFT_MASK = 1, RED = &HFF&

Dim Drawing As Integer

Sub Form_Load ()
    Drawing = False              'Drawing nothing at startup time
End Sub

Sub Form_MouseDown (Button As Integer, Shift As Integer,
 X As Single, Y As Single)
    If (Button And LEFT_BUTTON) <> 0 Then
        Drawing = True           'Draw as long as mouse button is held down
        CurrentX = X
        CurrentY = Y
    End If
End Sub

Sub Form_MouseUp (Button As Integer, Shift As Integer,
 X As Single, Y As Single)
    If (Button And LEFT_BUTTON) <> 0 Then
        Drawing = False          'Stop drawing
    End If
End Sub
```

Figure 7-14.   *(continued)*
Program code for the Line Drawing application.

Figure 7-14. *continued*

```
Sub Form_MouseMove (Button As Integer, Shift As Integer,
 X As Single, Y As Single)
    If Drawing Then
        If (Shift And SHIFT_MASK) = SHIFT_MASK Then
            Line -(X, Y), RED      'Draw red lines
        Else
            Line -(X, Y)            'Draw black lines
        End If
    End If
End Sub
```

When you run this application, the variable *Drawing* is initially set to False. When you press the left mouse button, however, the variable is set to True. When you release the mouse button, *Drawing* is set to False again. As you move the mouse with the button depressed, the program draws a line from the last known coordinate (*CurrentX, CurrentY*) to the current mouse location. If you hold down the Shift key while you are drawing, the line color will change to red until you release the key.

> *Note: For a single-button mouse, its one button is defined as the left button. If you have a two-button mouse and have used Windows' Control Panel to swap the left/right sensing of the mouse buttons, Visual Basic will pass the value LEFT_BUTTON when you press the right mouse button and the value RIGHT_BUTTON when you press the left mouse button.*

Keyboard Events

Chapter 6 introduced the KeyPress event, which is triggered for certain objects when the user is typing. Visual Basic also provides an even finer degree of control with the KeyUp and KeyDown events, which are triggered when the user presses and releases keys at the keyboard. Only very specialized applications require the use of these events, however; complete information is contained in the Visual Basic reference manual.

Forms have another useful feature related to user keystrokes. Normally, keystrokes (and their associated events) are sent directly to the object (a text box, for example) that is the current focus of attention. However, by setting the KeyPreview property of a form to True, you cause the form's *KeyPress, KeyUp,* and *KeyDown* event procedures to be triggered first. These procedures can then filter the information that is passed on to the object's *KeyPress, KeyUp,* and *KeyDown* procedures.

For example, to record every keystroke a user types, you could define the following function (assuming that *SaveAll* is declared as a form-level string variable):

```
Sub Form_KeyPress (KeyAscii As Integer)
    SaveAll = SaveAll + Chr$(KeyAscii)
End Sub
```

If the form's KeyPreview property is set to True and if the form-level key-handling procedure modifies the *KeyAscii* variable, the *KeyPress* event procedure of the currently selected object will see the modified keystroke. If the form-level procedure sets *KeyAscii* to 0, the object's *KeyPress* procedure is not called.

Drag and Drop

Visual Basic also provides special support for another form of user interaction, called drag and drop. The term *drag and drop* refers to using the mouse to drag a displayed object to some final resting place. You have seen this process in Windows' File Manager, which allows you to move files from one directory to another by dragging the file icons.

You enable dragging of a Visual Basic object (usually a picture box or an image control) by setting its DragMode property to 1. When DragMode is set to 1, a control no longer receives Click or MouseDown events. Instead, the object moves when the user clicks on it and begins dragging it. The item being dragged is called the *source object*, and the item that receives the DragDrop event is called the *target*. When the user releases the source object (by releasing the mouse button), Visual Basic signals a DragDrop event to the target. In addition, DragOver events are sent to any object that the source object has passed over.

The drag-and-drop feature allows you to design a simple, "hands-on" user interface in which tasks can be performed without commands, menus, or buttons. This method is very intuitive in many situations and is often much faster than other methods. Obvious examples include dragging file icons to a directory folder in Windows' File Manager and printing a file by dragging it to Windows' Print Manager.

To demonstrate drag and drop, let's write an application called Electronic Mail, which will simulate a desktop environment for electronic mail. It will let you create new messages and drag them to a mailbox from which they could be sent out over a network. (Only the drag-and-drop features of this example are presented here; the source code for an electronic mail system could fill an entire book.)

Start by creating a new form. Add two command buttons and seven small image controls, as shown in Figure 7-15. The three image controls at the bottom of the screen will hold master copies of icons, as some of the image controls did in the Slots application in Chapter 6. After you initialize these three controls, you can resize the form to hide them from view.

Set the properties of the bottom three image controls (Image5, Image6, and Image7) as listed in Figure 7-16. The Tag property is ignored by Visual Basic; you can use it to hold any identifying text you want. This application uses the Tag property to distinguish the letter icon from the other icons.

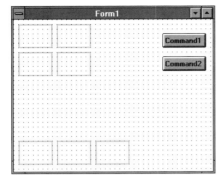

Figure 7-15.
The initial form design for the Electronic Mail application.

Object	Property	Setting
Image5	Name	imgMboxEmpty
	Picture	MAIL16A.ICO
Image6	Name	imgMboxFull
	Picture	MAIL16B.ICO
Image7	DragMode	1 - Automatic
	Index	0
	Name	imgLetter
	Picture	MAIL01A.ICO
	Tag	Letter

Figure 7-16.
*Property settings for the bottom three image controls
in the Electronic Mail application.*

Setting the DragMode property of Image7 (the letter icon) to 1 allows the user to drag letters around in the window. The Index property setting of 0 makes the letter icon a control array, although the array contains only a single element at this time. (In a moment, you'll see how the program code uses this.) Figure 7-17 on the following page shows you how the bottom row of images in the form should look after these properties are set.

Now set the properties of the other objects as indicated in Figure 7-18 on the following page. After you resize the form so that the bottom three images are no longer visible, your form should look like the one shown in Figure 7-19 on page 173. The image control that appears in the top left will serve as a mailbox into which letter icons can be dropped. The icons that you see on the desktop (the pencil, the phone, and the paperclip) cannot be mailed. The mailbox will display the empty mailbox icon (from Image5) when it is empty, and the full mailbox icon (from Image6) when the user drags letters into it. The command buttons will let the user create new letters (with the letter icon) and empty the mailbox.

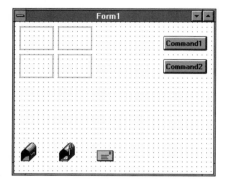

Figure 7-17.
The bottom three icons used in the Electronic Mail application.

Object	Property	Setting
Form1	BorderStyle	3 - Fixed Double
	Caption	Electronic Mail
Image1	BorderStyle	1 - Fixed Single
	Name	imgMailbox
Image2	DragMode	1 - Automatic
	Name	imgPencil
	Picture	POINT09.ICO
Image3	DragMode	1 - Automatic
	Name	imgPhone
	Picture	PHONE01.ICO
Image4	DragMode	1 - Automatic
	Name	imgPClip
	Picture	CLIP01.ICO
Command1	Caption	New Msg
	Name	btnNew
Command2	Caption	Empty Mbox
	Name	btnEmpty

Figure 7-18.
The remaining property settings for the Electronic Mail application.

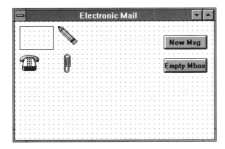

Figure 7-19.
The completed form design for the Electronic Mail application.

The code for this application template requires the following declaration:

```
Dim NextLetter As Integer
```

Two procedures are required at the form level. The *Form_Load* procedure initializes the mailbox icon and the *NextLetter* variable; the *Form_DragDrop* procedure moves control to the point the user specifies:

```
Sub Form_Load ()
    imgMailbox.Picture = imgMboxEmpty.Picture
    NextLetter = 1
End Sub

Sub Form_DragDrop (Source As Control, X As Single, Y As Single)
    Source.Move X, Y
End Sub
```

The basic window shows only three icons. To allow the user to create new letter objects, you must write the code for the New Msg button:

```
Sub btnNew_Click ()
    Load imgLetter(NextLetter)
    imgLetter(NextLetter).Left = btnNew.Left - 2000 + NextLetter * 100
    imgLetter(NextLetter).Top = btnNew.Top
    imgLetter(NextLetter).Visible = True
    NextLetter = NextLetter + 1
End Sub
```

The program first calls the *Load* procedure. Because *imgLetter* is a control array, *Load* creates a new control and gives it the index specified by *NextLetter*. After Visual Basic creates the new member of the control array (*imgLetter*), this new member is given a location in the window and becomes visible. Then the *NextLetter* variable is incremented so that a subsequent Click event will create a new letter.

The Empty Mbox button simply resets the icon (the Picture property) of the mailbox to the default value:

```
Sub btnEmpty_Click ()
    imgMailbox.Picture = imgMboxEmpty.Picture
End Sub
```

The mailbox requires its own drag-and-drop procedure. When a control is dropped on the mailbox, the program checks the tag of the source object. If the source object is not a letter, the procedure exits, and the source object is not moved. Otherwise, the Unload statement removes the letter, and the Picture property of the mailbox is set to the icon of imgMboxFull.

```
Sub imgMailbox_DragDrop (Source As Control, X As Single, Y As Single)
    If Source.Tag <> "Letter" Then
        Beep
        Exit Sub
    End If
    Unload Source
    imgMailbox.Picture = imgMboxFull.Picture
End Sub
```

Run this application, and try clicking on the New Msg button a few times to create new letters. Except for the mailbox, all of the images on the desktop can be dragged. Dragging a letter into the mailbox changes the mailbox's icon, and clicking on the Empty Mbox button resets the mailbox icon. Note that the program will not allow you to drag the telephone, the pencil, or the paperclip into the mailbox.

This sample program uses the variable *NextLetter* to specify a continually increasing index value for subsequent elements of the *Letter* control array. In a real-world version of the program, you would want to keep closer tabs on the index values. Visual Basic allows a maximum of 255 elements in a control array, which means that the program will fail if the user tries to create 256 or more letters. Ideally, the program would monitor the deletion of control-array elements and would reuse the index values of the unloaded elements.

8

Debugging and Error Handling

This chapter focuses on mistakes and what to do about them. No matter how experienced a programmer you are, your programs will rarely run perfectly on the first try. And no matter how skilled are the users who will be working with your program, they're bound to cause or encounter a certain number of runtime errors. We'll look first at the process of finding and removing bugs and then at ways to handle runtime errors as they occur.

Bugs are those insidious gremlins plaguing the programs that you "know" are correct, even though you aren't getting the right results. Interestingly, one of the first recorded computer bugs really *was* a bug. The Mark II computer was an electromechanical computer built in 1945. One day the computer mysteriously stopped working. An arduous search finally revealed a moth caught between the contact points of a relay. Grace Murray Hopper, one of the creators of the COBOL language and a pioneer in the computer industry, retrieved the unlucky lepidopteran and taped it into the project logbook with the notation "First actual bug found."

The bugs discussed in this chapter, however, are errors of logic in your program. You can, of course, make all sorts of mistakes that will prevent your program from running—trying to assign a string value to a variable of type double, for instance. But Visual Basic flags these fairly straightforward errors as soon as it encounters them, which makes them easy to find and fix. The really interesting bugs are the ones you must find and fix on your own.

Debugging is simply the process of finding and removing bugs. Unlike traditional pest extermination, debugging computer programs results in no toxic side effects, unless you count the sleepless hours and innumerable cups of coffee it can take to find a seemingly intractable bug.

Debugging a program can be interesting and even exciting. Tracking down and obliterating a software bug usually results in a feeling of real satisfaction, whether it derives from a sense of healing or repairing your program, a sense of accomplishment, or just the thrill of the hunt. The intellectual exercise can be enlightening as well, allowing you to examine and analyze your own thought processes.

Debugging Tools

Much as we hate to admit it, all bugs are really programmer errors. Sometimes, however, they appear so infrequently or under such unusual conditions that they seem to exhibit a malign intelligence that delights in taunting us. I have had experience with a bug that appeared only on alternate weeks and with a program that worked perfectly except when a particular application was run immediately before it. Much more common is the routine that simply doesn't work. When you encounter such a problem, you'll want to utilize some of the tools Visual Basic offers for debugging.

As you work with the various debugging tools, you'll find that some of the buttons on the Visual Basic Toolbar provide handy shortcuts. Figure 8-1 identifies the Toolbar buttons that are most useful in debugging.

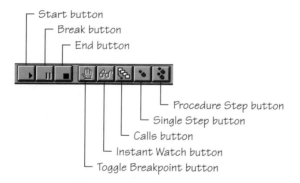

Figure 8-1.
The Toolbar buttons used in debugging.

The Debug Window

As you already know, you can press Ctrl-Break at any time while your program is running, to interrupt the application and activate the Debug window. If a particular procedure is running when you interrupt the program, you will also see the code window for that procedure. At this point, you can enter and execute Visual Basic statements in the Debug window. Each statement can be only one line long. The statement is executed within the Debug window when you press the Enter key. The code in the code window does not change.

Typically, you will want to simply print the values of variables and expressions that interest you, but you can do much more than that. In fact, you can execute nearly any Visual Basic programming statement; you could, for example, modify a variable or execute a procedure within the Debug window. Note, however, that you can modify only the local variables and parameters of the current procedure and the module-level and global variables; you cannot examine or change local variables from any procedure other than the current one. You can also change the values of any properties that can be modified at runtime.

As a demonstration, create a new project that contains a single command button. Add the general procedure *DoStuff* and the *Click* procedure for the command button, as shown in Figure 8-2.

```
Sub DoStuff ()
    Dim A As Single, B As Integer

    A = .5
    For B = 1 To 10000
        A = A + B
    Next B
End Sub

Sub Command1_Click ()
    Dim C As String, D As Integer

    C = "Hello, sailor"
    For D = 1 To 100
        DoStuff
    Next D
    C = "Good night, Gracie"
End Sub
```

Figure 8-2.
Program code for the Thumb Twiddler application.

Press F5 to start the application. Click on the command button, and then press Ctrl-Break to have Visual Basic halt the application and display the code window, which will resemble the one shown in Figure 8-3 on the following page. (The odds are good that the program will break in the *DoStuff* routine; if it does not, press F5 to restart the program, and try interrupting it again.)

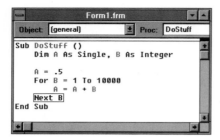

Figure 8-3.
The code window of an interrupted program.

In the code window shown in Figure 8-3, a box appears around the line *Next B*, which is the statement Visual Basic will execute next. In the Debug window, you could enter the statement *Print B* (or simply *? B*) to see how many times the *For* statement has looped. You could enter *Print A* to see the current value of *A*. You cannot, however, type *Print C* or *Print D* to examine the other variables in the application, even though they have values assigned to them, because the Debug window is limited to the scope of the executing procedure. If you did enter the statement *Print C* or *Print D*, Visual Basic would assume that you were simply using undeclared variables in the current procedure and would print a blank line. You do have access to all variables and properties of module-level or global scope, which allows you to execute statements such as *Print Command1.Caption* and *Print Form1.Height*.

> **Note:** *If you have included the statement* Option Explicit *in the general declarations section of your program, Visual Basic won't even print a blank line when you attempt to display the value of an undeclared variable in the Debug window. Instead, you'll see the message* Variable not defined.

If you want to try modifying a property or a variable within the Debug window, you can use the same statements and expressions you would use in a program. For example, you could shrink the size of the form window by executing the statement *Form1.Height = Form1.Height / 2.* Or you could execute any sub procedure or method by entering its name. When you type a *Print* statement, for example, you are calling the *Print* method for the object representing the Debug window (an object named Debug). You are not limited to Visual Basic's built-in procedures; you can also execute any of the procedures you have written.

Watch Expressions

When you want to simply check the value of a variable, Visual Basic offers a quick technique that doesn't involve any *Print* statements. Double-click on a variable name in the code window—try double-clicking on the variable *B* from the *DoStuff* procedure—and then choose Instant Watch from the Debug menu or click on the Instant Watch button on the Toolbar. The Instant Watch dialog box, shown in Figure 8-4, appears and displays the value of the variable you selected.

Figure 8-4.
The Instant Watch dialog box.

The selected variable is referred to as a *watch expression*. As its name implies, a watch expression can be more than a single variable. If you select *A + B* from the *DoStuff* procedure, the Instant Watch dialog box will display the value of the entire expression.

You can also add a watch expression to the Debug window so that you can check the value of the expression at any time without having to open the Instant Watch dialog box. To add a selected expression, click on the Add Watch button in the Instant Watch dialog box or choose Add ·Watch from the Debug menu. In the Add Watch dialog box, shown in Figure 8-5, click on the OK button to have the selected watch expression appear at the top of the Debug window.

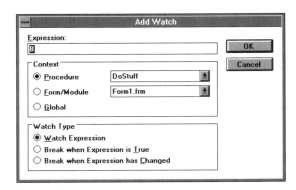

Figure 8-5.
The Add Watch dialog box.

You can even add a watch expression to the Debug window without first selecting it in your program code. Simply type the expression directly in the Expression text box of the Add Watch dialog box. The Context portion of the dialog box allows you to specify the procedure or module in which a variable in your expression is defined—which can be useful, for example, in case you have a form-level variable and a local variable with the same name. (We'll discuss the Watch Type portion of the dialog box in a later section.)

Figure 8-6 shows the Debug window after two watch expressions have been added. The expressions display the variable *D* in the *Command1_Click* procedure and the variable *B* in the *DoStuff* procedure.

Figure 8-6.
The Debug window with watch expressions.

If you want to edit or remove a watch expression that has been added to the Debug window, choose the Edit Watch command from the Debug menu and make the necessary changes in the resulting Edit Watch dialog box.

The Call Tree (Where Am I?)

In the simple example in the preceding section (the Thumb Twiddler application), it was pretty obvious what was happening when the program was interrupted. In a more complex application, however, the sequence of events might not be so clear. In that case, you can choose the Calls command from the Debug menu or click on the Calls button on the Toolbar to produce a dialog box showing the list of active procedure calls in the program.

Figure 8-7 shows the Calls dialog box for the Thumb Twiddler program. The first line of the dialog box displays the current procedure—in this case, the procedure *DoStuff*, which is in the Form1 module. This procedure was called by the event procedure *Command1_Click*, also in the module Form1. The call trace ends here because the call to the *Click* procedure was triggered by a user event. For a complex program, the Calls dialog box could display many entries indicating the nesting of the procedure calls. You can double-click on any of the entries (or select an entry and click on the Show button) to display the code for a particular procedure.

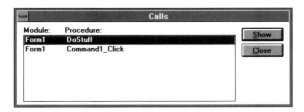

Figure 8-7.
The call tree for an interrupted program.

Breakpoints and *Stop* Statements

When you pressed Ctrl-Break to interrupt the Thumb Twiddler program, you didn't have much control over where the program stopped. Visual Basic will, however, allow you to explicitly mark one or more statements as *breakpoints,* points at which the program execution will stop, giving you a chance to poke and prod the program in an effort to diagnose its problems. You can set breakpoints either before you run your program or after you interrupt it. To set a breakpoint, open the code window to the appropriate procedure, and click on the statement at which the program should break. Then press F9, choose the Toggle Breakpoint command from the Debug menu, or click on the Toggle Breakpoint button on the Toolbar. Visual Basic will highlight the line to indicate the presence of the breakpoint.

To remove a breakpoint, simply click on the highlighted program line to select it, and then press F9, choose Toggle Breakpoint again, or click on the Toggle Break-point button. If you have set multiple breakpoints, you can choose the Clear All Breakpoints command from the Debug menu to remove them all at once.

You can achieve the same effect as setting a breakpoint by adding a *Stop* statement to your program. This technique is not as convenient as using a breakpoint because it means modifying the code. With a breakpoint, however, Visual Basic interrupts the program every time the breakpoint is reached. If you use a *Stop* statement, you can be much more specific, ensuring that your program will halt only under certain conditions. For example, the following code fragment containing a *Stop* statement would interrupt your program only after executing 10 times and then only if the value of the variable *A* was less than 0.

```
Static BrkCount As Integer

BrkCount = BrkCount + 1
If BrkCount > 10 And A < 0 Then
    Stop
End If
```

After your program has been interrupted by either a breakpoint or a *Stop* statement, you can continue execution by pressing the F5 key or by choosing the Continue command from Visual Basic's Run menu. If you used a *Stop* statement, you must remember to remove it from your program. Breakpoints are active only for a single Visual Basic session.

Using a *Stop* statement can be described as an *invasive* technique—that is, you must reach in and physically modify your program code. You might recall another invasive technique from an earlier chapter: writing to the Debug window from within the program. The statement *Debug.Print* followed by an expression causes the value of the expression to be written to the Debug window without interrupting the program in any way. By sprinkling a few such statements throughout an ailing program, you can often discover the point at which problems start to occur. Common uses include printing the name of a procedure as it begins to execute or printing the values of certain key variables.

Although invasive techniques allow you to carry out more sophisticated operations, *noninvasive* techniques such as setting breakpoints are usually preferable because they prevent you from leaving the programming equivalent of a sponge or scalpel inside your patient. If you forget to remove a *Stop* statement from a rarely called procedure before you compile a program, you (or worse yet, a customer using your program) could get a rude shock when the message *Stop statement encountered* appears in the middle of an application that promptly terminates, sending all your data away to never-never land.

Watchpoints

You can also use a noninvasive tool called a *watchpoint,* which tells Visual Basic to interrupt the program when a particular condition is met (in contrast to a breakpoint, which specifies an interruption when a particular line of code is reached) or when the value of an expression changes.

To set a watchpoint, highlight the specific expression in your code and choose the Add Watch command from the Debug menu, or choose the Add Watch command first and then type the expression in the text box of the Add Watch dialog box. In this dialog box (shown previously in Figure 8-5), move to the Watch Type section, select the option button marked Break When Expression Is True, and then click on the OK button. Visual Basic will add the expression to the Debug window. If you want your program to pause when the value of the watch expression changes, you should instead select the option button marked Break When Expression Has Changed in the Add Watch dialog box.

In either case, when you resume execution of the program, Visual Basic evaluates the watch expression after every single statement and stops execution when the specified condition occurs.

Watchpoints are very powerful tools, but they have a downside. Although they are noninvasive and thus make no changes to your code, they slow the execution of your program because the watch expressions must be continually tested. The best technique is to use breakpoints and watchpoints together: Set a breakpoint at the location in your program where you suspect something is going wrong. The program can run at full speed up to that point. Then you can turn on one or more watchpoints and continue execution more slowly.

Step by Step

Another helpful noninvasive debugging technique is the *single step,* which lets you execute your program a single statement at a time. It is essentially equivalent to setting a breakpoint one statement ahead of the current position, executing the current statement, and clearing the breakpoint. When you single-step through your code, you can examine the effect of every statement in the program.

Single-stepping is controlled by the F8 key or the Single Step button on the Toolbar (or the Single Step command on the Debug menu, although the function key or the Toolbar button is usually much handier). You can begin single-stepping whenever your program is not running. Each time you press F8, Visual Basic executes one statement, and the box marking the next line in the code window advances. If the statement that is executed contains a call to a user-written procedure, the code window changes, and the box appears around the first executable line of the new procedure. If you execute a statement that contains more than one call, you will step through the procedures in order. For example, consider the program shown in Figure 8-8 on the following page. (The reference numbers on the left have been added simply to identify various lines of the program.)

If you run this program with a breakpoint set at line 3 ($A = 4$), a box initially appears around line 3. When you press F8 to begin single-stepping, the box advances to lines 4, 8, 9, 12, 13, and 5. (Because lines 7 and 11 are considered declarations, not executable lines, the debugging tool bypasses them. If you set a breakpoint at a declaration, the box will appear around the next executable line when the program is interrupted.)

```
1    Sub Command1_Click ()
2        Dim A As Integer
3        A = 4                                 'Initial breakpoint
4        Debug.Print OneMore(A) + OneLess(A)   'Step through procedures
5    End Sub
6
7    Function OneMore (X As Integer) As Integer
8        OneMore = X + 1
9    End Function
10
11   Function OneLess (X As Integer) As Integer
12       OneLess = X - 1
13   End Function
```

Figure 8-8.
Program code that demonstrates single-stepping.

If you are single-stepping through a program and reach a procedure that has already been thoroughly debugged, you can avoid stepping through each statement of that procedure. If you hold down the Shift key while you press F8 or if you click on the Toolbar's Procedure Step button, Visual Basic restricts stepping to the current procedure and simply executes the procedure calls in that procedure as if each call were a single statement. If you use Shift-F8 to step through the program shown in Figure 8-8, you will move from line 3 to line 4 to line 5. Visual Basic executes lines 7 through 9 and lines 11 through 13, but you can avoid stepping through two function procedures that you know are correct.

You are free to alternate between single-stepping and procedure-stepping any time during your debugging session. Note that a breakpoint set inside a procedure will interrupt the program even if you are using procedure steps.

Try experimenting with these techniques in the Thumb Twiddler program shown in Figure 8-2. First use F9 to set a breakpoint at the statement *Next D* in the *Command1_Click* procedure. Press F5 to run the program, and click on the command button to reach the breakpoint. Press F9 again to clear the breakpoint. Then hold down the Shift key and press F8 a couple of times. You will stay in the *Command1_Click* procedure (although you might notice a pause while the *DoStuff* procedure is executed). When you return to *Next D*, press F8 twice without using the Shift key. These single steps will take you inside the *DoStuff* procedure, where you can continue single-stepping.

Debugging Strategies

Typically, the source of a problem in a program is easy to localize; it's often reasonably obvious that everything is working except one button or a certain computation. You can then employ the classic technique of decreasing granularity. The term *granularity* refers to the size of the program chunks that need to be executed. You might start out using breakpoints, which allow you to execute large portions of the program without interruption. As you near the point where things go wrong, you could switch to procedure-stepping and then to single-stepping to pinpoint the statement in which the error occurs.

Of course, the preceding paragraph optimistically assumes that a single statement is the source of all your problems. That is often not so. You might find that you have made assumptions about variable values or user input that simply aren't true and that will force you to rewrite portions of your program. Because you are likely to take these assumptions with you into your debugging session, it can sometimes be difficult to tell what is going awry. At times like these, you might find it profitable to code your assumptions into the program directly. For example, if you assume that a certain parameter will never have a value that is less than 10 or greater than 50, you might place the following code at the beginning of the procedure that includes the parameter:

```
If Param < 10 Or Param > 50 Then
    Debug.Print "Assertion about variable 'Param' violated"
    Stop
End If
```

Although it is an invasive technique, coding these assertions into your program can sometimes help you catch bugs more quickly than using breakpoints or stepping, especially if the program is long or complex.

Finally, for the times when you haven't the foggiest idea what is going wrong, you might be tempted to resort to the Elmer Fudd technique, in which you bring out your trusty 12-gauge and threaten to "Bwast that wascawy pwogwam to kingdom come" if it doesn't straighten up and fly right. Satisfying as that might sound, it is, alas, rather unproductive.

You do have another alternative, however: You can use a *binary search,* which is a variation on the decreasing granularity approach. The strategy of a binary search is the same as the strategy of a simple guessing game. If your opponent picks a number between 1 and 100, you can always determine the number with no more than eight guesses. Your first guess should always be 50. Your opponent must then tell you whether you guessed too high or too low. If you're too high, you should guess 25; if you're too low, you should guess 75. With each guess, you eliminate half of the remaining possibilities.

Similarly, when you have a complex program and no clear idea of where to look for a bug, set a breakpoint halfway through the application. When you reach the interrupt, examine the important variables. If everything seems in order, set the next breakpoint halfway between the current location and the program's end. Otherwise, set the breakpoint halfway between the starting point and the current breakpoint and restart the program. This technique should quickly get you into the vicinity of the bug, and you can then easily switch to single-stepping or another appropriate technique.

Don't hesitate to use Visual Basic's debugging features to test your theories about what has gone wrong with your program. For example, if you discover that you forgot to increment a variable, don't simply stop the debugging process and change the program. Use the Debug window to set the variable to the value you think is correct, and let the program continue running. You will sometimes discover that what seemed to be the source of the problem is in fact only a side effect or symptom of the real problem.

You can even use the debugging tools to experiment with the flow of control in your program. Let's say you interrupt your program partway through a procedure and realize that you should have put in an *If* statement to skip the next few lines. You can set the next statement to be executed by clicking on it and then choosing the Set Next Statement command from the Debug menu. You can select any statement within the current procedure, even one that appears before the current statement, but you cannot specify a statement in some other procedure as the next statement to be executed.

A Call for Help

Visual Basic's online Help system, which was introduced in Chapter 1, can give you some invaluable assistance in programming and debugging. To access Help quickly, press the F1 key any time you are designing or debugging an application, or choose an option from Visual Basic's Help menu.

Visual Basic provides context-sensitive help—that is, it tries to offer the most useful piece of information for the current situation. For example, if you want to use the *Format* function in a program but don't recall what parameters must be supplied, start typing your program statement. As soon as you have typed the *Format* keyword, press F1. Visual Basic will open a window that displays the Help text for the

Format function. Similarly, if your program generates a runtime error with a message such as *Subscript out of range*, you can press F1 when the message dialog box appears, and Visual Basic's Help system will tell you more about the error.

If you need to search for information, you can take one of several routes. When you choose the Contents command from the Help menu or click on the Contents button in the upper left portion of an open Help window, Help displays a complete list of its information categories, as shown in Figure 8-9.

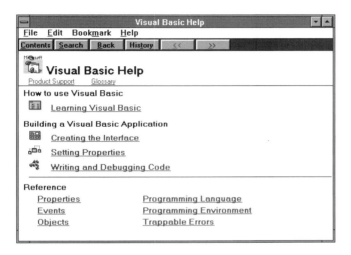

Figure 8-9.
Visual Basic Help Contents screen.

Each underlined phrase represents a hypertext link to another Help screen. For example, if you click on the phrase *Programming Language* (or tab to it and press Enter), the Help screen displays an index of all the Visual Basic language features, as shown in Figure 8-10 on the following page. In turn, you can click on any one of the underlined terms in this index to find specific information about that topic. For instance, Help might provide a statement's syntax, a description of the statement's operation, and sometimes even a code sample. If appropriate, you can even mark and copy sample code from the Help system and paste it into your program.

As you gather and check information, you might also find the Search option helpful. Clicking on the Search button in the Help window produces the Search dialog box, shown in Figure 8-11 on the following page. In the text box at the top of the dialog box, begin typing the keyword or concept that you want to investigate. With each letter you type, the Help system narrows your search to the items appearing in the list box immediately below the text box. You can then select an item in the list box and click on the Show Topics button, or simply double-click on the item. When you do this, the list box at the bottom of the dialog box will list all the related Help topics. You can view any of these Help screens by double-clicking on the topic or by selecting it and clicking on the Go To button.

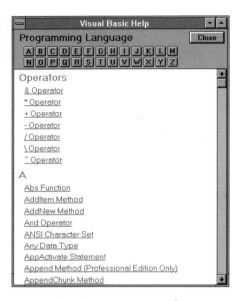

Figure 8-10.
Part of the Programming Language Help index.

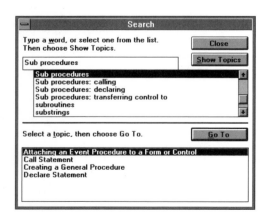

Figure 8-11.
Help's Search dialog box.

Many of the Help topics include example code that demonstrates the language element discussed. To view the example, simply click on the Example hyperlink at the top of the screen. If you want to try running the code, click on the Copy button at the top of the example code window. In the Copy window, select the code you're interested in, and click on the Copy button. When you return to Visual Basic, you can paste the selected code directly into your program's code window.

Sometimes it's useful to have the Help window available on the screen while you edit your code. To keep other windows from covering the open Help window, choose the Always On Top command from the Help menu in the Help window. A checkmark appears beside this option on the menu when it is active. To turn it off, simply choose it again. And if you want to print the current Help topic for later study, choose Print Topic from Help's File menu.

Error Handling

Thus far, this chapter has concentrated on programmer errors that can cause an application to fail or return invalid results. Another class of problems, called runtime errors, also can cause your program to fail. Runtime errors often arise from conditions you cannot control, such as a shortage of memory or disk space, a mistake by the user, an attempt to open a file that has already been opened by another application, and so on. Other runtime errors are bugs, indicative of logic errors in your program, such as indexing beyond the dimensioned bounds of an array.

When a runtime error occurs, Visual Basic usually displays a message dialog box and terminates the application. You can, however, take programmatic control over error handling. This technique, called *error trapping,* allows your program to detect and possibly fix the problem, or at least shut down the program in a user-friendly manner. You assert your control over the system by enabling error trapping. When you write a procedure that traps errors, its general structure should look like this:

```
Sub declaration
    [statements]
    On Error GoTo label
    [statements]
    Exit Sub
label:
    error-handling code
End Sub
```

The statement *On Error GoTo label*, in which *label* identifies the error-handling code, turns on error trapping. If a runtime error occurs in the statements following the *On Error GoTo label* statement, control is immediately transferred to the error-handling code designated by *label*. *Label* can be any identifier you choose and, when used to mark a particular location in your code, must end with a colon (:).

To turn off error trapping later in the same procedure, you can use the statement *On Error GoTo 0*. Any runtime errors that occur in the statements following *On Error GoTo 0* will be handled directly by Visual Basic, not by the error-handling code in the procedure. This ability to turn error trapping on and off is useful if only a small portion of your code is likely to encounter runtime errors.

Error trapping is active only within a procedure that contains an *On Error GoTo label* statement. When a procedure terminates, error trapping returns to the routine that originally called the procedure. If that routine has no error handler, error handling is disabled.

Once your program moves to the error-handling code in a procedure, you can test the value of the function *Err* to learn the cause of the error. *Err* returns an integer indicating the type of error—error 7, for example, indicates that you have run out of memory; error 53 tells you that the program cannot find the designated file; and so on. The complete list of error codes is included in Visual Basic's online Help and in the Visual Basic reference manual.

In all likelihood, your error handler won't test for every possible error. Error 53, for example, can occur only when you attempt to access a file. If your procedure makes no use of files, you don't have to test for error 53.

After you have determined which error has occurred, you have four choices of how to proceed. The simplest alternative is to hand the error back to Visual Basic. You can do this by using the *Error* statement. The *Error* statement takes a single parameter (the error number) and immediately forces a runtime error. By adding the line *Error Err* to the end of your error-handling code, you can neatly deal with any errors that you don't want to handle.

The other three choices involve resuming the program execution. Including the *Resume* statement in your error-handling code restarts a program after an error has been corrected. You can use any of these three variations:

Statement	Action
Resume	Continues the program by executing the statement that caused the error
Resume Next	Continues the program by executing the statement immediately following the one that caused the error
Resume *label*	Continues the program execution at a point specified by *label*

Consider the program code shown in Figure 8-12, which generates an error when it tries to divide by zero.

```
1    Sub Test ()
2        Dim XX As Integer, YY As Integer
3        XX = 0
4        YY = 10
5        On Error GoTo HandleIt
6        YY = YY / XX
7        Debug.Print YY
8    IQuit:
9        End
10   HandleIt:
11       XX = 2
12       Resume
13   End Sub
```

Figure 8-12.
Program code that includes error handling.

When you run this procedure, the statements are executed sequentially until the program reaches line 6. At that point, error 11 (division by zero) is triggered, and program control passes to line 10. The error-handling code sets the value of the variable *XX* to 2, and the *Resume* statement causes line 6 to be executed again. This time, the expression will not generate an error. The statement in line 7 will print the value 5, and the procedure will end.

If the *Resume Next* statement had been used in line 12, the program would have continued with line 7, which would have printed the value 10 (the unmodified value of *YY*) because line 6 did not execute successfully. Finally, if the statement in line 12 had been *Resume IQuit,* execution would have resumed with line 8, which would have ended the program without printing a value.

It is important to note that the *Resume* statement applies only to the procedure in which it appears. Let's take the example from Figure 8-12 and modify the code to include two procedures, as shown in Figure 8-13 on the following page, which demonstrates error handling across multiple procedures.

```
Dim XX As Integer

Sub Bugged ()
    Dim YY As Integer
    Debug.Print "Entering"
    YY = 10
    YY = YY / XX
    Debug.Print YY
    Debug.Print "Leaving"
End Sub

Sub Test ()
    On Error GoTo HandleIt
    Debug.Print "Start"
    XX = 0
    Bugged
    Debug.Print "Done"
    End
HandleIt:
    XX = 2
    Resume
End Sub
```

Figure 8-13.
Program code that demonstrates error handling across multiple procedures.

When you execute this code, you'll see the following output:

```
Start
Entering
Entering
5
Leaving
Done
```

If you change the *Resume* statement in the error-handling code to a *Resume Next* statement, the output changes as shown here:

```
Start
Entering
Done
```

In both cases, the error handler causes execution to resume within the procedure that contains the error handler, not at the statement that actually caused the error in the *Bugged* procedure. If you wanted your program to be able to resume normal execution within the *Bugged* procedure, you would need to add an error handler to that procedure.

9

File Input and Output

Files provide long-term storage for information. Values contained in variables are transitory, disappearing when an application is closed, recalculated when it runs again. To store persistent data that can be accessed and retrieved, you must save the data in a file.

This chapter looks at how Visual Basic handles some standard file operations, including locating, opening, saving, and closing files. It lets you create a sample application that demonstrates Visual Basic's file system tools. With these tools, you can produce dialog boxes that work like the File Open and File Save As dialog boxes created by the Common Dialog control.

We'll also look at two ways of storing and accessing data in files: a line-by-line method, which essentially treats information as text; and a record-oriented method. In addition, you'll learn how to store configuration information in INI files so that you can save startup and configuration information for your applications in the standard Windows manner.

File System Overview

As Chapter 2 described, your computer's microprocessor uses the bits of information stored in its memory as instructions and data. The design of a microprocessor's hardware gives it immediate access to RAM (random access memory) in the computer system. But even modern microcomputers with dozens of megabytes of RAM can't keep all the information they need in RAM. The system needs another storage location for the data that doesn't fit into RAM.

Computer systems have used various mechanisms for providing external storage, from punch cards to hard disks and floppy disks to CD-ROMs. These external media can store hundreds of megabytes or even gigabytes of data, at a cost that is hundreds of times less than the cost of adding RAM. Cost and capacity make external storage very attractive, even though it is slower and less convenient.

The large amounts of data handled by external storage also bring up the problem of organization. You need some way to say, "Well, here's my letter to Grandma," and "Over there is my word processing program," and "Here's where I keep all my fortune cookie fortunes." Early developers of computer systems approached the problem of organization with a business analogy, setting up the equivalent of a filing system and calling each separate collection of data a file. Graphical user interfaces continue to play on this analogy by using icons of file folders and filing cabinets.

Because disk storage is outside the main processor, the computer has to perform a certain set of activities to get information from or add information to a file. Visual Basic categorizes a file by the way in which the computer accesses it: sequential, random access, or binary.

- A *sequential file* is a plain text file. Visual Basic reads from and writes to a sequential file one line at a time; hence the name. Each line can be as long or as short as needed.

- A *random access file* is a file whose contents Visual Basic can read and write in any order needed. Every line (or *record*) must have the same length.

- A *binary file* is merely a collection of bytes—Visual Basic makes no assumptions as to how the data is organized, which allows your program to organize and access the data in any fashion required. This type of file provides great flexibility, but it means more work for your program. (Because of these greater demands, we won't cover binary files in this book.)

File Operations

When you open a file or save your work in a file, most Windows-based programs present a dialog box that lets you specify the file's name, directory, and drive. In Visual Basic, normally you would use the Common Dialog control to present the File Open dialog box or the File Save As dialog box. However, you may need to create a dialog box that is similar but has additional options. You can create such a dialog box using three of the tools in the Visual Basic Toolbox: the File List Box tool, the Directory List Box tool, and the Drive List Box tool, shown in Figure 9-1. These tools let you create three kinds of objects that are designed to interact with one another; most applications do not use these objects separately.

Figure 9-1.
The File List Box tool, the Directory List Box tool, and the Drive List Box tool.

Creating the TestFile Application

The TestFile application demonstrates how to create a dialog box using Visual Basic forms and the three file system tools. The TestFile code and the dialog box are reusable, which will allow you to copy them into other applications that require the same capabilities. This dialog box will be called Open File to distinguish it from the File Open dialog box produced by the Common Dialog control.

Begin by opening a new project. Set the Caption property of the form to Main, and set the form's Name property to frmMain. Place a command button in the middle of the form, and set the button's Name property to btnTest and its Caption property to Test. Double-click on the command button to open a code window, and define the button's *Click* procedure as shown here:

```
Sub btnTest_Click ()
    Dim Selected As String

    Selected = OpenFileDlg("*.TXT")
    If Selected = "" Then
        MsgBox "Canceled"
    Else
        MsgBox "File " + Selected + " selected"
    End If
End Sub
```

This procedure calls the function *OpenFileDlg* (as yet undefined), which displays a dialog box that allows the user to select a file based on the file specification *.TXT. If the user does not select a file and simply closes the dialog box, the function returns an empty string; otherwise, the procedure *btnTest_Click* displays the name of the selected file.

Adding a second form

The next step is to create the dialog box that the function *OpenFileDlg* will display. Choose the New Form command from the File menu or click on the New Form button on the Toolbar to place a second Visual Basic form on the screen. On the new form, add a file list box, a directory list box, a drive list box, and two command buttons. Set the properties of these objects as shown in Figure 9-2, and then arrange the objects on the form so that they resemble Figure 9-3 on the following page.

Object	Property	Setting
Form2	BorderStyle	3 - Fixed Double
	Caption	Open File
	Name	frmOpen

Figure 9-2. *(continued)*
Property settings for the second form in the TestFile application.

Figure 9-2. *continued*

Object	Property	Setting
File1	Name	filList
Dir1	Name	dirList
Drive1	Name	drvList
Button1	Caption	Open
	Default	True
	Name	btnOpen
Button2	Cancel	True
	Caption	Cancel
	Name	btnCancel

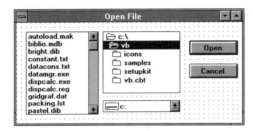

Figure 9-3.
The form design for the Open File dialog box in the TestFile application.

When you create a Visual Basic application that has more than one form, Visual Basic loads only one of the forms when the program starts up. To designate frmMain as the startup form, choose Project from the Options menu. In the Project Options dialog box, shown in Figure 9-4, select the item Start Up Form. The Setting drop-down list box at the top of the dialog box contains a list of all the forms in your application. Select frmMain and click on the OK button.

Figure 9-4.
The Project Options dialog box.

Note: *When you select the Start Up Form item in the Project Options dialog box, notice that the Setting list box includes the option Sub Main as well as a list of the forms in your application. Choosing the Sub Main option tells Visual Basic not to load a form when the program starts but instead to start the application by running the sub procedure named* Main *(which you must provide). You might want to use this option if, for example, the form your program opens depends on the day of the week or on certain initialization parameters.*

Adding a code module

Next you'll need to write the procedures that control the Open File dialog box, including the function *OpenFileDlg*. You might expect all this code to be in the frmOpen form, but one important consideration prevents this: The scope of all procedures in a form module is restricted to that module—that is, any procedure in frmOpen can be accessed only from another procedure in frmOpen. Because the call to *OpenFileDlg* is in frmMain, that function cannot be located in frmOpen.

One workable solution is to put the code for *OpenFileDlg* in frmMain. But we are interested in making the dialog box reusable, and the Test button in frmMain is clearly not needed in every application. A better solution is to create a separate code module containing the code that controls the dialog box. Because every procedure in a code module has global scope, the problem of accessibility will be solved. The code module will be a separate entity that can be loaded into any other Visual Basic application.

Add the code module by choosing New Module from Visual Basic's File menu or by clicking on the Toolbar's New Module button. Visual Basic will add a file named MODULE1.BAS to the list in the Project window and will open the module's code window. In the general declarations portion of the module, add the following statement:

```
Global SelectedFile As String
```

This statement declares a global string variable that will hold the filename selected by the user. The variable must be global because it will be accessed both by the *OpenFileDlg* function in the code module and by the event procedures in frmOpen.

Now add the following procedure to the code module:

```
Function OpenFileDlg (Wild As String) As String
    Load frmOpen
    frmOpen.filList.Pattern = Wild
    SelectedFile = ""
    frmOpen.Show 1
    OpenFileDlg = SelectedFile
End Function
```

This function is called with a wildcard file specification (such as *.TXT) as an argument. It first loads the frmOpen form into memory with the *Load* statement. The *Load* statement ensures that this form is available, but it does not make the form visible. The next line of code sets the Pattern property of the filList object (the file list box) to the wildcard pattern. The Pattern property of a file list box determines which files appear in the list—for example, the pattern *.* allows all files to be displayed. Note that the code is written as *form.object.property* instead of the typical *object.property* designation. Because the *OpenFileDlg* function is not in the form frmOpen, the function must explicitly name the form if it needs to access an object in frmOpen.

Next the *SelectedFile* variable is set to an empty string, indicating that no selection has yet been made. The following statement calls the *Show* method for frmOpen, which makes the form visible. *Show* can be called with an argument of 0 or 1. When *Show 0* is used, the form becomes visible, but processing continues in the procedure that called the *Show* method. When *Show 1* is used, as it is here, the specified form not only becomes visible but also is displayed *modally*—that is, no other form in the application can be used while this form is displayed on the screen. Processing is suspended in the calling procedure until the modal form is closed.

When the user closes the dialog box, effectively hiding frmOpen, the *OpenFileDlg* function continues with its final statement, which sets the return value of the function to the string *SelectedFile*. Program control then returns to the procedure that called the *OpenFileDlg* function.

Coding the event procedures

All that remains is to code the event procedures for the objects in frmOpen. Those procedures are defined in Figure 9-5. The comments in the code describe what happens as the program executes. As you can see, the operation of the file system objects is relatively simple, although you must carefully program the interaction among them. (You can use a similar technique to create a Save File dialog box, although you must do a little more programming to test for valid user input; the Visual Basic documentation provides further information.)

```
Sub filList_DblClick ()
    'Double-clicking on a filename is the same as
    'clicking on the Open button
    btnOpen_Click
End Sub
```

Figure 9-5. *(continued)*
Program code for event procedures in the TestFile application.

Figure 9-5. *continued*

```
Sub dirList_Change ()
    'When the directory list box changes, set a
    'new path for the file list box
    filList.Path = dirList.Path
End Sub

Sub drvList_Change ()
    'When the drive list box changes, set a
    'new path for the directory list box
    'Also causes a Change event for dirList
    dirList.Path = drvList.Drive
End Sub

Sub btnCancel_Click ()
    'No file selected; clear the string and hide the form
    SelectedFile = ""
    Hide
End Sub

Sub btnOpen_Click ()
    'Be sure a filename has been highlighted in the
    'file list box
    If filList.ListIndex >= 0 Then
        'Get the path of the selected file
        SelectedFile = filList.Path
        'Be sure the pathname ends with a backslash
        If Right$(SelectedFile, 1) <> "\" Then
            SelectedFile = SelectedFile + "\"
        End If
        'Append the selected filename to the path
        SelectedFile = SelectedFile + filList.List(filList.ListIndex)
    End If
    'Hide the form (close the dialog box)
    Hide
End Sub
```

Executing and Saving the TestFile Application

When you start the TestFile application, you will see only your designated startup form, which contains the Test button. Click on the Test button to display the Open File dialog box. Choose different directories and drives to see how the controls react. When you choose a file, a message box informs you of your choice. If you do not choose a file or if you click on the Cancel button, a message box notes that you have canceled the dialog box. You can click on the Test button and bring up the dialog box as many times as you like.

As you can see, it requires a fair amount of effort to duplicate the capabilities of the Common Dialog control (discussed in Chapter 5). The TestFile application could be programmed with a single form and about 10 lines of code in the btnTest_Click procedure if you were using the Common Dialog control.

Be sure to save the TestFile application because you can use the *OpenFileDlg* function in other projects. When you end the application, choose the Save Project command from the File menu. Use the filenames FRMMAIN.FRM, FRMOPEN.FRM, and FRMOPEN.BAS for the main form, the dialog box form, and the code module. Save the project file as TESTFILE.MAK.

Sequential Files

As mentioned earlier, the simplest method of processing data files involves reading or writing lines of textual data as if they were sequential lines of text in a book. A text editor such as Windows' Notepad application, for example, deals with documents in a sequential fashion: It reads the first line into memory and displays it, reads and displays the second line, and so on. When you tell the program to save your document, a similar process happens as the document is written to a file one line at a time. Figure 9-6 illustrates this process.

Bytes in file, stored on disk

Data displayed on screen

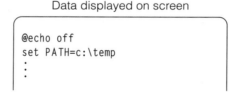

Figure 9-6.
A sequential file on disk and on screen.

Notice the symbols <CR> and <LF> in the illustration. These two characters, historical artifacts from the days of Teletype communication, are used to separate one line from another in a sequential file. Teletypes printed on rolls of paper, one line at a time. In addition to printing text, they also responded to certain nonprinting *control codes* such as Ctrl-G, which rang a bell on the machine. Starting a new line of text required two control codes: the carriage return (ASCII 13), which moved the print head to the beginning of the line; and the linefeed (ASCII 10), which advanced the paper one line. These codes were contained in the text files along with the text.

As newer output devices such as dumb terminals and daisywheel printers were developed, their manufacturers adopted some of these control-character conventions. The MS-DOS/Windows world has also inherited the carriage return/linefeed legacy. Thus, you'll often see this pair of characters abbreviated as CR and LF.

Opening and Closing Sequential Files

The *Open* statement tells Visual Basic which file to access. Typically, you use a standard dialog box such as the one you designed earlier in this chapter to get the name of a file. You then specify that filename in the *Open* statement using this syntax:

Open *fileName* For { Input ¦ Output } As *#fileNumber*

In addition to providing the filename, you must tell Visual Basic whether you want to read from the file (input) or write to it (output), and you must give it a file number. The file number must be an integer in the range 1 through 255. Here are some statements that open files:

```
Open "C:\CONFIG.SYS" For Input As #1

Doc$ = "A:\WWATCH1\BANZAI.DOC"
Open Doc$ For Input As #2

Open "RESULT.TXT" For Output As #15
```

If you attempt to open a file for input when the file does not already exist, Visual Basic generates an error. If you are opening the file for output, Visual Basic always creates a new file, overwriting any existing file with the same name. If you want to check for an existing file before opening a file for output, use the *Dir$* function. If you call the *Dir$* function with a filename as a parameter, the function either returns a copy of the filename (meaning that the file exists) or returns an empty string (meaning that no existing file has the specified name). This program fragment illustrates the *Dir$* function:

```
If Dir$("OEDIPUS.TXT") <> "" Then
    If InputBox("OEDIPUS.TXT already exists. Delete it?") <> "Yes" Then
        Exit Sub
    End If
End If
Open "OEDIPUS.TXT" For Output As #15
```

After you finish working with a file, you must close it. The Visual Basic *Close* statement has the following syntax:

Close *#fileNumber*

The file number in the *Close* statement corresponds to the number you assigned to the file in the *Open* statement. When you close a file, all data written to it (if any) is saved, and other programs are then free to access the file.

Reading from Sequential Files

Reading from a sequential file is remarkably easy. A single statement, *Line Input #*, reads each line of text. As you can see in the syntax for the statement, you must identify the file (by number) and provide a string variable in which to store the input text:

Line Input #*fileNumber, stringVariable*

The function *EOF* (which stands for end of file) lets you know when you've run out of data. It takes a single argument (a file number) and returns a value of True if all the information has been read. Here's an example of code that opens, reads, processes, and closes a sequential file:

```
Open FileVar For Input As #1
Do While Not EOF(1)
    Line Input #1, LineVar
    Process LineVar        'User procedure to handle a line of text
Loop
Close #1
```

This code assumes the existence of the string variables *FileVar* and *LineVar*. *FileVar* is initialized to the name of the file, and the code reads each line of the text file into the *LineVar* variable.

Writing to Sequential Files

Writing to a sequential file is just as easy as reading from one. The *Print #* statement writes to a sequential file, in much the same way that the *Print* method writes to a form. Here is the syntax for the *Print #* statement:

Print #*fileNumber* [, *expression* [{ , ¦ ; } *expression*]...] [{ , ¦ ; }]

The values of expressions separated by semicolons are written with no space between them, whereas the values of expressions separated by commas are written to separate *print fields,* which are 14 characters long. A carriage return and a linefeed are appended to the output unless the last character in the *Print #* statement is a comma or a semicolon.

The Configurator Application

Let's build a small sample program using sequential I/O. We'll call it the Configurator application because it will allow you to edit your CONFIG.SYS file.

Create a new project, and position a large text box and three command buttons on the form as shown in Figure 9-7. Set the properties of the objects as listed in Figure 9-8.

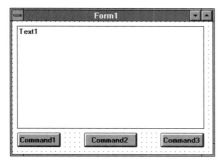

Figure 9-7.
The initial form design for the Configurator application.

Object	Property	Setting
Form1	BorderStyle	3 - Fixed Double
	Caption	Configurator
	Name	CEdit
Text1	MultiLine	True
	Name	txtContent
	ScrollBars	3 - Both
	Text	[none]
Command1	Caption	Open
	Name	btnOpen
Command2	Caption	Save
	Name	btnSave
Command3	Caption	Quit
	Name	btnQuit

Figure 9-8.
Property settings for the Configurator application.

In the general declarations section of the code, add the following declarations:

```
Dim TextChanged As Integer, ConfigFound As Integer, CRLF As String
```

Then, for the appropriate objects, enter the procedures shown in Figure 9-9 on the following page.

```
Sub Form_Load ()
    TextChanged = False
    ConfigFound = False
    CRLF = Chr$(13) + Chr$(10)
End Sub

Sub btnOpen_Click ()
    Dim CLine As String

    If ConfigFound Then
        Beep
        Exit Sub
    End If
    Open "C:\CONFIG.SYS" For Input As #1
    Do While Not EOF(1)
        Line Input #1, CLine
        txtContent.Text = txtContent.Text + CLine + CRLF
    Loop
    Close #1
    ConfigFound = True
End Sub

Sub btnSave_Click ()
    If Not (ConfigFound And TextChanged) Then
        Beep
        Exit Sub
    End If
    Open "C:\CONFIG.SYS" For Output As #1
    Print #1, txtContent.Text
    Close #1
End Sub

Sub btnQuit_Click ()
    End
End Sub

Sub txtContent_Change ()
    TextChanged = True
End Sub
```

Figure 9-9.
Program code for the Configurator application.

Notice that the string variable *CRLF* appears in the Configurator program code. Typically, the end-of-line implementation is hidden. The *Line Input #* statement reads up to the end of a line and then passes a string containing all the characters in the line except the line terminators. The *Print #* statement writes what you specify and automatically appends the end-of-line characters. In the sample program, however, the carriage return/linefeed that has been stripped out by the *Line Input #* statement is reinserted so that the text box knows where the end of the line is and can properly format the display.

Figure 9-10 shows how the Configurator application might look when you run the program and use it to edit your CONFIG.SYS file.

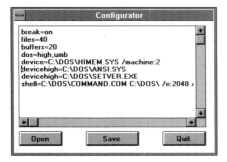

Figure 9-10.
Editing a CONFIG.SYS file with the Configurator application.

Ignoring Line Boundaries

Although the *Print #* statement is typically used to write only a single line or part of a line, you can use it to write out many lines at once, as you did in the Configurator program. The *Line Input #* statement, in contrast, is restricted to processing input one line at a time.

You can, however, use the Visual Basic function *Input$* to read an input file one character at a time. The *Input$* function returns a string of characters read from the file, including the carriage return/linefeed characters. Here is the syntax:

Input$(*charCount*, #*fileNumber*)

You can specify from 1 through 32,767 characters (*charCount*) to be read at one time. If the file contains fewer characters than the number you specify, Visual Basic will generate an *Input past end of file* error message.

The Configurator program could easily have been written using the *Input$* function. Here is the *btnOpen_Click* event procedure rewritten to use *Input$*:

```
Sub btnOpen_Click ()
    Dim CLine As String

    If ConfigFound Then
        Beep
        Exit Sub
    End If
    Open "C:\CONFIG.SYS" For Input As #1
    txtContent.Text = Input$(LOF(1), #1)      'Assume that file has fewer
                                              'than 32,767 characters

    Close #1
    ConfigFound = True
End Sub
```

This procedure reads the entire CONFIG.SYS file at once, which is acceptable because CONFIG.SYS is typically a small file. With a longer file, you would need a loop that checks for the end of the file (EOF). Notice that the rewritten procedure also uses the function *LOF* (which stands for length of file). This function takes a file number as a parameter and returns the number of bytes in the file.

Random Access Files

Most programmers eventually encounter two problems with sequential input as it has just been described. One problem is that it's not always efficient to represent data in a textual manner. For example, you can store the number 42.1596 in a 4-byte single-precision variable, but you would need to use 7 bytes to store the number as text in a sequential file. The other problem is that you sometimes need to process information in nonsequential ways.

Let us return once again to our friends the Bavarian Tufted Forest weasels. When last we left them, a database was being constructed to keep track of them. The assumption at that time was that all the information about the weasels would be held in program variables (an array). With this approach, however, changes to the data require changes to the program, a problem roughly equivalent to having to physically modify your word processor for every document you write.

The solution, of course, is to store the data in a file. You don't want to store the data as text, though; it's preferable to store it exactly as it is stored in the program: integers as integers, double-precision numbers as double-precision. In addition, you should be able to access any weasel's vital statistics at any time, without having to process the entire file in sequence until you find what you need. On the following pages, we'll construct the Weasel database to demonstrate a program that uses random access files.

Opening and Closing Random Access Files

The syntax for the *Open* statement for random access files is the following:

Open *fileName* For Random As *fileNumber* Len = *recordLength*

In this version of the *Open* statement, you do not specify input or output mode because you can read from and write to random access files without having to open and close the files each time. Additionally, you must provide a record length, which is the number of bytes to be read or written with each *Get* or *Put* statement (the statements used to read from and write to the file). For example, if you planned to use a file consisting of all integers, the record length would be 2. If every value in the file were type currency instead, the record length would be 8. If you don't specify a record length, Visual Basic assumes a record length of 128. (Odds are that this default value won't be appropriate for your file.)

To determine the record length for the Weasel database, you need to look at the data that you plan to read and write. In Chapter 6, you defined the data type BTFWeasel as follows:

```
Type BTFWeasel
    Name As String
    Color As String
    Weight As Integer
    Length As Integer
    Birthdate As Double
    TuftColor As String
    TuftLength As Integer
End Type
```

Assuming that each record looks exactly like this, you can add up all the component fields to get the record size. Unfortunately, three of the fields are strings, and you have no way of knowing their sizes.

To solve this problem, Visual Basic lets you declare fixed sizes for strings. If you use this capability and impose some restrictions on your data, you can compute a record length. For example, if you restrict weasel names to a maximum of 32 characters and color names to 12 characters, you can redefine the BTFWeasel type as follows:

```
Type BTFWeasel
    Name As String * 32
    Color As String * 12
    Weight As Integer
    Length As Integer
    Birthdate As Double
    TuftColor As String * 12
    TuftLength As Integer
End Type
```

The expression *String * 32* allots the fixed size of 32 bytes to each weasel name. If the name requires fewer than 32 characters, Visual Basic pads the name with blanks. Names that would require more than 32 characters are truncated. Thus, the total length of a BTFWeasel record is now 70 bytes (32 + 12 + 2 + 2 + 8 + 12 + 2).

Closing a random access file is simple: Use the *Close* statement exactly as you would to close a sequential file. For example, if you open a random access file as file #1, use the statement *Close #1* to close it.

Reading from and Writing to Random Access Files

The *Get* and *Put* statements are used to read from and write to random access files. The syntax for the two statements is simple:

> Get #*fileNumber*, [*recordNumber*], *variable*

> Put #*fileNumber*, [*recordNumber*], *variable*

The *Get* statement reads from the file and stores data in the variable, whereas the *Put* statement writes the contents of the specified variable to the file. In each case, you can optionally specify the record number. If you do not specify a record number, the next sequential position is used.

A random access file looks very much like an array of user-defined types. The main difference is that the data is stored on a disk instead of in memory, and thus the data will not vanish when the program ends. (Also note that records on a disk are indexed beginning with record 1, whereas the elements of an array are indexed beginning with 0.) Figure 9-11 shows how records are stored on a disk.

Record Number	Name	Color	Weight	Length	Birthdate	TuftColor	TuftLength
1	Siegmund	Brown	18	11	09/13/91	Brown	6
2	Sieglinde	Light brown	14	10	10/29/91	Black	6
3							
⋮							

Figure 9-11.
Records in a random access file.

The Weasel Database Application

Now let's begin constructing the Weasel database application, which will keep track of your Bavarian Tufted Forest weasels. Of course, if you don't happen to have any weasels, remember that this program can be easily modified to keep track of other kinds of data.

216

The basic plan for the Weasel database involves using a random access file to store the information about the weasels. When you run the application, it scans the file, collects the name of each weasel, and displays the list of names in a list box. When the user chooses a name from the list box, the program finds that weasel's record in the file and displays all the relevant data. In addition, command buttons will allow you to add a new weasel to the data file or remove a weasel from the file.

To start, create a new project. On the form, place one combo box, six text boxes, seven labels, and two command buttons. The initial layout is shown in Figure 9-12.

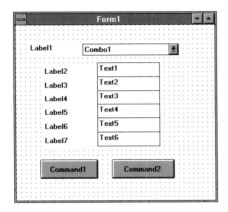

Figure 9-12.
The initial form design for the Weasel database application.

Set the properties of the screen objects as specified in Figure 9-13. When you are done, the form should look like the one shown in Figure 9-14 on the next page.

Object	Property	Setting
Form1	BorderStyle	3 - Fixed Double
	Caption	Weasels
	Name	Weasels
Label1	Alignment	1 - Right Justify
	Caption	Name:
Combo1	Name	cboName
	Style	2 - Dropdown list
Label2	Alignment	1 - Right Justify
	Caption	Color:
Text1	Name	txtColor
	Text	[none]

Figure 9-13.
Property settings for the Weasel database application.

(continued)

Figure 9-13. *continued*

Object	Property	Setting
Label3	Alignment Caption	1 - Right Justify Weight:
Text2	Name Text	txtWeight [none]
Label4	Alignment Caption	1 - Right Justify Length:
Text3	Name Text	txtLength [none]
Label5	Alignment Caption	1 - Right Justify Birthdate:
Text4	Name Text	txtBirthdate [none]
Label6	Alignment Caption	1 - Right Justify Tuft Color:
Text5	Name Text	txtTuftColor [none]
Label7	Alignment Caption	1 - Right Justify Tuft Length:
Text6	Name Text	txtTuftLength [none]
Command1	Caption Name	Add btnAdd
Command2	Caption Name	Remove btnRemove

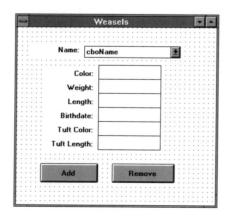

Figure 9-14.
The completed form design for the Weasel database application.

This application needs some global declarations. Because global variables and type declarations cannot be declared in a form module, you need to create a code module. Choose the New Module command from the File menu. In the code window, add the following declarations to the general declarations section:

```
Type BTFWeasel
    Name As String * 32
    Color As String * 12
    Weight As Integer
    Length As Integer
    Birthdate As Double
    TuftColor As String * 12
    TuftLength As Integer
End Type

Global Const WEASEL_RECLEN = 70
```

Defining the constant *WEASEL_RECLEN* will make your program easier to read; seeing the constant's name rather than the number 70 is a reminder of what the value really means. A more important reason for defining the constant, however, is the issue of upgrading your program.

Suppose that in the future you need to redefine the BTFWeasel type; perhaps you need to add a new field, or perhaps you decide that 32 characters are insufficient for names. If you had not used a constant name for the record length, you would have to examine every line of the program, looking for the number 70 and changing it to the new value. In addition, you would have to ensure that each 70 was truly a reference to the record size, not some other value. By using a constant name, you can simply change the constant's value, and the rest of your program is instantly upgraded to work with the newly defined record size.

The remainder of the declarations are local to the form. Close the code window for the code module, and open the code window for the form. Add the following lines to the general declarations section:

```
Dim CurrentWeaselIx As Integer      'Number of current weasel
Dim WeaselCount As Integer          'Total number of weasels
Dim RecordModified As Integer       'Boolean flag
```

These variables will hold an index number indicating which weasel's records are being displayed, will keep track of the total number of weasel records stored in the file, and will track whether or not the user has modified any of the data on the screen. (Note that this program uses the abbreviation *Ix* instead of the word *Index* because Index is the name of a Visual Basic property.)

To initialize the system, the program should read each record in the file and place the names of all the weasels in the list box. The user can then choose a name. The program will respond by fetching the entire record for that weasel and displaying it. If the user modifies the record, those changes are written back to the file.

To illustrate a style of programming that works well with large quantities of data, this program will not read all the records into an array but instead will work entirely with memory variables. An array, you'll recall, cannot have an index greater than 32,767. That's a lot of weasels and, at 70 bytes per record, would require more than 2 megabytes of RAM. By keeping only one record in memory at a time, you can greatly reduce memory requirements.

For simplicity's sake, the program requires that all the names fit in memory at once, but if the average name is eight or nine characters, this should not be a problem. Assuming that the data file exists in a predefined location on disk, you can then write the following initialization routine. (In this application, we won't use the *File-OpenDlg* function. Instead, we'll assume a fixed filename and path for the data. The pathname *C:\VB* designates the Visual Basic directory on my system; be sure to use a pathname that is valid for your system.)

```
Sub WeaselInit ()
    Dim Weasel As BTFWeasel, W As Integer

    Open "C:\VB\WEASEL.DAT" For Random As #1 Len = WEASEL_RECLEN
    WeaselCount = LOF(1) / WEASEL_RECLEN
    For W = 1 To WeaselCount
        Get #1, W, Weasel
        cboName.AddItem Weasel.Name
    Next W
End Sub
```

The *Open* statement opens or creates the file. The function *LOF* returns the total number of bytes in the file, which is divided by the record size to yield the total number of records. Then each existing record is read, and each weasel name is inserted in the list box.

When the initialization is complete, the user can choose a weasel name to display data about the weasel and can then edit some of the data. The procedures shown in Figure 9-15 will meet these needs.

```
Sub ShowWeasel (ByVal Ix As Integer)
    Dim Weasel As BTFWeasel

    Get #1, Ix + 1, Weasel
    CurrentWeaselIx = Ix
    cboName.ListIndex = Ix
    txtColor.Text = Weasel.Color
```

Figure 9-15. *(continued)*
The ShowWeasel *and* UpdateCurrentWeasel *procedures.*

Figure 9-15. *continued*

```
        txtWeight.Text = Str$(Weasel.Weight)
        txtLength.Text = Str$(Weasel.Length)
        txtBirthdate.Text = Format(Weasel.Birthdate, "mm/dd/yy")
        txtTuftColor.Text = Weasel.TuftColor
        txtTuftLength.Text = Str$(Weasel.TuftLength)
        RecordModified = False
    End Sub

    Sub UpdateCurrentWeasel ()
        Dim Weasel As BTFWeasel

        If Not RecordModified Then
            Exit Sub
        End If
        Weasel.Name = cboName.Text
        Weasel.Color = txtColor.Text
        Weasel.Weight = Val(txtWeight.Text)
        Weasel.Length = Val(txtLength.Text)
        Weasel.Birthdate = DateValue(txtBirthdate.Text)
        Weasel.TuftColor = txtTuftColor.Text
        Weasel.TuftLength = Val(txtTuftLength.Text)
        Put #1, CurrentWeaselIx + 1, Weasel
        RecordModified = False
    End Sub
```

The *ShowWeasel* procedure takes an index number as a parameter. It sets *Current-WeaselIx* to this value and fetches the data for that weasel, updating each display field. It then sets a flag indicating that the record has not yet been modified. The *UpdateCurrentWeasel* procedure checks to see whether the record has been modified. If it has not been modified, the procedure simply ends. If the user has modified the record, the current value of each field is read, and the resulting record is written back to disk.

The other main tasks of the program are creating new records and removing outdated ones. You can create new records with the function procedure shown in Figure 9-16 on the next page. (We'll discuss the removal procedures a bit later.) The *NewWeasel* function fills in a weasel record with the name passed to the function and with default values for the other fields. It increments *WeaselCount* to account for the new weasel, writes the new record to the data file, and adds the name to the list box. Because the new record is always written at the end of the file, its list box index is the same as the old value of *WeaselCount*, which is returned to the caller as the value of the function.

```
Function NewWeasel (NewName As String) As Integer
    Dim Weasel As BTFWeasel

    Weasel.Name = NewName
    'Assign default information
    Weasel.Color = "Brown"
    Weasel.Weight = 0
    Weasel.Length = 0
    Weasel.Birthdate = Now
    Weasel.TuftColor = "Brown"
    Weasel.TuftLength = 0
    'Assign index number to return
    NewWeasel = WeaselCount
    'Increment number of weasels
    WeaselCount = WeaselCount + 1
    'Write new record to disk
    Put #1, WeaselCount, Weasel
    'Add name to list of weasels
    cboName.AddItem Weasel.Name
    RecordModified = False
End Function
```

Figure 9-16.
The NewWeasel *function procedure.*

The procedures you have written thus far for this program have been defined in the general section of the form because each routine performs a specific task. These procedures can be called by any other procedures, including event procedures, so it is best to define them as independent units rather than coding them as part of a specific object's event procedure. It is better to do application-specific work in general procedures and have the code in the event procedures serve as a link from the user interface to the functional portion of the program.

The first important link is connecting program startup to the initialization of the database. When you start an application, the form's *Load* event procedure is the first procedure to be called:

```
Sub Form_Load ()
    WeaselInit
End Sub
```

You must also link the user's choice of a name from the list box to the program's display of a record, and you must link the creation of a new record with the Add button. These two routines make those connections:

```
Sub cboName_Click ()
    ShowWeasel cboName.ListIndex
End Sub

Sub btnAdd_Click ()
    Dim NewName As String

    NewName = InputBox("What is the new weasel's name?")
    If NewName = "" Then
        Exit Sub
    End If
    ShowWeasel NewWeasel(NewName)
End Sub
```

Setting up the record display is easy because simply adding 1 to the index of the name in the list box corresponds to the index position of the record in the file. With the second routine, the user is prompted for the name of a new weasel when the Add button is clicked. If no name is supplied, no record is added. If the user does supply a name, the procedure calls *NewWeasel* to create a record and passes the index value it returns directly to *ShowWeasel* so that the new record can be displayed.

To complete the application, you must implement support for editing the weasel records. Two simple routines are required for each text box: The *Change* procedure executes the statement *RecordModified = True*, and the *LostFocus* procedure updates the record by calling *UpdateCurrentWeasel*. The code for each text box appears in Figure 9-17.

```
Sub txtColor_Change ()
    RecordModified = True
End Sub

Sub txtColor_LostFocus ()
    UpdateCurrentWeasel
End Sub

Sub txtWeight_Change ()
    RecordModified = True
End Sub

Sub txtWeight_LostFocus ()
    UpdateCurrentWeasel
End Sub

Sub txtLength_Change ()
    RecordModified = True
End Sub
```

Figure 9-17.   *(continued)*
Event procedures for the text boxes in the Weasel database application.

Figure 9-17. *continued*

```
Sub txtLength_LostFocus ()
    UpdateCurrentWeasel
End Sub

Sub txtBirthdate_Change ()
    RecordModified = True
End Sub

Sub txtBirthdate_LostFocus ()
    UpdateCurrentWeasel
End Sub

Sub txtTuftColor_Change ()
    RecordModified = True
End Sub

Sub txtTuftColor_LostFocus ()
    UpdateCurrentWeasel
End Sub

Sub txtTuftLength_Change ()
    RecordModified = True
End Sub

Sub txtTuftLength_LostFocus ()
    UpdateCurrentWeasel
End Sub
```

It's best to simply set a flag in the *Change* procedure rather than calling the *Update-CurrentWeasel* routine directly, because the *Change* procedure is called by Visual Basic every time the content of a text box changes. For example, if you type the text *Black* in the Color text box, the *Change* procedure is called five times, once for each letter typed. But the record should not be updated until the value in the text box is complete, so the program instead calls the update routine in the *LostFocus* event procedure.

What is the LostFocus event? Any screen control can be the "focus of attention" at some time during the execution of an application. Windows keeps track of this with the events GotFocus and LostFocus. When you click in a text box, for example, the GotFocus event is triggered. The focus remains in the text box while you are typing. If you then press the Tab key or click on some other control, the text box receives a LostFocus event, and the new control receives GotFocus. Therefore, when a text box's *LostFocus* procedure is run, you know that the user has finished typing and that your program can safely call the update routine.

The Weasel database application is now ready to run. Press F5 to start it. Because this is the first time you've run the program, no entries will appear in the list box. Click on the Add button, and enter data for three or four weasels. Then press Alt-F4 to exit the program, and immediately start it up again. As illustrated in Figure 9-18, you should be able to choose from the names you entered in the previous session.

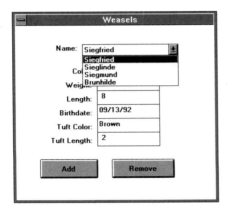

Figure 9-18.
Running the Weasel database application.

Deleting records

The logical model for this application is efficient and relatively easy to understand. But that simplicity has a price: You have no simple way to delete records.

Imagine that the database file WEASEL.DAT contains four records, for weasels that are unimaginatively named A, B, C, and D, as shown in Figure 9-19. Creating these records has produced a file that contains 280 bytes (4 × 70).

WEASEL.DAT

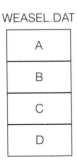

Figure 9-19.
A four-record data file for the Weasel database.

You cannot simply remove bytes from the middle of the file and "throw them away." If you want to delete the record for weasel B, for example, you have only two choices: copy all the records except B to a new file, or overwrite record B with some new data. If you make a copy, you can then delete the original file and rename the copy with the original filename. This solution is illustrated in Figure 9-20.

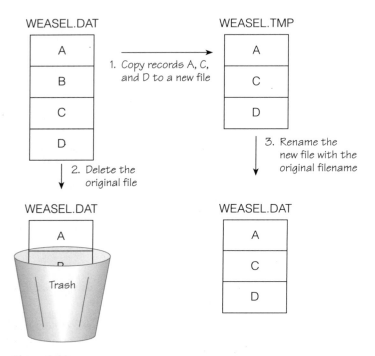

Figure 9-20.
Copying records and renaming the file.

If you overwrite record B with other data—a record containing all blanks, for example—the list box will eventually be full of blank entries. You might think that the initialization routine could simply omit any record with a blank name field. Unfortunately, if you skip records, the application will not be able to match a list box entry to the appropriate record. Figure 9-21 illustrates this problem.

The application as it is currently written requires a one-to-one mapping between the names in the list box and the records in the file. (Incidentally, this requirement also means that the Sorted property of the list box cannot be set to True because sorting would scramble the relationship between the index values of the list box and the record positions.) You can get around this problem, however, by maintaining a separate mapping between the list box index and the file positions. Figure 9-22 provides an example.

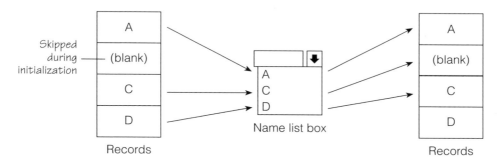

Figure 9-21.
Overwriting a record with blanks.

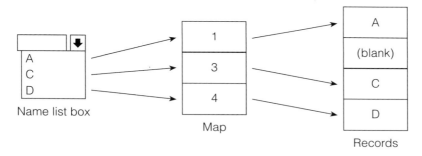

Figure 9-22.
Mapping the list box index.

Which solution is preferable? If you know that the data files for the application will always be small, the copy-and-rename method might be best. It can be implemented without affecting the code you have already written, and the application remains simple and easy to understand. In a data-intensive program, however, copying large files becomes time-consuming and requires enough free disk space for both the copy and the original to exist at one time; if disk space is tight, the program could fail. Creating a map allows your program to run more quickly, something end users appreciate. But that solution involves adding complexity (and possibly bugs) and rewriting some of the existing code.

As a programmer, you will often need to make decisions such as this. It is very important to thoroughly understand the tasks of your program and the nature of the data before making a decision. No matter how bug-free your code is, it will be worthless unless users can live with the design decisions you make.

Let's take a closer look at the two alternatives for deleting records from the Weasel database. The copy-and-rename solution requires no changes to the existing code. Simply add the procedure shown in Figure 9-23 to the program.

```
Sub btnRemove_Click ()
    Dim Weasel As BTFWeasel, W As Integer

    'Copy all but current record to temp file
    Open "C:\VB\WEASEL.TMP" For Random As #2 Len = WEASEL_RECLEN
    For W = 1 To WeaselCount
        If W <> CurrentWeaselIx + 1 Then
            Get #1, W, Weasel
            Put #2, , Weasel
        End If
    Next W
    'Delete and rename
    Close #1
    Close #2
    Kill "C:\VB\WEASEL.DAT"
    Name "C:\VB\WEASEL.TMP" As "C:\VB\WEASEL.DAT"
    'Clear list box and reload database
    cboName.Clear
    WeaselInit
End Sub
```

Figure 9-23.
The btnRemove_Click *procedure for the Weasel database application.*

The *btnRemove_Click* procedure opens a new file and copies every record except the current record into it. Both files are then closed. The *Kill* statement takes the original filename as a parameter, and that file is deleted. The *Name* statement then renames the copied file. When the data file has been taken care of, the list box is cleared, and the program calls the *WeaselInit* procedure again to reload the list box.

The second alternative, using an array as a map, is a bit trickier because it requires changes to the existing code. Figure 9-24 contains only the routines that must be modified to produce the mapped version; lines that have been added or changed are highlighted.

```
Function NewWeasel (NewName As String) As Integer
    Dim Weasel As BTFWeasel

    Weasel.Name = NewName
    'Assign default information
```

Figure 9-24.   *(continued)*
Revised program code for the Weasel database application, implementing a map array.

228

Figure 9-24. *continued*

```
        Weasel.Color = "Brown"
        Weasel.Weight = 0
        Weasel.Length = 0
        Weasel.Birthdate = Now
        Weasel.TuftColor = "Brown"
        Weasel.TuftLength = 0
        'Assign index number to return
        NewWeasel = cboName.ListCount
        'Increment number of weasels
        WeaselCount = WeaselCount + 1
        'Write new record to disk
        Put #1, WeaselCount, Weasel
        'Add name to list of weasels
        cboName.AddItem Weasel.Name
        cboName.ItemData(cboName.NewIndex) = WeaselCount
        RecordModified = False
End Function

Sub ShowWeasel (ByVal Ix As Integer)
        Dim Weasel As BTFWeasel

        Get #1, cboName.ItemData(Ix), Weasel
        CurrentWeaselIx = Ix
        cboName.ListIndex = Ix
        txtColor.Text = Weasel.Color
        txtWeight.Text = Str$(Weasel.Weight)
        txtLength.Text = Str$(Weasel.Length)
        txtBirthdate.Text = Format(Weasel.Birthdate, "mm/dd/yy")
        txtTuftColor.Text = Weasel.TuftColor
        txtTuftLength.Text = Str$(Weasel.TuftLength)
        RecordModified = False
End Sub

Sub UpdateCurrentWeasel ()
        Dim Weasel As BTFWeasel

        If Not RecordModified Then
            Exit Sub
        End If
        Weasel.Name = cboName.Text
        Weasel.Color = txtColor.Text
        Weasel.Weight = Val(txtWeight.Text)
        Weasel.Length = Val(txtLength.Text)
        Weasel.Birthdate = DateValue(txtBirthdate.Text)
        Weasel.TuftColor = txtTuftColor.Text
        Weasel.TuftLength = Val(txtTuftLength.Text)
        Put #1, cboName.ItemData(CurrentWeaselIx), Weasel
        RecordModified = False
End Sub
```

(continued)

Figure 9-24. *continued*

```
Sub WeaselInit ()
    Dim Weasel As BTFWeasel, W As Integer

    Open "C:\VB\WEASEL.DAT" For Random As #1 Len = WEASEL_RECLEN
    WeaselCount = LOF(1) / WEASEL_RECLEN
    For W = 1 To WeaselCount
        Get #1, W, Weasel
        'Skip deleted records
        If Mid$(Weasel.Name, 1, 1) <> " " Then
            cboName.AddItem Weasel.Name
            cboName.ItemData(cboName.NewIndex) = W
        End If
    Next W
End Sub

Sub btnRemove_Click ()
    Dim Weasel As BTFWeasel

    'Overwrite current record
    Weasel.Name = " "
    Put #1, cboName.ItemData(CurrentWeaselIx), Weasel
    'Update name list and mapping by removing item
    cboName.RemoveItem CurrentWeaselIx
End Sub
```

The changed program uses a property called ItemData, which is a built-in feature of the list box. ItemData is an array with a long integer entry for each element in the list box. This array is used to store the mapping—that is, it will hold the actual disk-file index for each entry. In the original version, the variable *CurrentWeaselIx* could refer either to the file position or to the index in the list box. In the new version, *CurrentWeaselIx* refers only to the index in the list box; the file position must be derived with the expression *cboName.ItemData(CurrentWeaselIx)*.

The changes to the procedures *NewWeasel*, *ShowWeasel*, and *UpdateCurrentWeasel* are trivial, simply ensuring that the mapping is correctly used and maintained. The changes to *WeaselInit* are relatively straightforward: As it reads each record in the file, it checks to see whether the first character of the name field is blank; if it is, that record is ignored. As the program reads the records, it writes the appropriate values into the ItemData map array. The property NewIndex contains the ListIndex value for the most recently added item. Because you no longer need a one-to-one relationship between the disk and the list box, you can set the Sorted property of the list box to True in this version of the program.

Finally, the *btnRemove_Click* procedure is completely different in the revised code. To remove the current record, the program overwrites it with a blank record. Then the name is removed from the list box.

One minor problem with the mapped version remains: Each deleted record requires space, and each new record is added to the end of the file. It would be nice if the *NewWeasel* procedure made use of deleted records, if any, rather than automatically extending the file. This change would prevent the data file from growing unnecessarily large. Implementing this change is left as an exercise to the reader. (I've always wanted to say that.)

Configuration

You might often want to save one or two important values from one application session to another—perhaps a configuration setting such as digital or analog mode for your clock program. Standard variables won't work because their values are lost when the program ends. You could create a data file, but this could be a lot of work for a small amount of data.

The standard solution to this problem for Windows-based applications is to store values in WIN.INI, the Windows initialization file. Each application can have its own section in the file, indicated by a name in square brackets. Following the section name are the variables and their values. Here are a few lines from my WIN.INI file:

```
[Paint Shop]
OpenDir=C:\DOCS
FileData=65,65,0,0,0,0
SaveDir=C:\DOCS\BOOK

[CorelDraw]
Dir=C:\WINDOWS\COREL

[Clock]
iFormat=0
```

The obvious way to process this information is to open the WIN.INI file, read each line looking for the right section, and then process each subsequent line. This would be a lot of work if you had to write all the code yourself. Fortunately, however, this operation is performed so frequently that the code for it is built into Windows itself. Although no Visual Basic functions can access that code, you can write your own functions.

Dynamic-Link Libraries

You can access functions that are built into Windows or built into Windows-based applications if the functions are part of a *dynamic-link library* (a DLL). If you scan through your Windows SYSTEM directory, you will see a number of files with the filename extension DLL. Some of these files came with Windows; others (such as VBRUN200.DLL) came with applications you've added. If you know the definitions of the functions in these files, you can call almost any of the functions from your Visual Basic applications.

To call these functions from Visual Basic, you need to know some fairly technical information about data types, parameter passing, and so on. Some of this information is provided in the discussion of the *Declare* statement in the Visual Basic reference manual. For specific information about individual callable functions, you must consult the programming manuals for the products that supply DLLs.

> **Warning:** *The* Declare *statement is very powerful. It gives you access to almost any Windows system function. But you must use it carefully. Because it calls the system directly, you do not have the benefit of Visual Basic's error checking. Potentially, you could crash your system if you mistyped a declaration or called a system function with illegal values.*

The Windows profile functions

The functions that read and write WIN.INI are part of KERNEL.DLL, a standard Windows dynamic-link library. These functions are named *GetProfileString* and *WriteProfileString*. To use these functions in a Visual Basic program, you must declare them. The declaration is much like a procedure declaration, but it tells Visual Basic that the procedure is found elsewhere and not in the Visual Basic application itself.

The declarations for the two functions *GetProfileString* and *WriteProfileString* are shown here. Note that each declaration must be entered as a single line (without carriage returns), although they are necessarily reproduced on several lines here:

```
Declare Function GetProfileString Lib "Kernel"
 (ByVal lpAppName As String, ByVal lpKeyName As String,
 ByVal lpDefault As String, ByVal lpReturnedString As String,
 ByVal nSize As Integer) As Integer

Declare Function WriteProfileString Lib "Kernel"
 (ByVal lpAppName As String, ByVal lpKeyName As String,
 ByVal lpString As String) As Integer
```

The declaration for *GetProfileString* tells Visual Basic that the function is found in KERNEL.DLL, that it has four string parameters and an integer parameter, and that it returns an integer. The first parameter of *GetProfileString* is a string that corresponds to the application name (section name) in WIN.INI. The second parameter is the keyword (the name of the "variable"). The third parameter is a default value that is returned if the keyword is not found. The fourth parameter is an empty string that will be overwritten with the value of the configuration variable. The fifth parameter is an integer defining the length of the empty string. The return value is the size of the configuration variable string.

The *WriteProfileString* declaration is similar but simpler. *WriteProfileString* also takes as its first parameter a string that names the WIN.INI section, and it uses the keyword as its second parameter. The third parameter is the value you want to assign to the keyword in WIN.INI.

Packaging the functions for Visual Basic

Create a new Visual Basic project, and choose New Module from the File menu. You will need to create two Visual Basic procedures, *GetIni* and *SetIni*, and place them in the new module. You can then include this module in any application you write, to give you access to WIN.INI variables.

In the general declarations section of the code window, enter the declarations for the *GetProfileString* and *WriteProfileString* functions as shown in the preceding section. Remember to type each one as a single line, with no carriage returns. Next enter the code for *GetIni* and *SetIni*, shown in Figure 9-25.

```
Function GetIni (AppName As String, Keyword As String) As String
    Dim ResultString As String * 128, Temp As Integer

    Temp = GetProfileString(AppName, Keyword, "", ResultString,
     Len(ResultString))
    'Return string up to but not including ASCII 0
    GetIni = Left$(ResultString, Temp)
End Function

Sub SetIni (AppName As String, Keyword As String, KeyVal As String)
    Dim Temp As Integer

    Temp = WriteProfileString(AppName, Keyword, KeyVal)
End Sub
```

Figure 9-25.
The GetIni *and* SetIni *procedures.*

The procedures *GetIni* and *SetIni* will now allow you to read from and write to the WIN.INI file with a simple Visual Basic interface. For example, the line of code *SetIni "Godzilla", "Color", "Green"* would result in the following lines being added to your WIN.INI file:

```
[Godzilla]
Color=Green
```

The Memory Application

You can test these functions with a small demonstration program. A classic use of configuration variables is to use them to store the last known location and size of an application's display window. When the user moves the window to a location on the screen, the window will appear in that location the next time the application is run. Similarly, if the user resizes the window, it will appear as that size the next time a user runs the program. The Memory application will perform exactly this task (and nothing else).

Close the code window of the code module in which you created *GetIni* and *SetIni*. Set the form's Name property and its Caption property to Memory. Then add the code shown in Figure 9-26. The *Form_Load* procedure reads the configuration variables; if they contain values, it uses those values to set the form's positional properties. The *Form_Unload* procedure, which is called when the application exits, writes the current position to the WIN.INI file.

```
Sub Form_Load ()
    Dim Fetch As String

    Fetch = GetIni("Memory", "Top")
    If Fetch <> "" Then
        Memory.Top = Val(Fetch)
    End If

    Fetch = GetIni("Memory", "Left")
    If Fetch <> "" Then
        Memory.Left = Val(Fetch)
    End If

    Fetch = GetIni("Memory", "Height")
    If Fetch <> "" Then
        Memory.Height = Val(Fetch)
    End If

    Fetch = GetIni("Memory", "Width")
    If Fetch <> "" Then
        Memory.Width = Val(Fetch)
    End If
End Sub

Sub Form_Unload (Cancel As Integer)
    SetIni "Memory", "Top", Str$(Memory.Top)
    SetIni "Memory", "Left", Str$(Memory.Left)
    SetIni "Memory", "Height", Str$(Memory.Height)
    SetIni "Memory", "Width", Str$(Memory.Width)
End Sub
```

Figure 9-26.
Program code for the Memory application.

Tip: It is not considered "polite" to have an application write more than nine or ten values to the WIN.INI file. If your program requires a great deal of configuration information, you should consider creating a private data file that is processed in your code.

Press F5 to start the application. When the empty form appears, use the mouse to move the form window or resize it. Now quit the application by double-clicking on the Control menu box in the upper left corner of the window or by choosing Close from the form's Control menu. (You must use the Control menu; choosing End from Visual Basic's Run menu terminates the application without unloading the form.) When you are back in design mode, you will see the form as you originally designed it. But if you press F5 again to rerun the application, the positional properties will be loaded from the WIN.INI file, and the window will appear as the same size and in the same location as when you last quit the application. Be sure to save this program so that the module containing the *GetIni* and *SetIni* procedures is available when you need these procedures.

10

Graphics Programming

This chapter is an introduction to Visual Basic graphics. Working with graphics can be fun, although it's not necessarily easy. Windows, of course, is at heart a graphical environment; remember that the best programs written for Windows make use of that strength.

Forms and Picture Boxes

Up to this point, most of the "drawing" you've done in Visual Basic has been done at design time. Visual Basic also supports a number of graphics methods that allow you to write to the screen at runtime, performing tasks such as printing text, drawing lines, sketching circles, changing colors, and so on. These methods are associated with forms, with picture boxes, and with a special object called the Printer object. The discussion that follows concentrates on forms, but the properties and methods described apply to picture boxes as well. Printing and the Printer object are discussed in the last part of this chapter.

Screen Management

The images on your display monitor are the direct reflection of the contents of *video memory,* a bank of RAM that belongs to the video controller card. The images on the screen consist of many individual dots called *pixels* (short for picture elements). The number of pixels that make up the screen determines how much video memory is required. A monochrome display requires a single bit per pixel. If the corresponding bit in video memory is set to 1, that pixel is lit on the screen. When the bit is set to 0, the pixel is dark. If the screen resolution is 640 pixels by 320 pixels, for example, a total of 204,800 (640 × 320) bits, or 25,600 bytes, of video memory are used to control the display.

In a color display, more than a single bit is needed to control a pixel because color is created by mixing varying intensities of red, green, and blue. Depending on the type of controller, it can take from 4 to 32 bits per pixel to control a color monitor. (The more bits, the more colors that can be simultaneously displayed.) In expensive systems with large color displays, the video RAM alone can sometimes be as large as 4 megabytes.

Displaying graphics

All screen images, from multicolored lines to simple text, are created by setting the proper bits in video memory. The Visual Basic graphics methods do all the bit setting for you. These graphics methods—which are named *Print, Line, Circle,* and *Pset*—draw text, lines, arcs, and individual points on the screen. In addition, a method called *Point* determines the color of a given point, and the *Cls* method clears the form to an empty display.

In an environment in which a single program controls the display, an image that is drawn on the screen stays there. Windows, however, is a multitasking environment. After you have drawn an image on a form, the user can switch to another application that will draw something else on the screen. The fun begins when the user switches away from the second application and expects to see the image created by your program, when in fact it has been obliterated by the second application.

Windows solves this problem with the Paint event, which is handled by a Visual Basic event procedure. If an application's display has been obscured by some other window, Windows sends a Paint event to the application when the application regains control of the display, allowing it to re-create the screen image. The same process occurs (without an interfering application) when you minimize a window containing pictures or controls and then restore it.

A simple application can demonstrate what's going on. Create a new project. Add the following code as the form's *Click* procedure, and then run the application:

```
Sub Form_Click ()
    Print "Hello"
End Sub
```

Click on the form a few times to place some text on the screen. Now minimize the form or move another application's window in front of it. When you restore the form as the topmost window, you'll see that the text has disappeared.

In this case, when the form was restored, Visual Basic called your *Form_Paint* procedure. Because you hadn't written it, nothing happened. Obviously, if you intend to write graphics applications, you must write a *Paint* event procedure that can reconstruct the screen. This takes some careful planning. The best approach is to place all of your graphics code in the *Paint* procedure itself. When you are ready to draw an image for the first time, call the *Paint* procedure directly. Then everything is in place so that if the screen needs to be refreshed, Visual Basic can automatically call your *Paint* procedure.

Try modifying the sample Hello program you just wrote by using this technique. First enter the following code in the general declarations section:

```
Dim ClickCount As Integer    'Initialized to 0 by Visual Basic
```

Then add these two event procedures:

```
Sub Form_Click ()
    ClickCount = ClickCount + 1
    Form_Paint
End Sub

Sub Form_Paint ()
    Dim I As Integer

    Cls                        'Clear screen; reset printing to top of form
    For I = 1 To ClickCount
        Print "Hello"
    Next I
End Sub
```

When you run this version of the program, try minimizing or hiding the form window. You will see that the display always returns when the form is restored.

The AutoRedraw property

Visual Basic also offers a simpler technique for screen repainting. Each form has an AutoRedraw property, which is set to False by default. If you set this property to True, Visual Basic itself will handle all the repainting.

To test this, use the original code for the sample Hello program (without including the *Form_Paint* procedure):

```
Sub Form_Click ()
    Print "Hello"
End Sub
```

Now set the AutoRedraw property to True, and press F5 to run the application. This time, the contents of the form will not be lost if the form is hidden or minimized, even though the program has no *Form_Paint* procedure.

There is, of course, a catch. When you set the AutoRedraw property to True, you simply pass the responsibility for managing the display to Visual Basic. Visual Basic handles this task by allocating a certain amount of memory (the number of bits required to duplicate the image on your form). When you draw to the form, Visual Basic keeps a copy in this backup memory. When it needs to restore the form, it writes its copy in backup memory to the system's video memory.

The trade-off, then, is the choice between a simple program that requires more memory and a complex program that requires less memory. As long as you are writing simple, single-form applications, setting the AutoRedraw property to True is probably adequate. When your applications become larger, however, you won't want to waste memory on backup copies of your forms, and thus you'll need to write *Form_Paint* procedures.

Note: In applications that do not use graphics methods, the AutoRedraw property should always be set to False. Text boxes, labels, list boxes, combo boxes, and other similar controls are not affected by Paint events, and therefore backup copies of the form are not needed.

Screen Coordinates

Visual Basic provides a default coordinate system that specifies the locations of objects within a form. This system, illustrated in Figure 10-1, assigns the coordinates (0, 0) to the upper left corner of a form, with values that increase as you move to the right along the horizontal axis and down along the vertical axis of the form. The Top and Left properties of an object specify its offset from the (0, 0) origin point (the upper left corner).

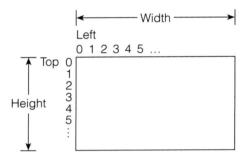

Figure 10-1.
The Visual Basic default coordinate system.

The Top, Left, Width, and Height properties are measured in twips. As you might recall from Chapter 5, a twip is a unit of measure equivalent to $\frac{1}{1440}$ inch, or $\frac{1}{20}$ point. (A point, which is approximately $\frac{1}{72}$ inch, is a standard typographic measure used in sizing fonts.) Thus, an object that is ½ inch high and 2 inches wide has its Height and Width properties set to 720 and 2880, respectively.

If you are more comfortable working with other units of measure, you can change the setting of your form's ScaleMode property to have Visual Basic report screen coordinates using other scales. Figure 10-2 describes the units of measure that correspond to the various ScaleMode settings.

You can easily see the effect of changing the ScaleMode setting. Place an object from the Toolbox on a form, and examine the object's Top, Left, Height, and Width property settings. Now modify the form's ScaleMode setting (not the object's ScaleMode setting), and reexamine the object's properties. If you change the form's ScaleMode setting to 5, a control whose Height property setting was originally reported as 720 (twips) will now have a Height setting of 0.5 (inches). If you set the ScaleMode property to 6, the Height setting will change to 12.7 (millimeters).

ScaleMode Property Setting	Unit of Measure
0	User-defined
1	Twips (20 per point, 1440 per inch)(default)
2	Points (72 per inch)
3	Pixels (monitor dependent)
4	Characters (6 per inch vertically, 12 per inch horizontally)
5	Inches
6	Millimeters
7	Centimeters

Figure 10-2.
Settings for the ScaleMode property.

The ScaleMode setting 4, which measures in characters, is a bit odd because it uses different scales for vertical and horizontal measurements. With other units of measure, an object that is *n* wide and *n* high is square. When you use characters as a unit of measure, an object with a height of 6 and a width of 12 is 1 inch square.

ScaleMode 0

If you set the ScaleMode property to 0, you can use your own scale of measures. To define the particular measurement system, you must then set the ScaleHeight and ScaleWidth properties. For example, if you set ScaleWidth to 500, you are telling Visual Basic to use a scale that contains 500 units across the entire width of the form. If you then set the Width property of a label object to 250, for instance, the label field will be exactly half the form's width, as shown in Figure 10-3. The ScaleHeight property can be set in a similar manner. The units of height do not need to bear any relation to the units of width.

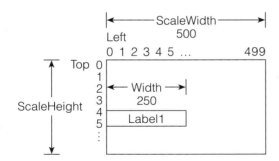

Figure 10-3.
Working with a user-defined unit of measure.

Besides setting the vertical and horizontal scales, you can also define an alternative origin point for the upper left corner. This corner is defined by the ScaleLeft and ScaleTop properties, which by default are both set to 0. By setting these two properties to new values, you define a new coordinate system. For example, setting ScaleLeft to 3 and ScaleTop to −4 changes the coordinates of the origin point (the upper left corner) from (0, 0) to (3, −4). The coordinates of the lower right corner are defined as (*ScaleLeft* + *ScaleWidth*, *ScaleTop* + *ScaleHeight*). Thus, if you set ScaleHeight to 17 and ScaleWidth to 10, the coordinates of the lower right corner become (13, 13) in the new measurement system, as shown in Figure 10-4.

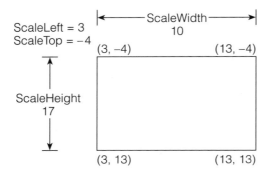

Figure 10-4.
A user-defined coordinate system.

If you would like to view the form as a standard Cartesian coordinate system with point (0, 0) in the center of the form, as pictured in Figure 10-5, set the ScaleTop property to a positive value and the ScaleLeft property to the corresponding negative value. Then define ScaleWidth as a positive value and ScaleHeight as the corresponding negative value. Figure 10-5 illustrates a coordinate system in which the upper left corner is defined as (−40, 40), the ScaleWidth property is set to 80, and the ScaleHeight property is set to −80.

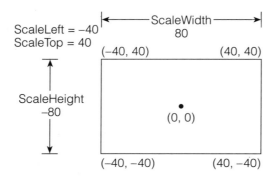

Figure 10-5.
A user-defined Cartesian coordinate system.

You can programmatically set the scale of a form either by setting properties individually or by using the *Scale* method. The syntax of this method is as follows:

[*object.*]Scale [(*left, top*)-(*right, bottom*)]

Notice that this syntax includes only the coordinates of the upper left corner and the lower right corner; Visual Basic computes ScaleHeight and ScaleWidth from these two points. Thus, the statement setting the scale for the form in Figure 10-5 would be *Scale (−40, 40)-(40, −40)*. Using the *Scale* method without parameters returns the scale to measurement in twips and resets the origin to the upper left corner, with coordinates (0, 0).

Equations and grids

If you're thinking that this information and a couple of bucks might get you a café latte but not much else, hang on. Actually, a user-defined measurement system can make your life much simpler. Let's assume that you are writing a program that graphs mathematical functions and that you want to graph the equation $y = x^2 − 3x + 12$ over a domain of −10 <= x <= 10. Using the standard origin and scale, you'd have to compute how many twips down and to the right to draw the axes, translate every x and y value into twips, and add the offset from the origin. But if you define a coordinate system appropriate to the problem, you merely need to compute x and y; Visual Basic does the rest. Figure 10-6 contains the program that draws this graph.

```
Function FofX (ByVal X As Single) As Single
    FofX = X ^ 2 - X * 3 + 12
End Function

Sub Form_Paint ()
    Dim X As Single

    'Set up display
    Cls
    Scale (-150, 150)-(150, -150)
    'Draw axes
    Line (-150, 0)-(150, 0)
    Line (0, -150)-(0, 150)
    'Draw graph
    CurrentX = -10
    CurrentY = FofX(-10)
    For X = -10 To 10
        Line -(X, FofX(X))
    Next X
End Sub
```

Figure 10-6.
Program code for graphing an equation.

Given a value for *X*, the function *FofX* computes *Y* according to the formula. Note that the rest of the program works regardless of the formula in *FofX*. The main code is in the *Form_Paint* procedure, which is called by Visual Basic every time it needs to update the display.

First the program sets the scale to a standard Cartesian coordinate system with the *Scale* statement. Next the axis lines are drawn using the *Line* method. In its simplest form, the *Line* method has the following syntax:

    [*object.*]Line [(*x1, y1*)]-(*x2, y2*)

It draws a line beginning at (*x1, y1*) and ending at (*x2, y2*).

Finally the program plots the graph using a variant of the *Line* method with no specified starting point. In this case, Visual Basic starts from the last known position, whose coordinates are stored in the CurrentX and CurrentY properties of the form. CurrentX and CurrentY need to be set only once in the program; after each *Line* statement executes, Visual Basic updates the property settings.

You can open a new form, enter this code, and run it with no additional controls or routines. A sample of the output is shown in Figure 10-7.

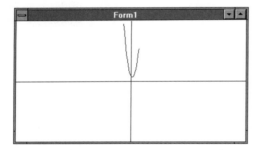

Figure 10-7.
The graph of the FofX *function.*

Note that the code shown in Figure 10-6 used the default value (1) for *Step*. To make the graph smoother, add a *Step* clause to the *For* statement, as shown here:

    For X = -10 To 10 Step 0.1

Even if you haven't plotted a graph since high school, you still might find a user-defined measurement system helpful for tasks such as drawing a chess board or constructing a grid for a game like Go. You can define a custom scale that is the size of your grid—for instance, 0 to 8 (or 1 to 9) for a chess board. Then, rather than having to compute the locations of the lines, you can simply draw the lines at locations 0, 1, 2, and so on. The code shown in Figure 10-8 draws the 8 by 8 grid that appears in Figure 10-9.

```
Sub Form_Paint ()
    Dim I As Integer

    'Set up display
    Cls
    Scale (0, 0)-(8, 8)
    'Draw grid
    For I = 1 To 7
        Line (0, I)-(8, I)        'Horizontal
        Line (I, 0)-(I, 8)        'Vertical
    Next I
End Sub
```

Figure 10-8.
Program code for drawing an 8 by 8 grid.

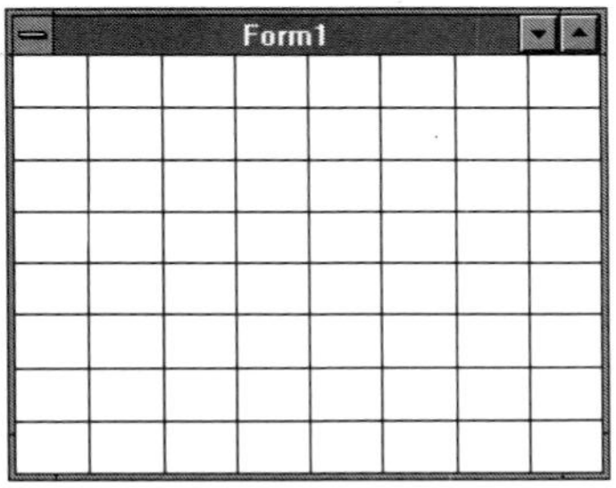

Figure 10-9.
An 8 by 8 grid drawn with the program code in Figure 10-8.

As mentioned earlier, all the properties and methods discussed here apply to picture boxes as well as to forms. Each picture box, for example, can have its own coordinate system defined by the scaling properties. You must include the name of the picture box control when you use these properties and methods; otherwise, the system defaults to the properties and methods of the form. For instance, if you have a picture box object whose Name property is set to MyPic, you can draw an 8 by 8 grid inside the picture box with the code shown in Figure 10-10.

```
Sub DrawGrid ()
    Dim I As Integer

    'Clear picture box
    MyPic.Cls
    MyPic.Scale (0, 0)-(8, 8)
```

Figure 10-10.
Program code for drawing an 8 by 8 grid inside a picture box.

(continued)

Figure 10-10. *continued*

```
    'Draw grid
    For I = 1 To 7
        MyPic.Line (0, I)-(8, I)      'Horizontal
        MyPic.Line (I, 0)-(8, 7)      'Vertical
    Next I
End Sub
```

Colors

Let's return for a moment to the graph shown in Figure 10-7. To distinguish the plotted line from the axes, it might be helpful to draw the axes in a different color. The *Line* method allows you to use an optional parameter to set the color of the line you are drawing. Alternatively, you can set the form's ForeColor property, which sets the color of anything drawn to the form (including text printed to the form). Both Figure 10-11 and Figure 10-12 contain code that draws the axes of the graph in green and the plotted line in the default color. The code in Figure 10-11 specifies the color with the *Line* method; the code in Figure 10-12 sets the ForeColor property of the form.

```
Sub Form_Paint ()
    Dim X As Single

    'Set up display
    Cls
    Scale (-150, 150)-(150, -150)
    'Draw axes
    Line (-150, 0)-(150, 0), RGB(0, 255, 0)
    Line (0, -150)-(0, 150), RGB(0, 255, 0)
    'Draw graph
    CurrentX = -10
    CurrentY = FofX(-10)
    For X = -10 To 10
        Line -(X, FofX(X))
    Next X
End Sub
```

Figure 10-11.
Program code for setting graph colors using the Line *method.*

Both routines use the *RGB* function to create a color value. This function (whose name is short for Red, Green, Blue) requires three arguments, each an integer in the range 0 through 255. The first argument specifies the strength of the color red, the second argument specifies the green intensity, and the third argument controls blue. A 0 argument indicates a total absence of that color; 255 indicates the greatest intensity. The function returns a long integer that represents an RGB color value. Figure 10-13 lists some common colors and their RGB settings.

```
Sub Form_Paint ()
    Dim X As Single, SaveColor As Long

    'Set up display
    Cls
    Scale (-150, 150)-(150, -150)
    'Draw axes
    SaveColor = ForeColor
    ForeColor = RGB(0, 255, 0)
    Line (-150, 0)-(150, 0)
    Line (0, -150)-(0, 150)
    'Draw graph
    ForeColor = SaveColor
    CurrentX = -10
    CurrentY = FofX(-10)
    For X = -10 To 10
        Line -(X, FofX(X))
    Next X
End Sub
```

Figure 10-12.
Program code for setting graph colors using the form's ForeColor property.

Color	RGB Setting
Black	RGB(0, 0, 0)
Red	RGB(255, 0, 0)
Green	RGB(0, 255, 0)
Blue	RGB(0, 0, 255)
White	RGB(255, 255, 255)
Yellow	RGB(255, 255, 0)
Magenta	RGB(255, 0, 255)
Cyan	RGB(0, 255, 255)

Figure 10-13.
RGB settings for some common colors.

> *Note: Although the* RGB *function theoretically allows a maximum of 16 million colors, your video hardware imposes certain restrictions. Standard VGA, for example, allows only 16 colors to be displayed simultaneously.*

In addition to setting the ForeColor property, you can also alter a form's background color by setting its BackColor property. If you change the value of this property at runtime, all existing graphics will be erased.

The file CONSTANT.TXT also includes special color constants that correspond to the settings in Windows' Control Panel. For example, the statement *ForeColor = ACTIVE_TITLE_BAR* sets the form's drawing color to be the color specified in Control Panel for the title bars of windows. The CONSTANT.TXT file defines these global constants as shown in Figure 10-14. (Notice that the definitions of the constants in Figure 10-14 begin with &H, indicating that the values appear in hexadecimal notation.) Using these constants instead of fixed colors ensures that your applications will fit into the color map defined by the user and also helps to make the applications look more professional.

Constant Name	Value	Description
SCROLL_BARS	&H80000000	Color of scroll bars' gray area
DESKTOP	&H80000001	Color of desktop
ACTIVE_TITLE_BAR	&H80000002	Color of title bar in active window
INACTIVE_TITLE_BAR	&H80000003	Color of title bar in inactive window
MENU_BAR	&H80000004	Background color of menu
WINDOW_BACKGROUND	&H80000005	Background color of window
WINDOW_FRAME	&H80000006	Color of window frame
MENU_TEXT	&H80000007	Color of text in menus
WINDOW_TEXT	&H80000008	Color of text in window
TITLE_BAR_TEXT	&H80000009	Color of text in title bar
ACTIVE_BORDER	&H8000000A	Color of active window border
INACTIVE_BORDER	&H8000000B	Color of inactive window border
APPLICATION_WORKSPACE	&H8000000C	Background color of multiple document interface (MDI) applications
HIGHLIGHT	&H8000000D	Color of selected item in a control
HIGHLIGHT_TEXT	&H8000000E	Color of text of selected item in a control
BUTTON_FACE	&H8000000F	Color of face shading on command buttons
BUTTON_SHADOW	&H80000010	Color of edge shading on command buttons
GRAY_TEXT	&H80000011	Color of grayed (disabled) text (set to 0 if current display driver does not support solid gray)
BUTTON_TEXT	&H80000012	Color of text on command buttons

Figure 10-14.
Global color constants defined in the CONSTANT.TXT file.

Hexadecimal Numbers

The hexadecimal (base 16) number system uses 16 symbols to represent numeric values: the digits 0 through 9 and the letters A (equivalent to decimal 10), B, C, D, E, and F (equivalent to decimal 15). As Chapter 2 explained in relation to other number systems, the value of each position in a hexadecimal, or hex, number increases by a power of 16. For instance, the hex number 1A3 represents the sum of 1×16^2 (256), 10×16^1 (160), and 3×16^0 (3); thus, its decimal equivalent is 419.

Hexadecimal notation is commonly used in programming as a compact way to represent the binary numbers used by a computer. Because any of the 16 digits can be represented in 4 bits, 2 hex digits (one for each 4 bits) can be represented in one of the 8-bit bytes on which computer memory and storage are based. Thus, 1 byte of storage can hold any of 256 different hex numbers (0 through FF).

You can use a hexadecimal value anywhere Visual Basic accepts a number. You must simply use the &H prefix to signal that the value is in hex notation.

Other Drawing Properties and Methods

The DrawWidth property determines the width of each line drawn. The setting for this property is always measured in pixels. Thus, a setting of 1 draws the narrowest line, with a width of 1 pixel. A setting of 2 draws a line that is thicker by an additional pixel, and so on.

The DrawStyle and DrawMode properties affect how lines appear on the screen. DrawStyle is similar to the BorderStyle property of a line object. Settings from 0 through 6 specify whether the drawn line is solid, dotted, dashed, or some combination of these styles.

The DrawMode property is a bit more complex. Its 16 settings determine how the image being drawn interacts with what is already on the screen. For example, the default setting of DrawMode (13 - Copy Pen) draws the image over the top of any existing graphics. With this setting, executing the statement *Line (0, .5)-(2, .75)* twice in succession would seem to draw only one line because the second line would directly overwrite the first. If, however, DrawMode was set to 6 - Invert, the first *Line* statement would draw a line in the inverse color of the background, and the second would invert it again, essentially making the line disappear. Other DrawMode settings combine colors in different ways and let you create special effects; see the Visual Basic reference manual for more information.

The FillColor and FillStyle properties affect the appearance of filled circles and polygons. These properties are similar to the FillColor and FillStyle properties of shape controls, described in Chapter 5.

Three Visual Basic methods support drawing: *PSet*, which sets a point (or pixel) to a specified color; *Line*, which allows you to draw lines and rectangles; and *Circle*, which lets you create circles, arcs, and ellipses. (We'll discuss these three methods in more depth in a moment.) In addition, the *Cls* method clears a form or a picture box; and the *Point* method, which operates like a function, returns the color of a specified point.

The *Cls* method erases, or clears, text and graphics from the specified object—more precisely, it sets every pixel to the background color (the color set by the BackColor property). Like the other methods discussed in this section, the *Cls* method acts on the current form by default if you do not specify an object.

The *Point* method has the following syntax:

[*object.*]Point (*x*, *y*)

It returns the RGB color value for the pixel located at the coordinates (*x*, *y*), where *x* is the horizontal axis position and *y* is the vertical axis position. The coordinates are measured in the units that are specified by the ScaleMode property of the form or the ScaleMode property of the picture box.

The *PSet* method

To set a single point to a particular color, use the *PSet* method. This method has the following syntax:

[*object.*]PSet [Step](*x*, *y*)[, *color*]

The coordinates (*x*, *y*) refer to an absolute location, measured in the units specified by the ScaleMode property of the object in which you are drawing. If these coordinates are preceded by the keyword *Step*, however, they are offset relative to the current position (given by the CurrentX and CurrentY properties). For example, *Step(2, 10)* refers to a location offset from the current position by 2 units horizontally and 10 units vertically—in other words, the location *(CurrentX + 2, CurrentY + 10)*.

You can set the point to any color. If you don't specify a color, the *PSet* method sets the point to the color setting of the ForeColor property. This method can be especially handy for clearing a single pixel: Simply set the pixel to the current background color (the setting of the BackColor property).

Note that the size and appearance of the point are affected by how you have set the DrawWidth and DrawMode properties. For example, when the DrawWidth property is set to 1, the *PSet* method sets the color of only 1 pixel. But when the DrawWidth setting is greater than 1, the point is correspondingly larger and is centered on the specified coordinates.

The *Line* method

The *Line* method, which draws a line or a rectangle, uses this syntax:

[*object.*]Line [[Step](*x1*, *y1*)]-[Step](*x2*, *y2*)[, [*color*][, B[F]]]

The first set of coordinates, (*x1, y1*), specifies the starting point of the line. If you omit the starting-point coordinates, the line simply starts at the current position. You must include the second set of coordinates, (*x2, y2*), which are the ending-point coordinates. You can also specify the color of the line with this method.

When you include the letter *B* (for box) in the *Line* statement, a rectangle is drawn instead of a line, with the two sets of coordinates representing opposite corners of the rectangle. The rectangle will be filled with the color set for the FillColor property and in the style set for the FillStyle property. If you also include the letter *F* in the *Line* statement, the rectangle will instead be filled with the color used to draw it. You cannot specify *F* unless you also include *B*.

Some examples of drawing with the *Line* method are shown here in Figures 10-15 and 10-16 and in Figure 10-17 on the following page. Each uses the statement *Scale (2, −2)-(−2, 2)* and the *Line* statement shown in the figure.

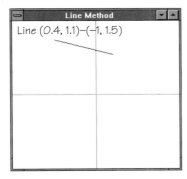

Figure 10-15.
Drawing a line with the Line *method.*

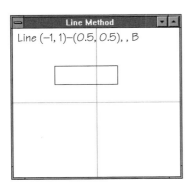

Figure 10-16.
Drawing a rectangle with the Line *method.*

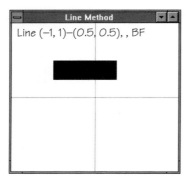

Figure 10-17.
Drawing a filled rectangle with the Line *method.*

The *Circle* method

The *Circle* method is the most complex of the drawing methods. You can use it to draw circles, ellipses, arcs, and "pie slices." (A *pie slice* is an arc with radius lines connecting the endpoints of the arc with the center.)

The full syntax for the *Circle* method is the following:

[*object.*]Circle [Step](*x, y*), *radius*[, [*color*][, [*start*][, [*end*][, *aspect*]]]]

You must always specify center coordinates (*x, y*) when using the *Circle* method; this method does not default to the current position. When the circle is drawn, CurrentX and CurrentY will be set to the center point.

To draw a circle, simply specify an origin and a radius. To "squish" the circle into an ellipse, you must change the *aspect ratio*. Circles have an aspect ratio of 1.0. Values of *aspect* greater than 1.0 create ellipses that are tall and narrow; *aspect* values less than 1.0 create ellipses that are short and wide. Thus, an *aspect* value of 4.0 draws a "Laurel" ellipse, and a value of 0.4 draws a "Hardy," as shown in Figures 10-18 and

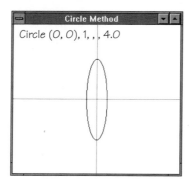

Figure 10-18.
Drawing a "Laurel" ellipse with the Circle *method.*

10-19. Note that you must type all the intervening commas in the *Circle* statement, even if you don't specify values for each parameter.

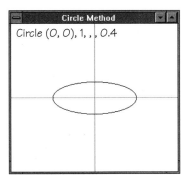

Figure 10-19.
Drawing a "Hardy" ellipse with the Circle *method.*

If you want to draw an arc rather than a complete circle or ellipse, specify *start* and *end* parameters in the *Circle* statement. These values must be provided in radians (dig out that geometry book) and can range from 0 to 2 *pi*. Figure 10-20 shows the value in radians of strategic points along a circle.

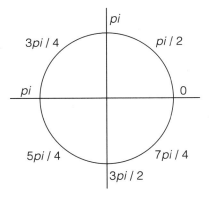

Figure 10-20.
Points along a circle, specified in radians.

If you are more comfortable using degrees than radians, define the constant PI and use the following function:

```
Function Degree2Radian(Degree As Single) As Single
    Degree2Radian = Degree * PI / 180.0
End Function
```

Now all you have to do is pass to *Degree2Radian* a value in degrees, and the function will return the corresponding value in radians.

To draw pie slices, you must use negative values for *start* and *end* in the *Circle* statement. Negative values for these parameters cause Visual Basic to draw a radius line at the angle specified by the absolute value of the parameter. Both *start* and *end* must be negative so that both radius lines are drawn. Visual Basic will not fill an arc or an "unclosed" pie slice. Some examples are shown in Figures 10-21 and 10-22.

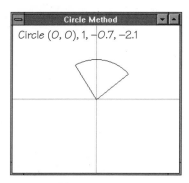

Figure 10-21.
Drawing a pie slice with the Circle *method.*

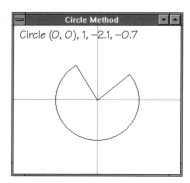

Figure 10-22.
Drawing a circle minus a pie slice with the Circle *method.*

The Printer Object

Using many of the same methods you use to write to a form, you can have your program write directly to a printer. Visual Basic supports methods for the Printer object that draw both text (the *Print* method) and graphics (the *Line*, *Circle*, and *PSet* methods). You can view writing to the printer as writing to a special form whose size is the size of a printer page.

Because you can apply the *Scale* method to the Printer object, you can work in any coordinate system you find comfortable. Of course, there is no *Cls* method, so you can't erase what you've written to the printer. Use the *NewPage* method to start a new page, and call the *EndDoc* method to tell Visual Basic to end the print task. You can read the Printer object's Page property to read the current page number.

In Figure 10-23, the graphing example first shown in Figure 10-6 has been modified to write to the printer.

```
Sub PrintGraph ()
    Dim X As Single

    Printer.Scale (-150, 150)-(150, -150)
    'Draw axes
    Printer.Line (-150, 0)-(150, 0)
    Printer.Line (0, -150)-(0, 150)
    'Draw graph
    Printer.CurrentX = -10
    Printer.CurrentY = FofX(-10)
    For X = -10 To 10
        Printer.Line -(X, FofX(X))
    Next X
    Printer.EndDoc
End Sub
```

Figure 10-23.
Program code for graphing an equation directly to the printer.

When you are drawing on a form on the screen and complete all the necessary drawing, you can simply call the form's *PrintForm* method to send a bitmap copy of the form to the printer. If you do this, you do not need to call *Printer.EndDoc*; the *PrintForm* method is a complete, single-page document process.

Hardware Considerations for Graphics Programs

If you are interested in writing graphics programs that will be truly useful for other people, you must carefully consider the design of your programs—and, in particular, you should take into account the hardware on which the programs are likely to be run. As discussed earlier in this chapter, for example, the issue of whether to use the AutoRedraw property or a *Paint* procedure to repaint the screen can be important. Remember that the amount of memory required for Visual Basic to back up your form images depends on the hardware on which the program is running. In an extreme case, for instance, you might develop the program on a monochrome system, but the user might have a 1280 by 1024 32-bit color display, whose memory requirements are substantially larger than those of your system. Using AutoRedraw on such a system could easily exhaust the available memory.

Or perhaps you develop your program on a computer with a high-resolution display. What happens if the user has a lower-resolution system? On your system, 6-point text might look just fine, but that size might not be readable on a low-resolution laptop. If you plan to write programs for distribution, you might want to examine the TwipsPerPixelX and TwipsPerPixelY properties of the Screen and Printer objects. (The Screen object represents the entire screen. Your program can examine the properties of the Screen object to determine such matters as which fonts to use and where to place dialog boxes.)

11

Databases and Grids

Chapter 5 introduced you to the Data tool and the Grid tool and described briefly how they are used to provide access to databases or to present data. This chapter describes each tool in more detail and provides examples for use. This chapter also covers more advanced concepts and complex programming techniques than you've used in previous chapters. If you are new to programming, you might want to skip the next two chapters and go on to Chapter 13, "A Complete Application for Windows."

What Is a Database?

Simply put, a database is any collection of information. In common computer usage, however, a database is a collection of related information that is stored in a structurally well-defined way. For example, the collection of information on the Bavarian Tufted Forest weasels in Chapter 9 is a database. It has columns that list different kinds of information about the subject and rows that describe all the attributes of a single instance of the subject. Each row is a *record,* in this case describing a weasel. In database terminology, a *table* is a collection of records that has this same structure. A group of related tables together make up the database. In Chapter 9, the database consisted of only a single table. Figure 11-1 illustrates the structure of the weasel database.

Record Number	Name	Color	Weight	Length	Birthdate	Tuft Color	Tuft Length	
1	Siegmund	Brown	18	11	09/13/91	Brown	6	
2	Sieglinde	Light brown	14	10	10/29/91	Black	6	
3	Siegfried	Brown	12	8	09/13/92	Brown	2	⎱ Record
4								
⋮								

Table

Figure 11-1.
Weasel database structure.

Keeping track of this kind of information is such a common chore that applications known as *database management systems* or *DBMSs* have been developed. They help to simplify the creation and maintenance of databases. Some DBMS programs of which you may be aware are Microsoft Access, Microsoft FoxPro, Borland Paradox, Borland dBase, and Claris FileMaker. Corporations often use DBMS programs to organize and update their employee records, payroll information, customer lists, and so on.

In this chapter, you'll work with a sample database that comes with Visual Basic—BIBLIO.MDB. It is a Microsoft Access database that contains bibliographic data about books relating to database topics and to Visual Basic. Figure 11-2 shows the structure of the database.

The BIBLIO database consists of three tables. The Authors table consists of names of authors and author ID numbers. The Publishers table is a collection of records describing publishers, including an ID code, the parent company name, the location, and the phone number. The Authors and Publishers tables contain actual source

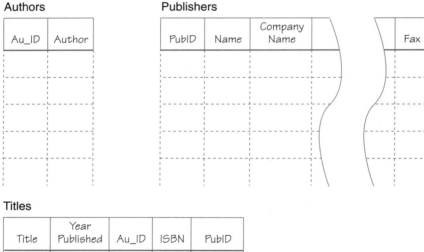

Figure 11-2.
The BIBLIO database.

data. The Titles table, although it looks no different from the other two in structure, is different. It holds a list of published books—the service data—and refers to the Authors table and the Publishers table for ID numbers. It contains some source data but also refers to the other tables for data through common fields, as illustrated in Figure 11-3.

The referral of one table to another via a common field is called a *relation*. It is this term that gives us the phrase *relational database*. Entire tables can be made up of relational fields, all referring to actual fields. Relational fields can also refer to other relational fields, which eventually refer to actual data.

In database language, a *query* is a request for information from the tables that make up a database. When you query a database (through a DBMS facility or through your own application) you need to define the set of data from which you plan to request information, thus narrowing the scope of the request.

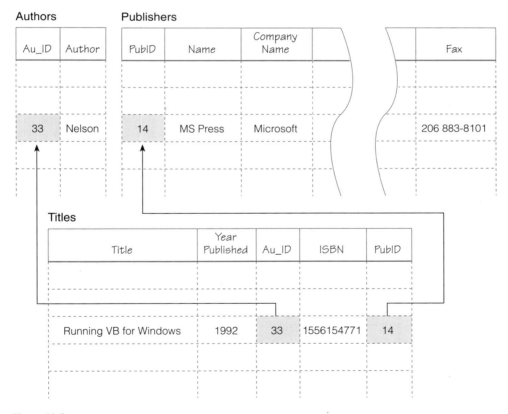

Figure 11-3.
The Titles table refers to the Authors and Publishers tables for the ID numbers of authors and publishers.

The result of a query is always something that looks like another table. It is a *virtual table*, or a *logical view*, of the data you requested. When you define the data set, you're actually setting up relations to the tables in the database. The resulting logical view doesn't exist in that form in the database but refers to the separate pieces of data, some of which might be tracked from other relations within the database tables, that do exist there. So it is the relations that let you construct logical views of data. Figure 11-4 shows a possible logical view of the BIBLIO database.

Accessing the data and displaying it are two different things. In the next section, you'll learn about creating a Visual Basic application that does both.

Title	Year Published	Au_ID	ISBN	Name	Company Name	
Running VB for Windows	1992	33	1556154771	MS Press	Microsoft	

Figure 11-4.
A possible logical view from the tables that make up the BIBLIO database.

Accessing and Displaying Data via Visual Basic

At some point, you might find yourself creating an application that makes use of information already contained in a database. It would be possible to duplicate that database information in a Visual Basic random access file; however, doing so would be both inefficient and potentially dangerous. It would be inefficient because it would mean that multiple copies of the data were taking up disk space. It would be dangerous because having more than one copy would mean that the sets of data might become out of sync with one another. That is, the information might be updated in one location, but the corresponding data in the copy might not be updated.

A far better solution is to keep only a single copy of the data in the database and have your Visual Basic application access it. This access can be set up by creating a Data control in your Visual Basic application. Figure 11-5 shows the Data tool button in the Toolbox and a Data control as it appears on a form.

Figure 11-5.
The Data tool button and a Data control as it appears on a form.

Note: *Before you use the Data tool in Visual Basic, you'll need to enable file sharing, unless you are using Windows for Workgroups. If file sharing is not enabled in your system, you must exit Windows and enter* share *at the MS-DOS prompt. You can then restart Windows and Visual Basic. You might want to put* share *in your AUTOEXEC.BAT file.*

The Data Control

The Data control has a number of properties that define the connection between your Visual Basic application and the database you want to access. An application can have more than one Data control; in fact, a separate Data control is required for each defined set of data. Each Data control always accesses a single record at a time. This is called its *current* record. After setting these properties, you can *bind* other Visual Basic controls to the Data control. As you change the current record (either by clicking directly on the Data control or by using program statements), those controls display data that is in the current record. The current version of Visual Basic supports exchanging data with the following DBMSs:

■ Microsoft Access

■ Microsoft FoxPro

■ Borland dBase

■ Borland Paradox

Making the Connection

Now let's create a new application in Visual Basic that can access the BIBLIO database. You'll set it up so that when you click on the Data control, the author ID number and book title for every record in the database are displayed one at a time. First place a Data control at the top of the form, and then place two labels and two Text Box controls on it. Set the properties as shown in the following table, and your form should resemble the one displayed in Figure 11-6 on the next page.

Object	Property	Setting
Form1	Caption	Database: BIBLIO
	Name	Biblio
Data1	Caption	Book Database
	Name	dtaBiblio
Label1	Caption	Author
Label2	Caption	Title
Text1	Name	txtAuthor
	Text	[none]
Text2	Name	txtTitle
	Text	[none]

At this stage, you have set up only the appearance of the form. To make the connection to the database, you must set a few additional properties of the Data control.

The properties listed below can be set either at design time or at runtime. Set them at design time if your application will always access the same database; Visual Basic will be able to do some additional error checking for you if you set the properties at design time.

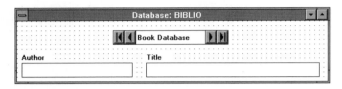

Figure 11-6.
The newly created Biblio form.

Choose the Data control (dtaBiblio) in the Properties window, and set the properties defined below:

Connect This property tells Visual Basic what format the data is in. For this example, set the property to the empty string, which indicates that the database is in Microsoft Access format. Other legal values include "foxpro 2.5;", "paradox;", and "dbase IV;". See the *Visual Basic Programmer's Manual* for all the database formats supported.

DatabaseName This property identifies the database file. Click on the ellipsis (...) in the Properties window and choose the file BIBLIO.MDB. It should be in the same directory as your Visual Basic installation.

RecordSource This property tells Visual Basic where to get the data. It can be the name of a table, or it can identify a logical view. For now, set RecordSource to "Titles" to get data from the Titles table.

Binding Display Controls to the Data Control

Your Visual Basic application now has enough information to retrieve data from the database. With one small addition, your application will display the data as well. Check Box, Image, Label, Picture Box, and Text Box controls can be bound directly to fields in the table accessed by a Data control. Image and Picture Box controls can be used to display pictures stored in the database, a Check Box control displays a Boolean value, and Label and Text Box controls can be used to present numeric or character information. For any of these controls, the DataSource property connects it to a Data control, and the DataField property identifies the name of the field in the table to which the control will be bound.

Click on the txtAuthor text box and set its DataSource property to dtaBiblio. Set its DataField property to Au_ID. Next click on the txtTitle text box, setting its DataSource to dtaBiblio and its DataField to Title. Run your application. As you click on the Data control, the records from the database will be displayed in the text fields, and you haven't had to write a single line of code!

You can also edit the data from your Visual Basic application, and the results will be written to the original database.

> *Note: It is important not to modify data that doesn't "belong" to you. If you are creating an application to access a corporate database, ensure that you grant update access only to those users who have permission to modify the table. See the* Visual Basic Programmer's Manual *for information on the Exclusive, Options, and ReadOnly properties.*

Defining the Recordset

The *recordset* refers to the records that are selected for access. It is defined by the RecordSource property of the Data control. In the current example, the recordset is the Titles table. Frequently, however, you'll want your application to access only a subset of the records in a database or access a view of the database that extends beyond a single table.

For example, the current application is somewhat less useful than it could be because it displays the author's ID number for a book rather than the author's name. We can take care of this problem by changing the recordset to be based on a relational view of the database. Stop the application, and in the Properties window set the RecordSource property of the Data control to the following text string:

```
select Author,Title from Authors,Titles where Authors.Au_ID =
    Titles.Au_ID
```

This is a SQL statement that creates a new view of the database (and defines a new recordset) by combining the Authors and Titles tables on the Au_ID relation and selecting out two columns: Author and Title. You must change the DataField property of the txtAuthor Text box to Author because the newly created view does not have a field named Au_ID. (You can learn more about SQL from your DBMS manuals, or browse the database to discover some of the books that have been published about it.)

Now run the application again. You will find that you now get the author's name rather than the ID in the Text box. When you access data where the recordset is defined by a query rather than a complete table, you might not be allowed to update the data.

Programmatic Control

In addition to choosing a record by using the Data control, you can use methods to programmatically accomplish the same things. In fact, you can set the Visible property of the Data control to False and perform all the data manipulations under program control. The following methods operate on the Data control:

Refresh The database is opened for use, or closed and reopened if it is already open.

MoveFirst The current record is set to the first record in the recordset.

MoveNext The current record is advanced to the next record in the recordset.

MovePrevious The current record is backspaced to the previous record.

MoveLast The current record is set to the last record in the recordset.

AddNew A new record is added to the recordset. (Only valid when the recordset is a table or a dynaset.)

Update Any edited fields are written back to the database. (Valid only for tables and dynasets.)

Delete The current record is deleted. This method is also valid only when the recordset is a table or a dynaset and must be immediately followed by one of the Move methods because the current record is rendered invalid after a Delete operation.

When moving about in the database programmatically, you will want to test the *BOF* (Beginning of File) and *EOF* (End of File) properties of the Data control. The BOF property is True when the current record is positioned before any data. This usually occurs when the first record has been deleted. The EOF property is true when the current record has been positioned past the end of the data. If either property is true, the current record is invalid. If both properties are true, then there is no data in the recordset at all.

Finding Specific Records

In addition to advancing sequentially through the recordset, you can set conditional match criteria and display only the records that meet the criteria. The methods FindFirst, FindNext, FindPrevious, and FindLast all operate much like the Move methods described above. The differences are that the Find methods operate on the recordset component of the Data control and they take a string parameter that expresses the search criteria as a Boolean expression.

For example, to loop through all the books whose titles begin with the letter "T" in the application above, you might code something like this:

```
Dim Criteria as String
Criteria = "Title >= 'T' And Title < 'U'"
dtaBiblio.Recordset.FindFirst Criteria
Do While Not dtaBiblio.Recordset.NoMatch
    Debug.Print dtaBiblio.Recordset.Fields("Title").Value
    dtaBiblio.Recordset.FindNext Criteria
Loop
```

The program fragment above also shows you how to use the NoMatch property after a Find operation and how to programmatically access a field of a recordset. If a Find operation fails (and the NoMatch property is True), the current record remains unchanged.

Creating a Rolodex-Style Application

Let's put everything we've discussed in this chapter together and extend the application to skip through the database based on the author's name. We'll take advantage of the fact that the database is sorted in alphabetic order by author.

Expand the form of the application and place a small command button in the lower left corner of the form, as shown in Figure 11-7. The button's Caption property has been set to "A" in the figure, and its Name property is cmdLetter.

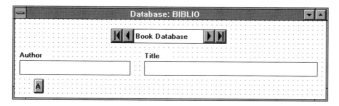

Figure 11-7.
Extending the application.

For a Rolodex look, we'd like a row of buttons from A through Z rather than just one button. However, drawing them all in and making them all just the right size could be a real pain, so we'll let Visual Basic do the work at runtime by making the command button a control array. Make the button a control array by setting its Index property to 0. Enter the following code as the form's Load procedure:

```
Sub Form_Load ()
Dim I As Integer

For I = 1 To 25
    Load cmdLetter(I)          'Create new control #I
    'Position it directly to the left of the previous one
    cmdLetter(I).Left = cmdLetter(I - 1).Left + cmdLetter(I - 1).Width
    'Compute its caption based on its position (A,B,C,D, ...)
    cmdLetter(I).Caption = Chr$(Asc("A") + I)
    cmdLetter(I).Visible = True
    Next I
End Sub
```

When this procedure executes at startup time, 25 new members of the Command Button control array will be created, each next to the other, and each with a succeeding letter of the alphabet as its caption. Now all you have to do is execute a Find method when the button is pressed. We'll use the Caption of the button as the search criteria. That is, if the "N" button is chosen, the criteria will be *Author > = 'N'*. Enter the following procedure as the *Click* procedure for the Command Button control array.

```
Sub cmdLetter_Click (Index As Integer)
    dtaBiblio.Recordset.FindFirst "Author >= '" +
    cmdLetter(Index).Caption + "'"
End Sub
```

Every time you click on one of the buttons, the current record will be positioned according to the search criteria. Because the table is stored in alphabetic order, pressing the Next and Previous arrows in the Data control will advance to the next author. When you run the application, it should look something like Figure 11-8.

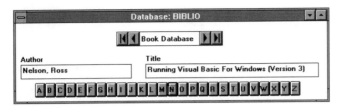

Figure 11-8.
The Rolodex version of the Biblio application.

Dynamically Accessing a Database

In the previous examples, the recordset was known at design time. Consequently, we were able to create linked controls that automatically displayed the fields of the recordset. You might want to write applications that open an unknown database selected by the user of the application. In this case, you will need to determine the fields of the database dynamically—that is, at runtime. This section tells you how to create an application that opens any database, presents the user with a list of tables, and, when a table is selected, displays it in a grid form.

In addition to the Recordset property of the Data control, Visual Basic offers objects that describe the database. The objects are accessed through properties of the Data control. For example, the Database property of the Data control accesses a database descriptor object. This object might, in turn, have properties of its own. Up to this point, most of the Visual Basic objects you have used have had properties of simple types; for example, a Command Button object has properties, such as Caption and Height, whose values are strings or integers. It is a simple extension to imagine a property that returns something more complex than a string or an integer, for example, a *collection,* which is described below. To access a property of an object that is itself the property of an object, you simply append another period (.) and property name to the original expression. So the expression X.Y.Z. would refer to the Z property of the object referenced as the Y property of X.

Collections

A collection is like a cross between a list box and an array. Like an array, it is purely programmatic, with no visual representation. Like a list box, however, a collection is an object with its own properties. Every collection has a Count property that tells how many other objects are contained in it. The contained objects can be accessed by a numeric index (from *0* to *Count-1*) or by the name of a contained object. In the loop example on page 264, you accessed the Fields collection of the Recordset object with the statement:

```
Debug.Print dtaBiblio.Recordset.Fields("Title").Value
```

In the statement above, the name "Title" is used to extract the desired field.

Sample Expressions

Here are some expressions that provide information about databases connected via a Visual Basic Data control. Assume the use of the dtaBiblio control in the previous example.

Expression	Value
`dtaBiblio`	The Data control itself
`dtaBiblio.Database`	The database descriptor object
`dtaBiblio.Database.Name`	The name of the database
`dtaBiblio.Database.TableDefs.Count`	The number of tables in the database
`dtaBiblio.Database.TableDefs(0).Name`	The name of the first table in the database
`dtaBiblio.Database.TableDefs(0).Fields.Count`	The number of fields in the first table
`dtaBiblio.Database.TableDefs(0).Fields(0).Name`	The name of the first field in the database
`dtaBiblio.Recordset`	The recordset currently being accessed by the control
`dtaBiblio.Recordset.Fields.Count`	The number of fields in the recordset
`dtaBiblio.Recordset.Fields(0).Name`	The name of the first field in the recordset
`dtaBiblio.Recordset.Fields(0).Value`	The value of the first field in the recordset

Once you know how to query the database for its description, you can dynamically create a display to present the information. Rather than creating separate text boxes for each field however, it might be more convenient to use the Grid control.

The Grid Control

A Grid is a two-dimensional array of display boxes, or *cells,* that is well suited to presenting database-style or spreadsheet-style information. The Toolbox icon for the Grid is shown in Figure 11-9 on the next page. The Grid control will not appear in the Toolbox unless the GRID.VBX file is added to the Project window.

Figure 11-9.
The Grid tool icon.

Two sample Grids are shown in Figure 11-10. The Grid on the left shows gray cells along the top row and the left column, and has scroll bars for horizontal and vertical positioning. The Grid on the right has no column of gray cells and no scroll bars. These display features are controlled by the following properties of the Grid:

Rows The total number of rows in the Grid. If there are more rows than will fit in the space allotted for the Grid on the form, a vertical scroll bar appears.

Columns The total number of columns in the Grid. A horizontal scroll bar will appear if the number of columns is too large for the size of the Grid.

FixedRows The number of rows, starting from the top, that are fixed in position. Fixed rows do not scroll and have a gray background. Fixed rows are usually used for titles.

FixedColumns The number of columns, starting from the left, that are fixed in position. Like fixed rows, they are useful for column headings, they do not scroll, and they are gray in color.

ColWidth The width of a particular column, measured in twips ($\frac{1}{20}$ of a point).

RowHeight The height of a given row, also measured in twips.

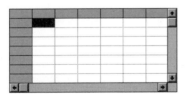

A Data Browser Application

Given what you've learned so far about controlling a Grid, you can create an application that opens any database, presents the user with a list of tables, and when a table is selected, displays it in the Grid. Begin by creating a new application. If your Project window does not contain GRID.VBX, choose the Add File command from the File menu and load it into your project. GRID.VBX should be in your Windows SYSTEM folder. Because we'll need a way to choose a database file to examine, add COMMDLG.VBX to your Project window in the same manner.

Place a command button, a combo box, a Data control, a Common Dialog control, and a Grid control on your form as shown in Figure 11-11. Next set the properties of the controls as detailed in the table below.

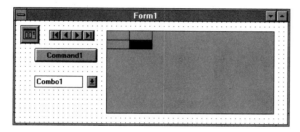

Figure 11-11.
Initial form layout.

Object	Property	Setting
Form1	Caption	Data Browser
	Name	Grid1
ComDlg1	Name	dlog
Data1	Name	dtaTable
	Visible	False
Command1	Caption	Open Database
	Name	cmdOpen
Combo1	Name	cboTables
	Text	[none]
Grid1	FixedCols	0
	Name	grdData

The Data control is set to be invisible because all the database access will be programmatic. The FixedCols property of the Grid is set to 0 because there are no row labels—only column headings in a fixed row across the top of the Grid.

Add the first line below to the form's general declarations section. Then define the *Click* procedure for the command button as shown. (The definition for the OFN_FILEMUSTEXIST constant comes from the CONSTANTS.TXT file.)

```
Const OFN_FILEMUSTEXIST = &H1000&

Sub cmdOpen_Click ()
    cboTables.Clear            'Empty the combo box list
    dlog.DefaultExt = "MDB"    'Extension for MS Access databases
    dlog.Filename = ""
    dlog.Filter = "Access databases (*.MDB)|*.MDB|Any file (*.*)|*.*"
    dlog.Flags = OFN_FILEMUSTEXIST
    dlog.Action = 1            'Open file dialog
    If dlog.Filename = "" Then Exit Sub
    OpenDataFile dlog.Filename
End Sub
```

When you click on the command button, the program will present the Open File dialog box and allow the user to select a database file. This program is set up to handle files in the Microsoft Access file format that have the extension MDB. When a file is selected, the program calls a routine named openDataFile, passing it the name of the database file. The code for this routine is shown below:

```
Sub OpenDataFile (ByVal Datafile As String)
    Dim I As Integer

    dtaTable.Connect = ""              'Access format
    dtaTable.DatabaseName = Datafile
    dtaTable.ReadOnly = True           'For faster access
    dtaTable.Exclusive = True          'For faster access
    dtaTable.Refresh                   'Load the database

    For I = 0 To dtaTable.Database.TableDefs.Count - 1
        'Place each table name in the combo box
        cboTables.AddItem dtaTable.Database.TableDefs(I).Name
    Next I

    cboTables.Text = "(none)"          'Nothing currently selected
End Sub
```

The *OpenDataFile* routine initializes the Data control and then queries the Database object for the names of all the tables in the database. These names are inserted in the Combo Box list. The code that controls the Combo Box is quite simple; it calls a routine that fills the Grid. Set the *Click* procedure for the Combo Box as follows:

```
Sub cboTables_Click ()
    FillGrid cboTables.Text
End Sub
```

All that's left to do is write the routine that fills in the Grid, as shown on the next page. It will accept the name of the selected table as a parameter, query the database to get the field names in the table, and place those names in the fixed row of the Grid. Then it will walk through the table, getting values from every record and placing them in the appropriate rows and columns of the Grid.

```
Sub FillGrid (ByVal TableName As String)
    Dim I As Integer, CellWidth As Integer

    'Initialize the recordset
    dtaTable.RecordSource = TableName

    'Set up column headers
    grdData.Cols = dtaTable.Database(TableName).Fields.Count
    grdData.Row = 0

    For I = 0 To dtaTable.Database(TableName).Fields.Count - 1
        grdData.Col = I
        grdData.Text = dtaTable.Database(TableName).Fields(I).Name
        grdData.ColWidth(I) = TextWidth(grdData.Text) + 100
    Next I

    dtaTable.Refresh

    'Determine the number of records and set Grid size
    dtaTable.Recordset.MoveLast
    grdData.Rows = dtaTable.Recordset.RecordCount + 1

    'Fill the Grid beginning with the first record
    dtaTable.Recordset.MoveFirst
    grdData.Row = 0

    Do While Not dtaTable.Recordset.EOF
        grdData.Row = grdData.Row + 1
        For I = 0 To dtaTable.Database(TableName).Fields.Count - 1
            grdData.Col = I

            'Store blank if data field is null
            If IsNull(dtaTable.Recordset(I).Value) Then
                grdData.Text = ""
            Else
                grdData.Text = dtaTable.Recordset(I).Value
            End If

            'Ensure all the data is visible
            CellWidth = TextWidth(grdData.Text) + 100
            If CellWidth > grdData.ColWidth(I) Then
                grdData.ColWidth(I) = CellWidth
            End If
        Next I

        dtaTable.Recordset.MoveNext
    Loop

End Sub
```

Note: *This application assumes that all the records from a given table will fit into memory. Some databases have tables with hundreds of thousands of records. To make this application truly general, you would want to read in only 100 records or so at a time and then read in the next set after the user scrolled past the first 100, and so on. You might want to extend this application if you work with large databases.*

There are two things to note about the *fillGrid* procedure: To determine the number of rows the Grid should have, the procedure skips to the end of the table (the *MoveLast* method) and checks the RecordCount property of the last record. It then resizes the Grid and begins loading the data from the top of the table. When loading the database, the procedure checks for fields that have no information in them by calling the *IsNull* function. If the *IsNull* function encounters a null field, a blank space is put into the Grid. As the Grid is filled, the procedure also sets the ColWidth of each column that needs to be expanded to display all the data. To determine how wide the column should be, the procedure calls the form's *TextWidth* method. Note that calling *TextWidth* assumes that the font information for the form is the same as it is for the Grid; if this were not the case, the *TextWidth* method would return the wrong value.

After the application is complete, you can run it. Figure 11-12 shows the application after the user has opened the BIBLIO.MDB database and selected the Publishers table.

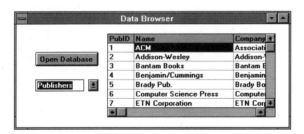

Figure 11-12.
The Grid1 Application.

12

Object Linking and Embedding

This chapter introduces the concept of object linking and embedding (OLE) and describes methods for using OLE in Visual Basic applications. The concepts and programming techniques presented in this chapter are somewhat more complex than in earlier chapters. If you are new to programming, you might want to go on to Chapter 13.

OLE in Visual Basic

In Chapter 11, you saw how Visual Basic can take advantage of data created, sorted, and maintained by a DBMS application. Although the Data control is part of Visual Basic, it relied on work done by the database management program. With OLE, you can take similar advantage of other applications.

OLE enables cooperation between Windows applications. Using OLE, your Visual Basic applications can display and control data from other applications. The means for using OLE in Visual Basic is the OLE control. It lets the user display data from another application and edit that data from within the application in which it was created. Figure 12-1 shows the OLE tool in the Visual Basic Toolbox.

> *Note:* The OLE control will not appear in the Toolbox unless you have the file MSOLE2.VBX loaded into your Project window. If you edited your AUTOLOAD.MAK file, you'll need to choose the Add File command from the Visual Basic File menu and find MSOLE2.VBX. It is installed in your Windows SYSTEM directory.

Figure 12-1.
The OLE tool.

Before you can fully understand the OLE control, you'll need to be familiar with some of the specific terms related to object linking and embedding.

Some OLE Terms

OLE object. An object is a discrete entity of data. Objects can be text, spreadsheets, a few cells in a spreadsheet, graphics, sounds, video segments, and anything else that can be displayed or controlled by an application. An OLE control can contain only one object at a time.

Linked object. The data in an OLE object can be linked to an application. When you link an object, you insert a placeholder, not the actual data, for the linked object into your application's OLE control. For example, when you link a graphic, such as a logo, into a Visual Basic application, the data associated with it is stored in another file; only a path to the actual data and an image of the data is stored in the OLE control. While using the Visual Basic application, the user can select the linked object, and the linked application starts automatically. The user can then edit the graphic using the associated application. You can set up other links with the same object, and when the graphic is changed in the source application, it will also be changed in all the applications to which it is linked.

Embedded object. The data in an OLE object can be embedded in an application. When you embed an object, you insert the actual data for the embedded object in your application's OLE control. For example, when you embed a graphic, such as a logo, into a Visual Basic application, all the data associated with it is contained in the OLE control. While using the Visual Basic application, the user can select the embedded object, and the associated application starts automatically. The user can then edit the graphic using the associated application. When the user exits the associated application, the object is automatically updated, and the new data is stored in the OLE control. Unlike a linked object, when an object is embedded in an application, no other application has access to the data in the embedded object.

Container application. A container application references objects that are created by another application. For example, a Visual Basic application that contains an embedded graphic from a drawing program is a container application.

Source application. A source application is the original application that creates an object. For example, a drawing program that creates a graphic object is a source application.

An OLE Example: Embedding an Object at Design Time

Suppose you wanted your Weasel database to play "Ride of the Valkyries" every time you started it up. Because Visual Basic has no sound capabilities beyond that of the

Beep command, you might expect to have to learn the direct Windows calls and create DLL declarations the way you did for the Profile functions in Chapter 9. But why should you have to bother learning all that when there is an application that can produce the sound you want? The Windows Sound Recorder application can play any sound stored as a WAV file. OLE comes into play here because you can embed the sound file in an OLE control. Then you can set the application so that it plays the sound when opened.

Click on the OLE tool in the Toolbox, and place the control on an empty form. As soon as you have placed the control on the form, the Insert Object dialog box appears, as shown in Figure 12-2. The contents of the dialog box will vary from system to system, depending on which applications you own and which support OLE.

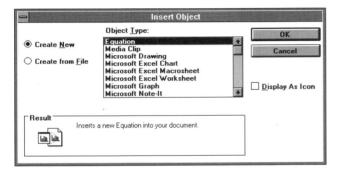

Figure 12-2.
The Insert Object dialog box.

Scroll through the list box until you find the Sound entry. Select it and click the OK button. An icon representing the Sound Recorder will appear in the OLE control area, and the Windows Sound Recorder application will be started and brought to the foreground, as illustrated in Figure 12-3.

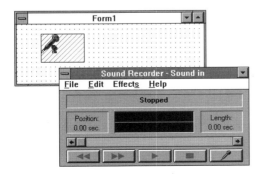

Figure 12-3.
An OLE control and the Sound Recorder application.

In the Sound Recorder, choose the Insert File command from the Edit menu. You will be prompted with an Insert File dialog box from which to select a sound file. Because you probably don't have a recording of "Ride of the Valkyries" on your system and I can't distribute mine, you'll have to make do with one of the Windows system sounds for now. Select CHIMES.WAV from your Windows directory. The sound will be loaded into the Recorder; you can play it back if you want to hear what it sounds like first. Next choose Exit from the File menu. The Sound Recorder will ask whether you want to update the embedded object before exiting. Click on Yes.

Select the OLE control on your form, and then switch to the Properties window and set the Visible property to False. Because we want the sound to play at startup, you don't need to display the OLE control. Double-click on the form to display the code window. Define the constant in the declarations section as shown below:

```
Const OLE_ACTIVATE = 7
```

Finally, set the form's Load procedure to the following routine so that the sound plays when the application is opened:

```
Sub Form_Load ()
    OLE1.Action = OLE_ACTIVATE
End Sub
```

Press F5 to start the application. When the form appears, you should also hear the chimes sound, compliments of the Sound Recorder application.

Linking vs. Embedding

You just created an embedded object; that is, a copy of the sound data is stored directly in your application. You also could have linked the sound file, in which case a pointer to the data (in this case, the CHIMES.WAV file) would have been stored instead of the actual data. Figure 12-4, on the next page, illustrates the difference between linking and embedding.

Object linking's main advantage is that it takes up far less space because only one instance of the data exists. It has the disadvantage of potentially losing the link if the original copy of the data is lost or moved or if the application is run on another computer. With object embedding, you never have to worry about losing the data, but some objects might take up a lot of space. Just 10 seconds of sampled sound can run over 100 KB, depending on the desired quality.

Clearly, linking is the best choice when it is safe. If you are linking to objects on a network server or running an application that will always reside on your computer, you can stick with linking. However, if you are going to distribute the application or if the source might be modified and you want to keep the original data, you should embed objects. In our Chimes example, we embedded the sound, which means that you could distribute this application without having to include a separate WAV file.

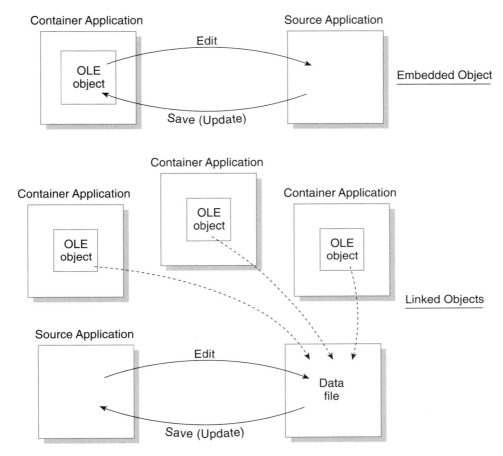

Figure 12-4.
Embedded and linked objects.

What Is Available for Linking and Embedding?

Whenever you install an application in Microsoft Windows, an entry will be added to the OLE registry if that application supports OLE. When you want to create an OLE control, you can see a list of supported objects in the Insert Object dialog box. Depending on the applications you own, you might be able to include formatted text, charts, spreadsheets, video clips, and more in your Visual Basic applications.

The next example application makes use of Microsoft Graph, a small utility that is shipped with a number of Microsoft programs, including Microsoft Word for Windows and Microsoft Access. If you do not have Graph on your system, try to adapt the example that follows to one of the objects your environment supports.

An OLE Example: Manipulating the OLE Control at Runtime

In the first example, you used OLE to embed a specific object at design time. OLE can also be controlled programmatically so that the user of your application can specify the object to link or embed. In this example, you'll tie the OLE control to the Graph application without embedding any data and present the user of the application with various choices on how to deal with the information.

The OLE control operates similarly to the Common Dialog control in that setting its Action property to certain values causes associated operations to be performed. For example, setting the Action property to OLE_INSERT_OBJ_DLG (which has the value 14) would display (at runtime) the Insert Object dialog box you saw when creating the OLE object (at design time) in the previous example. In this example, however, you won't allow any object to be inserted except objects created by the Graph application.

Open a new Visual Basic project. Select the OLE control, and draw a fairly large box on the empty form. When the OLE Insert Object dialog box appears, click on the Cancel button. The OLE control will be empty of any data when the application is run. Add a command button, a frame with two option buttons inside, a combo box, and a Common Dialog control, as shown in Figure 12-5. Then set the properties of the controls as shown in Figure 12-6.

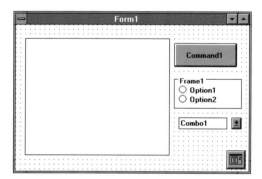

Figure 12-5.
The OLEGRAPH Form.

The first thing you need is the definition of the constants that are associated with the OLE control. You can enter the definitions as shown in Figure 12-7 or paste them in from the CONSTANTS.TXT file. (Note that in the CONSTANTS.TXT file, they are defined as global. The keyword *Global* has been edited out here.)

Control	Property	Value
Form1	Caption	OLE Graph
	Name	OLEGraph
OLE1	AutoActivate	0 - Manual
	SizeMode	1 - Stretch
Command1	Caption	Insert Graph
	Name	cmdInsert
Frame1	Caption	[none]
Option1	Caption	Linked
	Name	optLinked
Option2	Caption	Embedded
	Name	optEmbed
	Value	True
Combo1	Name	cboVerbs
	Text	[none]
ComDlg1	Name	dlog

Figure 12-6.
The property settings for the OLEGRAPH application.

```
'OLE Control
'Actions
Const OLE_CREATE_EMBED = 0
Const OLE_CREATE_LINK = 1
Const OLE_COPY = 4
Const OLE_PASTE = 5
Const OLE_UPDATE = 6
Const OLE_ACTIVATE = 7
Const OLE_CLOSE = 9
Const OLE_DELETE = 10
Const OLE_SAVE_TO_FILE = 11
Const OLE_READ_FROM_FILE = 12
Const OLE_INSERT_OBJ_DLG = 14
Const OLE_PASTE_SPECIAL_DLG = 15
Const OLE_FETCH_VERBS = 17
Const OLE_SAVE_TO_OLE1FILE = 18

'OLEType
Const OLE_LINKED = 0
Const OLE_EMBEDDED = 1
Const OLE_NONE = 3
```

Figure 12-7.
Defining the constants for the OLEGRAPH application.

(continued)

Figure 12-7. *continued*

```
'OLETypeAllowed
Const OLE_EITHER = 2

'UpdateOptions
Const OLE_AUTOMATIC = 0
Const OLE_FROZEN = 1
Const OLE_MANUAL = 2

'AutoActivate modes
Const OLE_ACTIVATE_MANUAL = 0
Const OLE_ACTIVATE_GETFOCUS = 1
Const OLE_ACTIVATE_DOUBLECLICK = 2

'SizeModes
Const OLE_SIZE_CLIP = 0
Const OLE_SIZE_STRETCH = 1
Const OLE_SIZE_AUTOSIZE = 2

'DisplayTypes
Const OLE_DISPLAY_CONTENT = 0
Const OLE_DISPLAY_ICON = 1

'Update Event Constants
Const OLE_CHANGED = 0
Const OLE_SAVED = 1
Const OLE_CLOSED = 2
Const OLE_RENAMED = 3

'Special Verb Values
Const VERB_PRIMARY = 0
Const VERB_SHOW = -1
Const VERB_OPEN = -2
Const VERB_HIDE = -3

'VerbFlag Bit Masks
Const VERBFLAG_GRAYED = &H1
Const VERBFLAG_DISABLED = &H2
Const VERBFLAG_CHECKED = &H8
Const VERBFLAG_SEPARATOR = &H800
```

When the application runs, the user will be allowed to insert a new object into the space provided. The object can be linked or embedded, depending on the setting of the Option buttons. The source code for creating the object is in the *Click* procedure of the cmdInsert control, as shown in Figure 12-8.

```
Sub cmdInsert_Click ()
    OLE1.Class = "MSGraph"        'Application to invoke
    If optLinked.Value Then       'Linked button selected
        'Graph uses Excel chart files; find one to link to
        dlog.Filter = "Chart(*.XLC)|*.XLC|Any file(*.*)|*.*"
        dlog.FilterIndex = 1
        dlog.Action = 1
        If dlog.Filename = "" Then
            MsgBox "No file selected"
            Exit Sub
        End If
        'Create OLE link
        OLE1.SourceDoc = dlog.Filename
        OLE1.Action = OLE_CREATE_LINK
    Else                          'Embedded button selected
        OLE1.Action = OLE_CREATE_EMBED
    End If
    'Do the OLE stuff
    OLE1.Action = OLE_ACTIVATE
    'Create list of operations
    AddVerbs
End Sub
```

Figure 12-8.
The cmdInsert_Click *procedure for the OLEGRAPH application.*

The final action performed by the procedure above is to call the *AddVerbs* sub-program. This routine will create a list of all the actions supported by the object just inserted. The names of the verbs will be placed in the combo box. The code for AddVerbs is as follows:

```
Sub AddVerbs ()
    Dim I As Integer

    'Query the ObjectVerbs array to find all the actions
    'supported by this object and place them in the combo box
    cboVerbs.Clear
    cboVerbs.AddItem "(no op)"
    For I = 1 To OLE1.ObjectVerbsCount - 1
        cboVerbs.AddItem OLE1.ObjectVerbs(I)
    Next I
    cboVerbs.ListIndex = 0
End Sub
```

After the combo box has been loaded with the object's verb names (plus a special no-operation entry), you'll need to define the combo box's Click routine as follows to invoke any action selected by the user.

```
Sub cboVerbs_Click ()
    If cboVerbs.ListIndex > 0 Then
        OLE1.Verb = cboVerbs.ListIndex
        OLE1.Action = OLE_ACTIVATE
    End If
End Sub
```

You need to code one more routine that will save the data that the user loads into the OLE object. When you create an object at design time, all the OLE data is stored in your Visual Basic form. When the object is created at runtime, however, you must save the data to a binary file. Just as any text entered into a text box would be lost if not squirreled away somewhere, the same is true of the OLE data. The OLE control contains data for both linked and embedded styles of the control. Although it is obvious that the embedded style would have data, the linked style does as well, but it has less. The linked style must store the name of the linked document and the type of the information.

To save the data that is stored in an OLE control, you must create a module-level variable and write two small subprograms, as follows:

```
Dim NeedToWrite As Integer

Sub OLE1_Updated (Code As Integer)
    NeedToWrite = True
End Sub

Sub Form_Unload (Cancel As Integer)
    Dim FileNum As Integer

    If Not NeedToWrite Then ExitSub
    FileNum = FreeFile
    Open "OLEGRAPH.DAT" For Binary As #FileNum
    OLE1.FileNumber = FileNum
    OLE1.Action = OLE_SAVE_TO_FILE
    Close #FileNum
End Sub
```

This brings up another point before you finish. If you saved the OLE data on exit, you'll need to load it up again when you next start the application. Here's the final routine for loading the OLE data. It must check to see whether the file exists before it attempts to load the data; if the file didn't exist, an error would result.

```
Sub Form_Load ()
    Dim FileNum As Integer

    If Dir$("OLEGRAPH.DAT") = "" Then Exit Sub
    FileNum = FreeFile
    Open "OLEGRAPH.DAT" For Binary As #FileNum
    OLE1.FileNumber = FileNum
    OLE1.Action = OLE_READ_FROM_FILE
    Close #FileNum
End Sub
```

After the OLE data is loaded or saved, the file is positioned immediately after the data. It would be possible, therefore, to load and save several OLE objects in a row as long as you maintained the same order when loading and saving. Figure 12-9 shows the application being run.

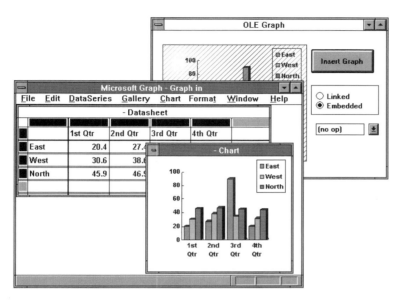

Figure 12-9.
The OLEGRAPH application.

Direct Object Control

In Chapter 11, you were able to get information about a database and control access to the database via a number of special objects such as the TableDef object and the Database object. The latest version of OLE supports the ability of any application to define objects and object protocols that can be manipulated outside of the application.

For example, a word processor might provide access to its spelling checker as an object, and you could, from Visual Basic, spell-check the text that a user entered in a text box. The user would never see the word processor application because access to its objects would be completely programmatic. This feature, called *OLE Automation,* is supported by Visual Basic. However, at the time of this writing, this capability is so new that very few applications support OLE Automation.

Every Object Is Different

Programming using OLE Automation is very much like communicating with the objects in the Data control. Each application supporting OLE Automation will expose some of its capabilities in the form of objects. To get access to the objects in Visual

Basic, you call the *CreateObject* function, passing the name of the object type as a string parameter. The documentation for each application that supports OLE Automation will list the names of objects that can be created.

Once you have created the object, you communicate with it via the methods that are appropriate for that particular object. Because each application supports different features, there is no common set of methods, no strictly defined syntax that I can pass on to you at this point. I'm afraid that sounds rather nebulous, and in fact it is, but there's not much else I can say in general about OLE Automation. It is so open-ended because it is essentially unlimited. Every application designer can create new objects, from spreadsheet cells to spelling checkers, from charts to CAD layers. You choose the ones that will enhance your application and make use of them.

An OLE Automation Example: The Calculator Application

To illustrate the basic capabilities of OLE Automation, the Visual Basic programming team included a special application that supports OLE Automation. Because I can't provide general information about OLE Automation, we'll make use of this specific demo application in this section. The demo is called DISPCALC, and, when run on its own, it operates as a simple hand calculator. DISPCALC can also be controlled programmatically via OLE Automation. It exports a number of objects and actions that can be manipulated by Visual Basic. The calculator performs the actions specified by Visual Basic.

The program you will write uses DISPCALC to multiply 19 by 57. Admittedly, this is something that could be done without resorting to OLE, but it will illustrate the basic principles. The first step is to check out the documentation for the objects supported by DISPCALC. It tells us, among other things, that DISPCALC must be registered with the system before use and that the application supports an object called *dispcalc.ccalc*. This object has the following properties and methods:

Property or Method	Explanation
Accum	The calculator's accumulator
Opnd	The calculator's operand
Op	A code indication of the operation the calculator is to perform
Eval	A method that performs the operation selected by Op
Display	A method that shows the result of the calculation on the screen of the calculator

To register the application, open the Windows File Manager to the Visual Basic directory. Double-click on the filename DISPCALC.REG. This will add an entry in the Windows OLE registry for the DISPCALC application. Most applications register themselves with Windows as part of their setup or installation processing. However, because DISPCALC is just a simple demo, it requires manual registration.

Create a new project and add a single command button to the form. For an application this simple, that's all you need. Note that you do not need an OLE control to use OLE Automation. The OLE control is for linked or embedded objects only.

Open a code window and enter the following text in the form's general declarations section:

```
Const OP_PLUS = 1
Const OP_MINUS = 2
Const OP_TIMES = 3
Const OP_DIVIDE = 4

Dim Calc As Object
```

The constants are the application-specific codes that can be assigned to the Op property. The variable *Calc* will hold the object once it has been created. Now enter the following routine as the Command button's *Click* procedure:

```
Sub Command1_Click ()
    Set Calc = CreateObject("dispcalc.ccalc")
    Calc.Accum = 19
    Calc.Opnd = 57
    Calc.Op = OP_TIMES
    Calc.Eval
    MsgBox "Calculations indicate that 19 * 57 is" + Str$(Calc.Accum)
    Calc.Quit
End Sub
```

Please note that in the line where the object is created, the Set statement is used to assign the object to the variable *Calc*. The Set kind of assignment should be used with all objects, including Visual Basic objects such as forms or controls. Normal assignment works by copying; that is, if you have a variable *A* to which you assign the string "Beethoven" and then you issue the statement *B = A*, both variables *A* and *B* have separate copies of the string, and if you modify one, the other is unchanged. The Set kind of assignment merely creates a *reference* to the thing being assigned so that if you execute *Set A = MyForm*, *A* refers only to the form object *MyForm*, and if you subsequently execute *B = A*, the *B* variable also points to the same form and any changes made to the form are visible through either variable.

In the program above, therefore, the first line tells Windows to find the application that can create a *dispcalc.ccalc* object and to create the object. A reference to that object is then stored in the Visual Basic variable *Calc*. The program sets the Accum, Opnd, and Op properties, calls the method *Eval*, and displays the resulting value of the Accum property. The *Quit* method effectively destroys the object.

Press F5 to run your program. When you click on the Command button, the DISPCALC application is called. Notice that it is actually displayed on the screen. This is not typical of most OLE Automation applications, but it is done here to illustrate the effects of OLE programming. If you look closely at the calculator display before you dismiss the message box, you will see that the display reads 0 even though the accumulator value returned the correct result. This is because the calculator's readout is controlled by the *Display* method, which was not called. Exit your program and edit the *Click* procedure to read as follows:

```
Sub Command1_Click ()
    Set Calc = CreateObject("dispcalc.ccalc")
    Calc.Accum = 19
    Calc.Opnd = 57
    Calc.Op = OP_TIMES
    Calc.Eval
    Calc.Display          'Update the readout
    MsgBox "Calculations indicate that 19 * 57 is" + Str$(Calc.Accum)
    Calc.Quit
End Sub
```

Now, when you run your program, the calculator's readout will match the result that was returned by the accumulator, as shown in Figure 12-10.

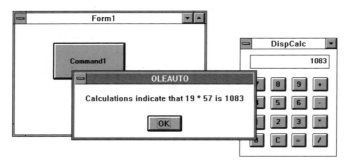

Figure 12-10.
Controlling the DISPCALC application with OLE Automation.

A Note About DDE

If you like the idea of making other programs work for you and aren't afraid of some more complicated programming, you might want to investigate Dynamic Data Exchange (DDE). DDE allows you to send and receive messages from other applications. For example, most setup programs use DDE to tell the Windows Program Manager to create new program groups and icon entries.

Microsoft Word and Microsoft Excel can create DDE links to your Visual Basic programs, and you can pass information through the links. DDE programming is not simple—typically you must program both sides of the conversation. For example, you'd need to program a WordBasic macro to open a link to your application and request data, and you'd also need to program your Visual Basic application to field the request and send the requested information. Consult the reference manuals for your applications to see what DDE facilities they support.

13

A Complete Application for Windows

You've climbed the mountains and braved the stormy seas—or, at least, you've learned enough about Visual Basic to solve some of your programming problems. But before you relax and call out, "The sun's over the yardarm. Fetch the cooking sherry," as San Francisco columnist Stanton Delaplane was wont to do, you should try your hand at putting it all together.

This chapter helps you build an application that includes many of the features and capabilities that have been discussed in the previous chapters: multiple forms, controls, files, menus, and even some graphics. You will also need the *GetIni* and *SetIni* procedures developed in Chapter 9.

General Design

To describe it simply, this application, which we'll call Project Timer, is a project accounting program. Here's how it works: While you are working at your computer, you tell the program which project you are working on. When you switch to another project, go to lunch, or finish your work at the end of the day, just let the program know. At the end of the week (or month), the program can display an accounting of all your time. You can set up Windows to load the program automatically when you start Windows.

All the data for your project times will be stored in a file and can be cumulatively updated. Statistics derived from the data can be either displayed on the screen or printed on paper. The name of the project file will be stored in an initialization variable in your WIN.INI file so that you won't have to specify the project file each time you run the application.

Figure 13-1 presents the general plan of action for the initial processing. After initialization, the program is controlled by user actions: choosing an item from a menu, clicking on a button, exiting the program. In Figure 13-2, a set of actions is defined for each of two of these possible events.

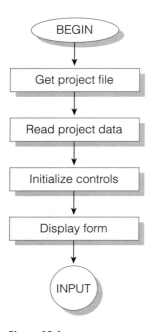

Figure 13-1.
A plan for initial processing in the Project Timer application.

You'll find that sketching such diagrams before designing a program is extremely useful, even when the task boxes are fairly high-level (that is, nondetailed), as they are in Figures 13-1 and 13-2. Putting a plan on paper helps to crystallize vague ideas into specific steps. It is also easier to identify areas that are missing or incomplete, and you can often find common processes that are good candidates for sharing code. If your design is sufficiently high-level, you can implement each box as a do-nothing procedure and then implement the details after the main program structure has been defined, as you'll be doing in this chapter.

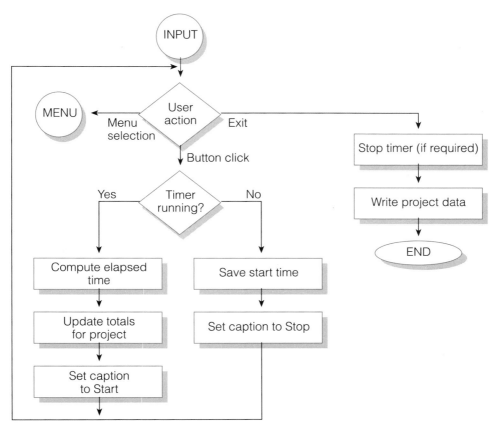

Figure 13-2.
A plan for the most-used portion of the Project Timer application.

Menu Design

Let's start the implementation by programming the menu system. You'll need two menus, which we'll call File and Project, to give the user basic control over the application. On the File menu, the item New allows a new project file to be created, and Open lets the user open an existing file. The Print command on the File menu writes the current statistics to the printer, and the Exit command ends the program. The Project menu lets the user work with the currently open project file to add or remove projects, to zero the project time counts, and to show all the projects' statistics. Figure 13-3 on the following page sketches the processing that some of these commands will perform.

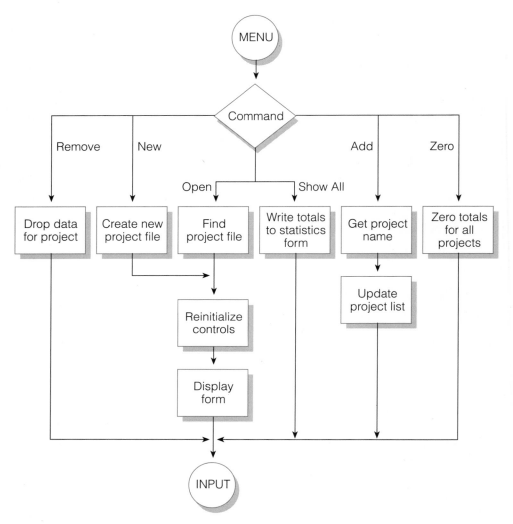

Figure 13-3.
A plan for menu options in the Project Timer application.

By working out the overall structure of your program before you begin writing code, you can often save yourself time by noting which procedures can be used more than once. For example, note that a box labeled *Reinitialize controls* appears in Figure 13-3 and that a similar box labeled *Initialize controls* appears in Figure 13-1. Because you now know that similar processing occurs in both cases, you can write a single procedure instead of two separate procedures.

Begin by starting a new project in Visual Basic and opening the Menu Design window. Figure 13-4 shows the menu design hierarchy after all the captions have been entered. Note that hyphens are added to the hierarchy list to create separator bars on the File menu. In the Name text box of the Menu Design window, type the name of each menu item as indicated in Figure 13-5.

Figure 13-4.
The menu design hierarchy for the Project Timer application.

Caption	Name
&File	mnuFile
&New	mnuFilNew
&Open	mnuFilOpen
-	mnuNULL1
&Print	mnuFilPrint
-	mnuNULL2
E&xit	mnuFilExit
&Project	mnuProject
&Add	mnuProAdd
&Remove	mnuProRemove
&Zero	mnuProZero
&Show All	mnuProShowAll

Figure 13-5.
Menu item names for the Project Timer application.

Form Design

The main form for the application is relatively simple. As shown in Figure 13-6, it contains 10 label controls, a combo box, a picture box control, a timer, a common dialog control, and a command button. After you've completed the initial layout, set the properties of the form and the controls as listed in Figure 13-7.

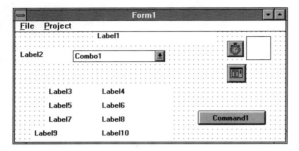

Figure 13-6.
The initial design for the main form of the Project Timer application.

Object	Property	Setting
Form1	BorderStyle	3 - Fixed Double
	Caption	Project Timer
	Name	TimerMain
Label1	Caption	[none]
	Name	lblDateTime
Label2	Alignment	1 - Right Justify
	Caption	Project:
Combo1	Name	cboProjectList
	Style	2 - Dropdown List
Label3	Alignment	1 - Right Justify
	Caption	Start:
Label4	BorderStyle	1 - Fixed Single
	Caption	[none]
	Name	lblStart
Label5	Alignment	1 - Right Justify
	Caption	End:
Label6	BorderStyle	1 - Fixed Single
	Caption	[none]
	Name	lblEnd

Figure 13-7.
Property settings for the Project Timer application.

(continued)

Figure 13-7. *continued*

Object	Property	Setting
Label7	Alignment	1 - Right Justify
	Caption	Elapsed:
Label8	BorderStyle	1 - Fixed Single
	Caption	[none]
	Name	lblElapsed
Label9	Alignment	1 - Right Justify
	Caption	Total for project:
Label10	BorderStyle	1 - Fixed Single
	Caption	[none]
	Name	lblTotalTime
Picture1	Name	picStatus
	ScaleHeight	−2
	ScaleLeft	−1
	ScaleMode	0 - User
	ScaleTop	1
	ScaleWidth	2
Command1	Caption	Start
	Name	btnControl
Timer1	Name	tmrTick
CMDialog1	Name	Dlog

After you have set the properties, your form should resemble the one shown in Figure 13-8.

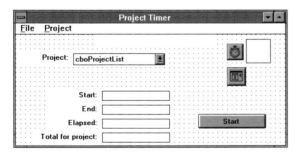

Figure 13-8.
The completed design for the main form of the Project Timer application.

The user will be able to select a project from the drop-down list in the Project combo box. The calculations of starting time, ending time, and elapsed time will be similar to those used in the Stopwatch application from Chapter 1. A single command button will both start and stop the timing, and the button's caption will change as appropriate. Finally, the timer control and the picture box will help to jazz up the application a bit.

Global Declarations

Choose the New Module command from Visual Basic's File menu, and add the code shown in Figure 13-9 to the module. This code module contains the global declarations and routines that are shared by the multiple forms that will eventually make up the application.

```
Global Const PI = 3.1415926
Global Const WIN_ICONIZED = 1

'MsgBox parameters
Global Const MB_OK = 0                    'OK button only
Global Const MB_OKCANCEL = 1              'OK and Cancel buttons
Global Const MB_ABORTRETRYIGNORE = 2      'Abort, Retry, and Ignore buttons
Global Const MB_YESNOCANCEL = 3           'Yes, No, and Cancel buttons
Global Const MB_YESNO = 4                 'Yes and No buttons
Global Const MB_RETRYCANCEL = 5           'Retry and Cancel buttons
Global Const MB_ICONSTOP = 16             'Critical message

'MsgBox return values
Global Const IDOK = 1                     'OK button pressed
Global Const IDCANCEL = 2                 'Cancel button pressed
Global Const IDABORT = 3                  'Abort button pressed
Global Const IDRETRY = 4                  'Retry button pressed
Global Const IDIGNORE = 5                 'Ignore button pressed
Global Const IDYES = 6                    'Yes button pressed
Global Const IDNO = 7                     'No button pressed

'Application-specific types
Type ProjRec
    Name As String * 30
    TotalTime As Double
End Type

Global Const PROJ_REC_SIZE = 38

'Application globals
Global ProjectList() As ProjRec           'Array of project information
Global NumProjects As Integer             'Number of projects
Global ProjectFileName As String          'Project data file
Global CRLF As String                     'Multicharacter constant

Global TimerRunning As Integer            'Timer status
Global StartTime As Double, EndTime As Double
Global SumProjectTime As Double
```

Figure 13-9.
Global declarations for the Project Timer application.

The constants that control the *MsgBox* function come from the CONSTANT.TXT file. ProjRec is the type definition for a project record, which includes a name and the amount of time recorded for each project. The constant PROJ_REC_SIZE defines the number of bytes in each project record.

Finally the code declares the variables that will be used by the program. *ProjectList* is a dynamic array that will contain the project records. *NumProjects* will hold the number of projects that the application is currently tracking. *CRLF* will be used as a string constant that will store the carriage return/linefeed characters. *TimerRunning* will contain a Boolean value indicating whether or not the program is currently timing a project. *StartTime* and *EndTime* will hold the current timer values, and the variable *SumProjectTime* will contain the cumulative sum of all the time charged to all of the projects.

Ancillary Forms

This application requires two additional forms, both very simple. The first, named the Query form, serves as an alternative to the *InputBox* function, which tends to create rather ungainly dialog boxes. The Query form must be large enough to contain a simple prompt (in a label) and a simple response (in a text box).

Create this form by choosing the New Form command from Visual Basic's File menu or by clicking on the New Form button on the Toolbar. Draw the label, the text box, and two command buttons, and set the properties of the form and the objects as indicated in Figure 13-10. Figure 13-11 on the next page shows the completed form.

Object	Property	Setting
Form2	BorderStyle	1 - Fixed Single
	Caption	Project
	ControlBox	False
	Name	Query
Label1	Caption	[none]
	Name	lblQuery
Text1	Name	txtQuery
	Text	[none]
Command1	Caption	OK
	Default	True
	Name	btnOK
Command2	Cancel	True
	Caption	Cancel
	Name	btnCancel

Figure 13-10.
Property settings for the Query form and its controls.

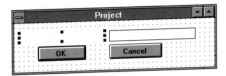

Figure 13-11.
The completed design for the Query form.

To control this form, you must write a function procedure that displays the form and returns whatever information the user types in. To be accessible to the entire application, this function must be in a module; place it in the code module that contains the global constants:

```
Function QueryText (S As String) As String
    Query.lblQuery.Caption = S
    Query.txtQuery.Text = ""
    Query.Show 1
    QueryText = Query.txtQuery.Text
End Function
```

This function accepts a string parameter, which it places in the Query form's label. It then clears the form's text box and displays the form using the *Show* method. The parameter 1 indicates that the *Show* method will display the form modally—that is, the *QueryText* function will be suspended until the user closes the Query form. When the Query form has been closed, the function returns any text that the user entered in the text box.

Although this function is sufficient for displaying the form and returning a value, the form itself must handle the OK and Cancel buttons. Double-click on the OK button and add this procedure:

```
Sub btnOK_Click ()
    Hide
End Sub
```

When the user clicks on the OK button, the *Hide* method closes the Query form, and control is returned to the *QueryText* function. A similar procedure is needed for the Cancel button:

```
Sub btnCancel_Click ()
    txtQuery.Text = ""
    Hide
End Sub
```

The code for the Cancel button takes the additional step of clearing the contents of the text box. This ensures that the *QueryText* function will always return an empty string when the Cancel button is clicked. (Note that this implementation does not distinguish between the case in which the user fails to enter text but clicks on OK and the case in which the user might or might not enter any text and then clicks on Cancel.)

The second ancillary form, named ProjStat, provides a place to display the statistics for all projects. Its only control is a single text box. The properties of the form and the text box should be set as shown in Figure 13-12. The completed form is illustrated in Figure 13-13.

Object	Property	Setting
Form3	Caption	Project Timer Statistics
	Name	ProjStat
Text1	MultiLine	True
	Name	txtStats
	ScrollBars	2 - Vertical
	Text	[none]

Figure 13-12.
Property settings for the ProjStat form and its control.

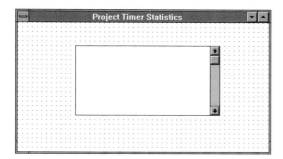

Figure 13-13.
The completed design for the ProjStat form.

The ProjStat form is not modal—that is, the user can switch back to the main form without closing the statistics window—and therefore does not require a special control routine. You can, however, define a routine that makes it easier for the program to put data in the text box. This procedure, which is placed in the code module, allows the program to send lines to the text box one at a time instead of having to send all the information at once:

```
Sub AddStatLine (L As String)
    ProjStat.txtStats.Text = ProjStat.txtStats.Text + L + CRLF
End Sub
```

The *AddStatLine* procedure appends a line of text to the existing text in the text box and then adds a carriage return/linefeed to advance to the next line.

To improve the appearance of this form, you can ensure that the text box is always the same size as the form, with no unused space. Double-click on the form to bring up its code window, and enter this *Resize* event procedure:

```
Sub Form_Resize ()
    txtStats.Left = ScaleLeft
    txtStats.Top = ScaleTop
    txtStats.Width = ScaleWidth
    txtStats.Height = ScaleHeight
End Sub
```

Whenever the form is resized (including the first time it is displayed), this procedure sets the size of the text box to match the internal dimensions of the form.

The *Main* Procedure

In a project that contains many forms or in a project in which initialization must occur before the form is displayed, it's often useful to have your Visual Basic program start by executing a specific procedure instead of simply displaying the first form. If you choose this route, you must give the procedure the name *Main* and place it in a module file. Open the window for your code module, and enter this procedure:

```
Sub Main ()
    CRLF = Chr$(13) + Chr$(10)
    ProjectFileName = FindProjFile()
    InitProject
End Sub
```

In this case, the *Main* procedure initializes the *CRLF* string variable, calls a function to find the project data file, and then continues with the procedure *InitProject* (which you haven't written yet). Remember the flow diagrams in Figures 13-1 and 13-3? They showed that this initialization would be common to the New and Open menu selections as well as to the main startup code, so you'll want to be able to access the initialization code from all three locations—hence the call to a separate initialization procedure.

You will also need to instruct Visual Basic to start the application by executing the *Main* procedure. Choose the Project command from the Options menu, and set the Start Up Form option to Sub Main.

Event Structure

The program code shown in Figure 13-14 implements the basic functions for each user event that can occur within the main form. This code implements the events as high-level procedure calls, with the detailed work saved for later.

298

```
Sub btnControl_Click ()
    If TimerRunning Then
        StopTimer
    Else
        StartTimer
    End If
End Sub

Sub Form_Load ()
    Dim I As Integer

    'Load list box with project names
    For I = 0 To NumProjects - 1
        cboProjectList.AddItem RTrim$(ProjectList(I).Name)
        cboProjectList.ItemData(cboProjectList.NewIndex) = I
    Next I
    cboProjectList.Enabled = True
End Sub

Sub Form_Unload (Cancel As Integer)
    If TimerRunning Then StopTimer
    Unload Query
    Unload ProjStat
    WriteProjFile ProjectFileName
End Sub

Sub mnuFilExit_Click ()
    Unload TimerMain
    End
End Sub

Sub mnuFilNew_Click ()
    Unload TimerMain
    ProjectFileName = NewProjFile()
    InitProject
End Sub

Sub mnuFilOpen_Click ()
    Unload TimerMain
    ProjectFileName = FindProjFile()
    InitProject
End Sub

Sub mnuFilPrint_Click ()
    ShowStatistics True
End Sub
```

Figure 13-14.   *(continued)*
Event procedures for the Project Timer application.

Figure 13-14. *continued*

```
Sub mnuProAdd_Click ()
    Dim NewName As String

    NewName = QueryText("Project name:")
    If NewName <> "" Then AddProject NewName
End Sub

Sub mnuProRemove_Click ()
    If cboProjectList.Text <> "" Then RemoveProject
End Sub

Sub mnuProShowAll_Click ()
    ShowStatistics False
End Sub

Sub mnuProZero_Click ()
    ZeroProjectTotals
End Sub

Sub cboProjectList_Click ()
    lblStart.Caption = ""
    lblEnd.Caption = ""
    lblElapsed.Caption = ""
    lblTotalTime.Caption = TimeStr(ProjectList(cboProjectList.ItemData
    (cboProjectList.ListIndex)).TotalTime)
End Sub
```

Note the use of the *Form_Load* and *Form_Unload* event procedures in Figure 13-14. In this program, the *Main* procedure receives initial control, and no form is loaded automatically. The *Form_Load* procedure can therefore serve as the initialization procedure for the list box, and *Form_Unload* is used to ensure that all the current data is written to disk.

The task remaining is to define the procedures that implement all the details of the program. These procedures can be divided into two groups: the ones that deal primarily with the main form and the ones that deal primarily with data handling. The procedures that interact with the main form, which are shown in Figure 13-15, should be entered in the general section of the form's code.

```
Sub AddProject (ProjName As String)
    'Add name to list box
    cboProjectList.AddItem ProjName
    cboProjectList.ItemData(cboProjectList.NewIndex) = NumProjects
```

Figure 13-15.   *(continued)*
General procedures for the main form of the Project Timer application.

Figure 13-15. *continued*

```
        'Add record to project totals
        ProjectList(NumProjects).Name = ProjName
        ProjectList(NumProjects).TotalTime = 0
        NumProjects = NumProjects + 1
        'Select new project
        cboProjectList.ListIndex = cboProjectList.NewIndex
    End Sub

    Sub RemoveProject ()
        Dim Answer As Integer

        Answer = MsgBox("Remove project " + cboProjectList.Text + "?",
        MB_YESNO, "Project")
        If Answer = IDYES Then
            cboProjectList.RemoveItem cboProjectList.ListIndex
        End If
    End Sub

    Sub StartTimer ()
        If cboProjectList.Text = "" Then
            MsgBox "No project selected", MB_ICONSTOP
            Exit Sub
        End If
        StartTime = Now
        TimerRunning = True
        'Update display information
        Caption = "Project Timer (running)"
        btnControl.Caption = "Stop"
        lblStart.Caption = TimeStr(StartTime)
        lblEnd.Caption = "-running-"
        lblElapsed.Caption = ""
        'Disable form objects
        cboProjectList.Enabled = False
        mnuFile.Enabled = False
        mnuProject.Enabled = False
    End Sub

    Sub StopTimer ()
        Dim ElapsedTime As Double

        EndTime = Now
        TimerRunning = False
        'Update display information
        Caption = "Project Timer"
        btnControl.Caption = "Start"
        lblEnd.Caption = TimeStr(EndTime)
        ElapsedTime = EndTime - StartTime
        lblElapsed.Caption = TimeStr(ElapsedTime)
```

(continued)

Figure 13-15. *continued*

```
    'Update data structures
    ProjectList(cboProjectList.ListIndex).TotalTime =
     ProjectList(cboProjectList.ListIndex).TotalTime + ElapsedTime
    lblTotalTime.Caption =
     TimeStr(ProjectList(cboProjectList.ListIndex).TotalTime)
    SumProjectTime = SumProjectTime + ElapsedTime
    'Enable form objects
    cboProjectList.Enabled = True
    mnuFile.Enabled = True
    mnuProject.Enabled = True
End Sub

Sub ZeroProjectTotals ()
    Dim Answer As Integer, I As Integer

    Answer = MsgBox("Zero all project totals?", MB_OKCANCEL, "Project")
    If Answer = IDOK Then
        For I = 0 To NumProjects - 1
            ProjectList(I).TotalTime = 0
        Next I
        SumProjectTime = 0
        cboProjectList_Click
    End If
End Sub
```

In Figure 13-16, you'll find the final routines necessary to make the application work. Place them in the code module that contains the *Main* procedure.

```
Function FindProjFile () As String
    Dim F As String, Answer As Integer

    F = GetIni("Project Timer", "Projects")
    If F = "" Then
        Answer = MsgBox("No project file specified. Create one?",
         MB_OKCANCEL, "Projects")
        'Can't continue without project file
        If Answer <> IDOK Then End
        F = NewProjFile()
    Else
        If Dir$(F) = "" Then
            Answer = MsgBox("Can't find " + F, MB_OK, "Projects")
            F = NewProjFile()
```

Figure 13-16. *(continued)*
General procedures for data handling in the Project Timer application.

Figure 13-16. *continued*

```
        End If
    End If
    FindProjFile = F
End Function

Sub InitProject ()
    ReadProjFile ProjectFileName
    TimerRunning = False
    Load TimerMain
    TimerMain.Show
End Sub

Function NewProjFile () As String
    Dim F As String

    TimerMain.Dlog.DialogTitle = "New Project File"
    TimerMain.Dlog.CancelError = True
    TimerMain.Dlog.DefaultExt = "DAT"      'Append .DAT by default
    TimerMain.Dlog.FileName = "PROJ.DAT" 'Start with this filename
    TimerMain.Dlog.Filter = "Data file (*.DAT)|*.DAT|Any file (*.*)|*.*"
    TimerMain.Dlog.FilterIndex = 1         'Start with .DAT filter
    TimerMain.Dlog.Flags = OFN_OVERWRITEPROMPT Or OFN_PATHMUSTEXIST
    On Error GoTo ErrTrap                  'Handle CANCEL
    TimerMain.Dlog.Action = 2             'Display the dialog
    On Error GoTo 0                        'Restore standard error handler
    F = TimerMain.Dlog.FileName
    SetIni "Project Timer", "Projects", F
    NewProjFile = F
    Exit Function

ErrTrap:
    MsgBox "No data file selected.  Program terminated."
    End

End Functions

Sub ReadProjFile (FileName As String)
    Dim Ix As Integer

    Open FileName For Random As #1 Len = PROJ_REC_SIZE
    NumProjects = LOF(1) / PROJ_REC_SIZE
    ReDim ProjectList(NumProjects + 100) 'Allow room for expansion
    For Ix = 0 To NumProjects - 1
        Get #1, , ProjectList(Ix)
        SumProjectTime = SumProjectTime + ProjectList(Ix).TotalTime
    Next Ix
    Close #1
End Sub
```

(continued)

Figure 13-16. *continued*

```
Sub ShowStatistics (OnPaper As Integer)
    Dim I As Integer, J As Integer, LineOut As String

    Load ProjStat
    ProjStat.txtStats.Text = ""
    For I = 0 To TimerMain.cboProjectList.ListCount - 1
        J = TimerMain.cboProjectList.ItemData(I)
        LineOut = ProjectList(J).Name + " " +
         TimeStr(ProjectList(J).TotalTime)
        If OnPaper Then
            Printer.Print LineOut
        Else
            AddStatLine LineOut
        End If
    Next I
    LineOut = "Total monitored time: " + TimeStr(SumProjectTime)
    If OnPaper Then
        Printer.Print LineOut
        Printer.EndDoc
    Else
        AddStatLine LineOut
        ProjStat.Show
    End If
End Sub

Function TimeStr(ByVal T As Double) As String
    TimeStr = Format$(T, "hh:mm:ss")
End Function

Sub WriteProjFile (FileName As String)
    Dim I As Integer, J As Integer

    'Delete old file and write new data to avoid dealing
    'with blank records from projects that have been removed
    Kill FileName
    Open FileName For Random As #1 Len = PROJ_REC_SIZE
    For I = 0 To TimerMain.cboProjectList.ListCount - 1
        J = TimerMain.cboProjectList.ItemData(I)
        Put #1, , ProjectList(J)
    Next I
    Close #1
End Sub
```

Before you can run the Project Timer program, you must include the *GetIni* and *SetIni* routines that you wrote in Chapter 9. Choose Add File from Visual Basic's File menu, and load the code module in which you saved these procedures.

As you can see in the code shown in Figure 13-16, the *FindProjFile* function uses the *GetIni* function to obtain the name of your project file from WIN.INI. If *GetIni* can't find the information, *FindProjFile* calls the *NewProjFile* function, which prompts you for the name of a new project file and then calls *SetIni* to save your answer.

The *InitProject* sub procedure is called when the program begins running and is called again each time you choose either New or Open from the application's File menu. It calls the *ReadProjFile* sub procedure, which opens the project file and reads all the saved project information.

The *AddProject* sub procedure (shown in Figure 13-15) inserts a new project name in the combo box and initializes the project's name and time in the *ProjectList* array. Using the ItemData property of the combo box allows the program to link a project name with the matching information in the *ProjectList* array.

When you're finished with a particular project, the *RemoveProject* sub procedure (shown in Figure 13-15) deletes the project name from the combo box. This procedure doesn't bother to modify the contents of the *ProjectList* array because the *WriteProjFile* procedure will ignore removed projects when it saves the project information to disk.

You can display the contents of the current project file in a window by selecting Show All from the application's Project menu, or you can print the same information by selecting Print from the File menu. Because the processes are so similar, the *ShowStatistics* sub procedure handles both tasks. If the *OnPaper* parameter is True, *ShowStatistics* sends the information to the Printer object; otherwise, the procedure displays the information on the screen.

Finally, the *WriteProjFile* sub procedure saves all the project data in a fresh file, neatly avoiding the problem of dealing with the blank records that result when you remove projects from the project list. *WriteProjFile* is called by the TimerMain form's *Form_Unload* event procedure, which ensures that all your information is saved when you exit the program. In addition, the event procedures for the New and the Open commands on the File menu explicitly unload the form, thus saving the current project file before opening a new file.

Your application is now ready to run. Before you start the program, however, let's go one step further.

A Little Flash

Finally, you can add a couple of small routines that are technically unnecessary but that give the program a little "flash." With these routines, the user will see a continuously changing image in the picture box when the timer is running, providing visual feedback that the program is executing. The image will be a segment of a circle that rotates much like the sweep hand of a stopwatch.

You can use the Visual Basic timer object and have the graphic advance around the circle with every timer tick. The graphic is a "pie slice" (or should that be *pi* slice?) one-eighth the area of the circle. The variable *WhichSlice* will cycle from 0 to 7 (in reverse order) to determine which slice to paint next. Because it must retain data between calls, *WhichSlice* must be declared with the *Static* keyword, as shown in Figure 13-17.

```
Sub tmrTick_Timer ()
    If TimerRunning Then NextSlice
End Sub

Sub NextSlice ()
    Static WhichSlice As Single

    picStatus.FillColor = picStatus.BackColor
    picStatus.Circle (0, 0), 1
    picStatus.FillColor = picStatus.ForeColor
    picStatus.Circle (0, 0), 1, , PI * -(WhichSlice + .0001) / 4,
     PI * -(((WhichSlice + 1) Mod 8) + .0001) / 4
    WhichSlice = WhichSlice - 1
    If WhichSlice < 0 Then WhichSlice = 7
End Sub

Sub Form_Resize ()
    'Ensure that caption is correct
    lblDateTime.Caption = Format$(Now, "dd MMMM yyyy")
    'Turn off timer when project is iconized; no need to waste
    'time drawing graphics when they can't be seen
    If TimerMain.WindowState = WIN_ICONIZED Then
        tmrTick.Interval = 0
    Else
        tmrTick.Interval = 60
    End If
End Sub
```

Figure 13-17.
"Extra" procedures for the Project Timer application.

In this code, the *Circle* method is called to create the slice, with parameters that are always $n\pi/4$ and $(n+1)\pi/4$ to keep the slice's shape the same. Because of the way Visual Basic draws the radius lines of the slice, you must offset the slice by a small value (such as 0.001). To create the radius lines of a pie slice, you must call the *Circle* method using negative numbers. When n is 0, $n\pi/4$ is also 0, which is not a negative number. Adding the small offset guarantees that the start and stop values will always be negative.

Figure 13-18 illustrates the finished Project Timer application in action.

Figure 13-18.
Running the completed Project Timer application.

A Look Ahead

You now know everything there is to know about Visual Basic, right? Not quite, I'm afraid. Although you now should be confident of your ability to create applications with Visual Basic, this programming system has many other advanced features that we didn't cover in this book. For example, Visual Basic allows you to harness the power of DDE (dynamic data exchange) to accomplish tasks such as exporting a value to a Microsoft Excel spreadsheet, importing the resulting pie chart, and displaying the chart within your application. Or you can create an MDI (multiple document interface) application, in which one form contains other forms, in a manner similar to Windows' Program Manager or File Manager. And you can add online Help to your applications to make them as easy to use and understand as any commercial application. You're limited only by your imagination—well, that and your spare time. Now where'd I put that cooking sherry?

Index

naming, *continued*
    function procedures, 165
    menu items, 125–26
    objects, 8–9, 10–11, 75
    variables and constants, 39–40
nested expressions, 53
nested statements, 134
New Form button, 203
New Form command, 203
New Module button, 205
New Module command, 205, 233
NewPage method, 255
NoMatch property, 264
noninvasive debugging techniques, 190
notation
    hexadecimal, 249
    syntax, 36, 72–73
NoteEdit application, 89–90
not equal to operator (<>), 59
Not logical operator, 60
Now function, 15, 68
numbers
    binary, 24
    converting, to strings, 59, 145
    converting strings to, 145
    hexadecimal, 249
    systems, 24–25
numeric data types
    floating-point, 35–36
    overview, 33–34
    range of, 34–35

O

Object box, in Properties window, 7–8
object linking and embedding (OLE)
    direct object control with OLE
        Automation, 283–86
    embedding objects at design time,
        274–76
    embedding objects at runtime,
        278–83
    linking vs. embedding, 276–77
    overview, *xvii*, 6, 115, 273–74
    registering applications for, 277, 284
    terms, 274

objects. *See also* Toolbox
    collections, 266
    control arrays, 153–55
    creating, 9–11
    database (*see* databases)
    defined, 5
    and event procedures (*see* event
        procedures)
    and events (*see* events)
    and methods (*see* methods)
    moving, 10
    naming, 8–9, 10–11, 75
    OLE, 274 (*see also* object linking
        and embedding (OLE))
    overview, 71–73
    as parameters, 172–75 (*see also*
        parameters)
    Printer, 254–55, 256
    properties, 6–7 (*see also* properties)
    recordsets, 263
    resizing, 10
    Screen (*see* screens)
    selecting, 10
    Toolbox and, 5–6, 9–10
OLE. *See* object linking and embedding
    (OLE)
OLEGRAPH application, 278–83
OLE tool, 6, 115, 273
On Error GoTo statement, 197–200
online help system, 3, 194–97
Open dialog boxes, 116–18
opening files
    Open dialog boxes for, 116–18
    random access, 215–16
    sequential, 209–10
Open Project button, 4, 21
Open Project command, 21, 31, 115
Open statement, 209, 215
operands, defined, 52
operators
    arithmetic, 53–57
    assignment, 51
    common mistakes in using, 63–65
    comparison, 59–60
    defined, 52

Ross Nelson is the author of *Microsoft's 80386/80486 Programming Guide* (Microsoft Press, 1991) and one of the coauthors of *Extending DOS* (Addison-Wesley, 1992). He also contributed to the *Microsoft Press Computer Dictionary* (1991) and has written articles for *BYTE* and *Dr. Dobb's Journal*.

Nelson has been programming in California's Silicon Valley for more than a dozen years. After earning his degree in computer science from Montana State University in 1979, he joined Intel Corporation, where his division produced some of the first working code for the 80286 and 80386 microprocessors. He is currently manager of software engineering for Answer Software, a company producing object-oriented database software for the Macintosh and Microsoft Windows. Nelson is also an active member of Computer Professionals for Social Responsibility (CPSR).

The manuscript for this book was prepared and submitted to Microsoft Press in electronic form. Text files were processed and formatted using Microsoft Word.

Principal editorial compositor: Cheryl Whiteside
Principal proofreader/copy editor: Shawn Peck
Principal typographer: Katherine Erickson
Interior text designer: Kim Eggleston
Principal illustrator: Lisa Sandburg
Cover designer: Rebecca Geisler-Johnson
Cover illustrator: Henk Dawson
Cover color separator: Color Service, Inc.
Indexer: Shane-Armstrong Information Systems

Text composition by Microsoft Press in Garamond Light with display type in Futura Heavy, using the Magna composition system. Composed pages were delivered to the printer as electronic prepress files.

Printed on recycled paper stock.

Information—
Direct From the Source

Running Microsoft Access™

John L. Viescas

Authoritative guide on Microsoft Access. Database expert John Viescas worked
closely with the Microsoft Access development team to bring you this example-packed,
hands-on user's guide and reference. Discover how to use Microsoft Access to effectively
run your business or office and how to create customized database applications using.
You'll also find tips and strategies not covered in the product documentation.
544 pages, softcover $29.95 ($39.95 Can.)   ISBN 1-55615-507-7

Code Complete

Steve McConnell

This practical handbook of software construction covers the art and
science of the most important part of the development process. Examples are
provided in C, Pascal, Basic, Fortran, and Ada—but the focus is on programming
techniques. Topics include upfront planning, applying good design techniques to
construction, using data effectively, reviewing for errors, managing construction
activities, and relating personal character to superior software.
880 pages, softcover $35.00 ($44.95 Canada)   ISBN 1-55615-484-4

Object Linking and Embedding
Programmer's Reference

Microsoft Corporation

Object Linking and Embedding (OLE) is a powerful way to extend the functionality
of your applications. This *Programmer's Reference* of previously undocumented
information for Windows is both a tutorial and the application programming interface
for OLE. The first half of the book lays the foundation for programming with OLE,
describing the creation of OLE client and server applications. The second half offers
a comprehensive and detailed reference to such topics as callback functions and
data structures, DLL functions, the registration database, and error codes.
448 pages, softcover $27.95 ($37.95 Canada)   ISBN 1-55615-539-5

Great Resources
from Microsoft Press